Culture and Customs of China

Culture and Customs of China

∽o∾

Richard Gunde

Culture and Customs of Asia
Hanchao Lu, Series Editor

GREENWOOD PRESS
Westport, Connecticut • London

Library of Congress Cataloging-in-Publication Data

Gunde, Richard, 1944–
  Culture and customs of China / Richard Gunde.
     p. cm.—(Culture and customs of Asia, ISSN 1097–0738)
  Includes bibliographical references and index.
  ISBN 0–313–30876–4 (alk. paper)
     1. China—Civilization. 2. China—Social life and customs. I. Title. II. Series.
  DS721.G89 2002
  951—dc21   2001023331

British Library Cataloguing in Publication Data is available.

Library of Congress Catalog Card Number: 2001023331
ISBN: 0–313–30876–4
ISSN: 1097–0738

First published in 2002

Greenwood Press, 88 Post Road West, Westport, CT 06881
An imprint of Greenwood Publishing Group, Inc.
www.greenwood.com

Printed in the United States of America

The paper used in this book complies with the
Permanent Paper Standard issued by the National
Information Standards Organization (Z39.48–1984).

10 9 8 7 6 5 4 3

To Sayuri and Wakana

Contents

Illustrations

Series Foreword

GEOGRAPHICALLY, Asia encompasses the vast area from Suez, the Bosporus, and the Ural Mountains eastward to the Bering Sea and from this line southward to the Indonesian archipelago, an expanse that covers about 30 percent of our earth. Conventionally, and especially insofar as culture and customs are concerned, Asia refers primarily to the region east of Iran and south of Russia. This area can be divided in turn into subregions commonly known as South, Southeast, and East Asia, which are the main focus of this series.

The United States has vast interests in this region. In the twentieth century the United States fought three major wars in Asia (namely, the Pacific War of 1941–45, the Korean War of 1950–53, and the Vietnam War of 1965–75), and each had profound impact on life and politics in America. Today, America's major trading partners are in Asia, and in the foreseeable future the weight of Asia in American life will inevitably increase, for in Asia lie our great allies as well as our toughest competitors in virtually all arenas of global interest. Domestically, the role of Asian immigrants is more visible than at any other time in our history. In spite of these connections with Asia, however, our knowledge about this crucial region is far from adequate. For various reasons, Asia remains for most of us a relatively unfamiliar, if not stereotypical or even mysterious, "Oriental" land.

There are compelling reasons for Americans to obtain some level of concrete knowledge about Asia. It is one of the world's richest reservoirs of culture and an ever-evolving museum of human heritage. Rhoads Murphey, a prominent Asianist, once pointed out that in the part of Asia east of Afghanistan and south of Russia alone lies half the world, "half of its people and far more than half of its historical experience, for these are the oldest living civilized traditions." Prior to the modern era, with limited interaction and mutual influence between the East and the West, Asian civilizations developed largely independent from the West. In modern times, however, Asia and the West have come not only into close contact but also into frequent conflict: The result has been one of the most solemn and stirring dramas in world history. Today, integration and compromise are the trend in coping with cultural differences. The West—with some notable exceptions—has started to see Asian traditions not as something to fear but as something to be understood, appreciated, and even cherished. After all, Asian traditions are an indispensable part of the human legacy, a matter of global "common wealth" that few of us can afford to ignore.

As a result of Asia's enormous economic development since World War II, we can no longer neglect the study of this vibrant region. Japan's "economic miracle" of postwar development is no longer unique, but in various degrees has been matched by the booming economy of many other Asian countries and regions. The rise of the four "mini dragons" (South Korea, Taiwan, Hong Kong, and Singapore) suggests that there may be a common Asian pattern of development. At the same time, each economy in Asia has followed its own particular trajectory. Clearly, China is the next giant on the scene. Sweeping changes in China in the last two decades have already dramatically altered the world's economic map. Furthermore, growth has also been dramatic in much of Southeast Asia. Today war-devastated Vietnam shows great enthusiasm for joining the "club" of nations engaged in the world economy. And in South Asia, India, the world's largest democracy, is rediscovering its role as a champion of market capitalism. The economic development of Asia presents a challenge to Americans but also provides them with unprecedented opportunities. It is largely against this background that more and more people in the United States, in particular among the younger generation, have started to pursue careers dealing with Asia.

This series is designed to meet the need for knowledge of Asia among students and the general public. Each book is written in an accessible and lively style by an expert (or experts) in the field of Asian studies. Each book focuses on the culture and customs of a country or region. However, readers should be aware that culture is fluid, not always respecting national boundaries. While every nation seeks its own path to success and struggles to maintain its own identity, in the cultural domain mutual influence and integration among Asian nations are ubiquitous.

Each volume starts with an introduction to the land and the people of a nation or region and includes a brief history and an overview of the economy. This is followed by chapters dealing with a variety of topics that piece together a cultural panorama, such as thought, religion, ethics, literature and art, architecture and housing, cuisine, traditional dress, gender, courtship and marriage, festivals and leisure activities, music and dance, and social customs and lifestyle. In this series, we have chosen not to elaborate on elite life, ideology, or detailed questions of political structure and struggle, but instead to explore the world of common people, their sorrow and joy, their pattern of thinking, and their way of life. It is the culture and customs of the majority of the people (rather than just the rich and powerful elite) that we seek to understand. Without such understanding, it will be difficult for all of us to live peacefully and fruitfully with each other in this increasingly interdependent world.

As the world shrinks, modern technologies have made all nations on earth "virtual" neighbors. The expression "global village" not only reveals the nature and the scope of the world in which we live but also, more importantly, highlights the serious need for mutual understanding of all peoples on our planet. If this series serves to help the reader obtain a better understanding of the "half of the world" that is Asia, the authors and I will be well rewarded.

Hanchao Lu
Georgia Institute of Technology

Acknowledgments

TO PARAPHRASE A PROVERB, any attempt to treat as large and complicated a subject as the culture and customs of a country within the brief span of a few hundred pages cannot end in success, but only in one degree or another of failure. If this book is not too miserable a failure it is because of the help, guidance, and assistance I have received from many individuals.

Hanchao Lu, the editor of this series, read every page of every draft and was always available for consultation in person, by e-mail, or by telephone. His encyclopedic knowledge has saved this book from many a potentially embarrassing error. More than that, Professor Lu provided the inspiration for this book: his scholarship on the everyday life of the common people of China is filled with respect and affection for his subjects. In Professor Lu's writings and talks I hear in the background the strains of Aaron Copeland's "Fanfare for the Common Man." I hope the reader of this book may hear at least a few measures.

Clayton Dube, Karen L. Hung, Douglas R. Reynolds, and Yunxiang Yan also read the manuscript and offered invaluable comments, criticisms, and suggestions. Moreover, they did so within the unreasonably short deadline I pressed upon them. I am particularly in their debt. Wendi Schnaufer of Greenwood Press, in unusual dedication for an editor, read the draft of each chapter as it was finished and gave prompt, sensible, and useful advice. I am grateful for her care and encouragement.

Many others also contributed to this book in various ways. I would like to acknowledge in particular the kind help of Maxwell Hearn, Perry Link, Stanley Rosen, Shu-mei Shih, and Lothar von Falkenhausen. Finally, at the start of this project Richard J. Smith sent me a small library of journal articles, notes, and various other source materials, as well as his own unpublished manuscripts. This treasure trove was of inestimable value in writing this book. The words "thank you" are much too puny to convey the magnitude of my appreciation for Professor Smith's generosity.

Guide to Pronunciation

THIS BOOK uses the *pinyin* system of romanization, which is now generally accepted as the international standard for rendering written Chinese. Pinyin is intended to convey the sounds of the standard, Mandarin dialect, which is based on pronunciation in Beijing. In a few instances, this book uses older spellings that are still conventional in the West, most of which are based on non-Mandarin dialects of Chinese (e.g., Sun Yat-sen, Chiang Kai-shek, Hong Kong).

	Approx. English equivalent	*Pronounced as in*	*Example/Note*
a	*a*	**fa**ther	
c	*ts*	ha**ts**	*cang* (pronounced "tsahng")
ch	*ch*	**ch**urch	almost same as *q* (see below)
e	*u*	**u**p	
i	*ee*	s**ee**	
j	*j*	**j**eep	
o	*o*	w**a**ll	
q	*ch*	**ch**urch	*Qing* (pronounced "ching")
x	*sh*	**sh**e	*xing* (pronounced "shing")

ü	*ew*	**few**, French **tu**	
ue (or üe)	*wea*	s**wea**t	*que* (pronounced "ch-wea"); *lüe* ("lwea")
ui	*way*	**way**	*sui* (pronounced "sway")
y	*y*	**y**ea	
z	*ds*	rea**ds**	
zh	*j*	**j**udge	

EXCEPTIONS

a	*eh*	**y**en	in the words *yan, yuan, juan, quan, xuan,* and in all syllables that end in *−ian*
e	*eh*	b**e**d	after *i* or *y*
i	*ir*	b**ir**d	in the words *chi, ri, shi,* and *zhi* only
i	*uh*	f**oo**t	in the words *si* and *zi* only

The *u* in the following words is pronounced as if it had an umlaut (*ü*):

ju	xun
qu	yu
qun	yun
xu	

Chronology

MAJOR PERIODS

Xia dynasty	ca. 2205–1766 B.C.
Shang dynasty	ca. 1766–1122 B.C.
Zhou dynasty	ca. 1122–221 B.C.
Spring and Autumn period	770–476 B.C.
Warring States period	475–221 B.C.
Qin dynasty	221–206 B.C.
Han dynasty	206 B.C.–A.D. 220
Three Kingdoms	220–280
Western and Eastern Jin	265–420
Southern and Northern dynasties	420–589
Sui dynasty	581–618
Tang dynasty	618–907
Five Dynasties and Ten Kingdoms	907–960
Song dynasty	960–1279
Yuan dynasty (Mongol)	1279–1368

Ming dynasty	1368–1644
Qing dynasty (Manchu)	1644–1911
Republic of China	1912– (after 1949 on Taiwan)
People's Republic of China	1949–

MODERN CHRONOLOGY

1911, Oct. 10	Outbreak of the Republican Revolution and downfall of the last dynasty
1912	Republic of China established, with Sun Yat-sen as provisional president
1913–27	Sun Yat-sen replaced as president by General Yuan Shikai; China divided among competing warlords
1921, July	Chinese Communist Party (CCP) founded
1923–27	CCP and Nationalists form United Front to combat warlords
1925	Sun Yat-sen dies
1927	Chiang Kai-shek expels Communists from United Front; Nationalists establish government in Nanjing
1931	Japan seizes Manchuria
1937–45	War with Japan
1946–49	Civil War between Communists and Nationalists; Nationalists flee to Taiwan in 1949
1949, Oct. 1	People's Republic of China (PRC) founded
1949–57	Land Reform, followed by gradual collectivization
1950–53	Korean War
1958–60	Great Leap Forward; "high tide" of the People's Communes

1966–76	Cultural Revolution; death of Mao Zedong in 1976
1971	PRC admitted to United Nations
1972	U.S. President Richard Nixon visits China; Japan establishes formal diplomatic relations with PRC
1978–	Economic reform period begins
1979, Jan.	United States establishes formal diplomatic relations with the PRC, and ends formal relations with the Republic of China (on Taiwan)
1989, June 4	Tiananmen Square Incident
1997	Hong Kong returned to China
1997, Feb. 19	Death of Deng Xiaoping, architect of the reform movement
1999, Dec. 20	Macao returned to China, ending the last colony in China
2001	China's entry to the World Trade Organization (WTO) pending

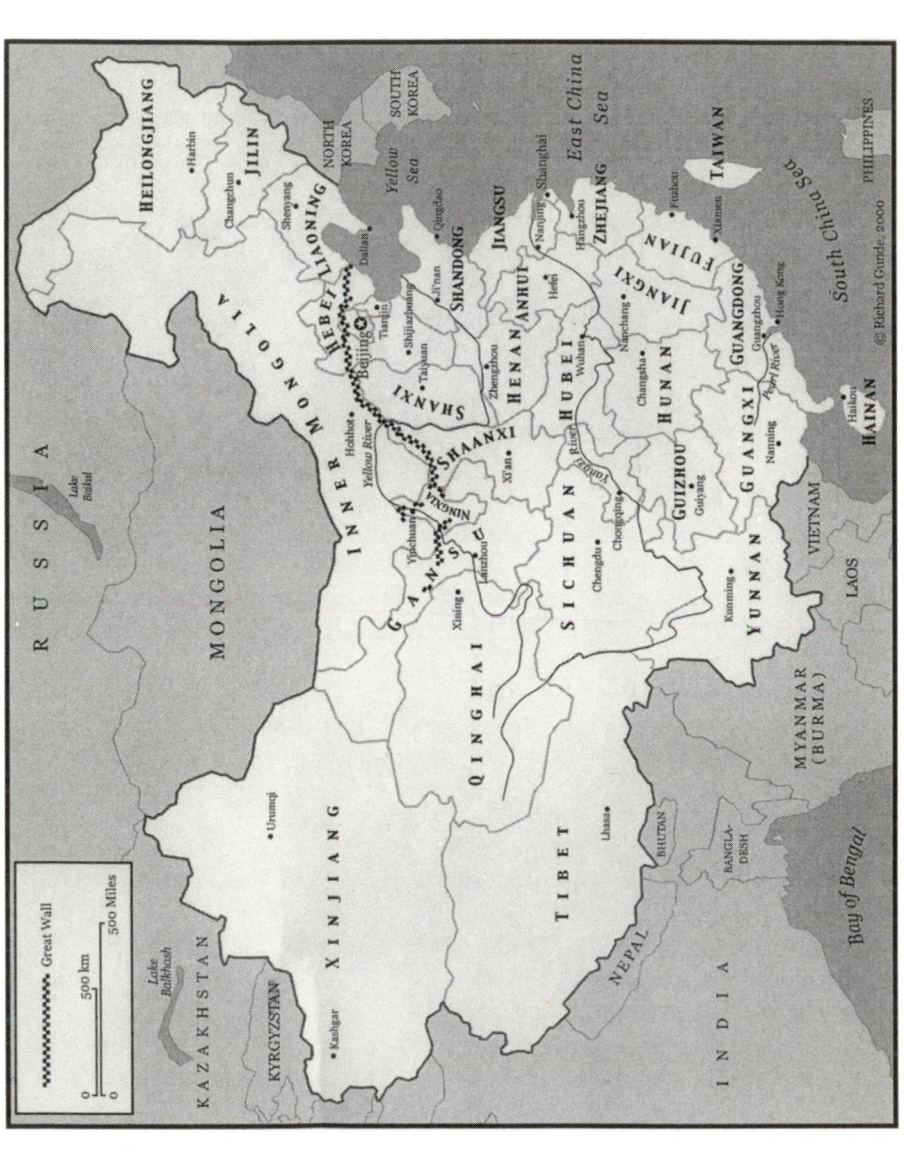

Map of China.

1

Land, People, and History

AMERICAN CHILDREN once fancied that if one digs straight down and keeps on digging, eventually one would emerge on the opposite side of the earth—in China. However geographically inaccurate this may be, it neatly epitomized an unshakable belief that China is not merely different from the United States, or more generally from the Western world, but so *completely different* that it is in all respects the polar opposite.

There is reason to think this way: take names, for instance. In China, the surname comes first. Thus, Mao Zedong was Mr. Mao, *not* Mr. Zedong. Or, consider how a letter is addressed. If one were sending a letter to Dr. Jane Smith in Boston and addressed the envelope the Chinese way, it would look like this:

USA
Massachusetts, Boston
Main Street 125
Smith Jane Dr.

But differences are far from the whole story. After viewing the many historical monuments in Charleston, South Carolina, a Chinese visitor quipped, "Southerners and Chinese are really quite alike: both eat rice and worship ancestors."[1] In this humorous statement is encapsulated an obvious but important truth: those who are sensitive to the human condition can find even in the most unexpected places the similarities that make cross-cultural understanding possible.

LAND

Many people concentrated on little useful land—that in a nutshell describes the core reality of China's geography. China is a vast country (at 3.7 million square miles it is the world's third largest, just slighter bigger than the United States), with a diverse geography. But in many respects it is a classic case of uneven distribution of natural resources and unbalanced economic development. Its arable land, its population (around 1.3 billion, the world's largest), and its industry are heavily concentrated toward the eastern seaboard, with the result that while the east is densely populated and relatively developed, the larger part of the country is sparsely populated and little developed.

Resources

China is home to about 22% of the world's population, but has just 7% of the world's arable land. Its forests and wilderness areas per capita are only 15% of the world average, and its range land per capita is less than half the world average.

Aside from productive land, other natural resources are also in short supply. Among major nations, China has the second lowest water resources per capita. The north in particular suffers from a chronic shortage of water. Compared to Canada, which is virtually afloat with 98,462 cubic meters per capita of water resources, and the United States with 9,413 cubic meters, China has but 4,200 cubic meters per capita, and of that, northern China accounts for only 750 cubic meters. Since around 70% of China's grain harvest is grown on irrigated fields, water resources are crucial. Even if China vigorously conserves water in the north, there seems to be no alternative in the future to moving people and industry to the south on a massive scale, or moving huge amounts of water from the south to the north—or both.

As for energy, natural gas deposits are scattered and oil is inadequate to meet the demand. China, which has been a net importer of petroleum since 1993, has about 2% of the world's known oil reserves, about the same as the United States. Coal, on the other hand, is abundant: China has a 300- to 400-year supply at current consumption rates, and coal now accounts for about 75% of the country's energy needs, compared to 26% in the United States. The problem with coal, of course, is that it is dirty. Coal-fired electric-generating plants contribute to the eye-smarting, filthy pall of smog that engulfs many of the country's cities. The dependence on coal could be reduced since China's potential for hydroelectric power is the greatest of any country, although today such power accounts for just 6% of the nation's primary energy.

Electric-generating capacity will increase by around 5% in one fell swoop with the completion of the Three Gorges Dam on the Yangzi River, scheduled for the year 2009—if the project works as planned. The dam is intended not only to generate a huge amount of electricity but also to control the frequent flooding of the Yangzi River, which causes great suffering and loss. The Three Gorges Dam has been described as China's largest construction project since the building of the Great Wall, centuries ago. It will be about four times bigger than any other dam now in existence, and will require technological solutions for which there is no precedent anywhere in the world. Almost 2 million people will have to be relocated as dozens of towns and hundreds of thousands of acres of farmland will be inundated. No one is quite sure of the environmental consequences of this massive dam. Some observers have predicted it will be an unmitigated disaster. Even if they are wrong, serious problems appear unavoidable. For instance, the city of Chongqing, upriver from the dam, now dumps 1.2 billion tons of wastewater into the Yangzi River annually: 900 million tons of industrial wastewater, of which only a third is treated, and 300 million tons of sewage, of which almost none is treated. All that wastewater is now carried down the river, but once the dam is in place and a 375-mile-long lake forms behind it, the pollution will be trapped. If nothing is done, it is inevitable that the Yangzi, where it runs right by Chongqing, will become a huge, vile, stinking cesspool. Alarmed by the prospect, the city is hurrying along plans to build 23 sewage treatment plants (with a loan of $100 million from the World Bank)[2]—but these are only plans, and even if carried out, the plants will treat only part of the sewage and none of the industrial effluent.[3]

Experts have pointed out that instead of the Three Gorges project, if China were to build four dams—each a quarter of the size of the Three Gorges Dam—along the Yangzi and its tributaries, it would be dealing with proven technology, the results insofar as power generation and flood control would be the same, *and* the environmental impact would be much more predictable and manageable. Why then is China going forward with this risky, and potentially disastrous, venture? The answer encompasses several key issues in life and politics in China today. The godfather of the Three Gorges Dam is Li Peng (b. 1928), the chairman of the Standing Committee of the National People's Congress (China's parliament), and also a leading figure in the seven-man Standing Committee of the Political Bureau, the highest organ of the Chinese Communist Party (CCP). The Party and the government are theoretically separate, but at the highest levels the same individuals are leaders in both. Jiang Zemin (b. 1926), for example, is both China's president (the formal head of the government) and the general secretary (the top leader) of the CCP. Also in theory—and in practice—the government is little more than an arm of the Party; it is the Party that really rules.

Li Peng, probably the second most powerful figure in the CCP, is the leader of an informal wing of the Party generally described as hard-liners. Li, who was trained as a hydraulic engineer in the Soviet Union in the 1950s, apparently took his education to heart and remains enamored of Stalinist-style megaconstruction. The fate of his pet project and of he himself as one of the most influential figures in the Party are now inextricably linked, whether he intended it or not. For the dam to be scrapped at this point would likely demolish his prestige and signal an end to his political career, something he presumably is unwilling to accept. Instead, one suspects that when Li Peng goes to bed at night he dreams that posterity will remember him as a latter-day Yu the Great. Yu, a semi-legendary ruler, supposedly founded the Xia dynasty (traditionally dated to 2205 B.C.), but is best remembered as a cultural hero who "tamed the waters" (of the Yellow River) by building catch basins, levees, and canals and so brought an end to the great floods that ravaged the land.

Building the Three Gorges Dam is also a matter of national pride. Nationalism is an extremely potent force in China today, as it has been for the past 150 years or so. Although many Chinese, frustrated by the corruption that is pervasive today or dispirited by being left behind in the current march to prosperity, are critical of their culture, it is also true that a great many take pride in the greatness of Chinese civilization and recognize that for centuries China was the world's wealthiest and most powerful country. That the West, and later Japan, spurted ahead of China in the past three centuries, and became richer, more developed, and more powerful is something which, as a country, China has found hard to accept. Building this monumental dam, larger and grander than any comparable project in contemporary times, is thus a way for China to demonstrate its greatness or, to some minds, its superiority. For those who think this way, the dam will be evidence that China really is the Central Country (Zhongguo), which is what the Chinese call their nation.

There are other people in China, however, who are very much opposed to the dam. Hydrologists, journalists, and some minor political figures have publicly spoken out against this grandiose project. However, these critics are like gnats buzzing around the Party-state elephant—the elephant may tolerate the gnats, but if and when they become too annoying, it may smack them. If there is also opposition to the dam within the top ranks of the Party, we could not be sure of it since the highest leaders strive to keep disagreements out of the public eye.

Yet, we certainly do know that the construction of the dam is tainted with corruption, a problem that has spread like cancer throughout Chinese society today. Several officials have been implicated in scandals. In 2000, one was sentenced to death for embezzling $1.45 million, and another absconded with several million dollars, leaving behind hundreds of angry and unpaid workers. Just how widespread the corruption is, and how high up it runs, is not known with certainty. President Jiang has declared that corruption must be hunted out and that the trail to malefactors must be followed, no matter how high it leads. But at the same time, the Party strives to maintain strict control over the flow of information and will permit absolutely no independent investigation.

The Three Gorges Dam project, then, is in many respects a microcosm of the troubles facing Chinese society today: dictatorial decision making, unbridled nationalism, corruption, and mistreatment of the environment. This list by no means exhausts all of China's problems, many of which are so complex and overwhelming as to seem beyond solution. Any thought that democracy, or a completely free-market economy, could be a magic wand that suddenly causes China's problems to disappear is simply a dream. Yet, looking at China in the context of its long history, what impresses is its great cultural strength and remarkable success in the face of adversity. When it comes to thinking about China's future, there is ample justification for the most disheartened pessimism and also for the most starry-eyed optimism.

Climate and Physical Geography

China embraces a vast and varied geographical area extending from Siberia to the equator and from the shores of the Pacific Ocean to the heart of the Eurasian continent. Most of the country is subject to two monsoons, or great movements of air, one in summer and the other in winter. The summer monsoon, loaded with moisture from the South China Sea, brings heavy rainfall with it as it moves northward. The eastern and southern regions of China in particular have frequent summer downpours. A large swath of the country, extending from the middle and lower Yangzi River Valley to around Fujian province, each year from around mid-June to mid-July experiences "plum rains," intermittent drizzles that follow one after the other, keeping everything perpetually damp. This is rice-transplanting time, and the sprouts thrive in all the moisture. But everything else just gets moldy—the food in the cupboard, the clothes in the closet, even the fences, which never get a chance to dry. It is often joked that if people stand around too long without moving, they too will grow moldy. By the time the monsoon reaches the North China Plain, it has already released most of its precipitation. Rainfall in North China averages 20 to 25 inches a year, barely adequate to sustain cultivation without irrigation. The winter monsoon is the opposite in just about every respect. It begins in the north—in Siberia and Mongolia—and as it moves southward it brings a flow of dry, cold air. Thus, in the areas of China subject to the monsoon, which encompass about 46% of the landmass and 96% of the population, summers are humid and hot and winters are dry and cool (or, in the far north, cold). Because of the monsoon, most places in China are hotter in the summer and colder in the winter than places elsewhere in the world at a similar latitude. For instance, the average August temperature in Shanghai is around 82°F, while in San Diego, California, at nearly the same latitude, it is around 70°F. In January, the average temperature in Shanghai is a chilly 38°F, while in San Diego it is 55°F. The sparsely populated far west of China, extending into Central Asia, is not subject to the monsoon, and has a dry, continental climate.

To escape the oppressive summer heat and humidity people like to go into the hills and mountains. Usually they do not have far to travel because more than half of China's counties contain mountainous areas. In fact, hills, mountains, and plateaus cover two-thirds of the country. The highest mountains are in the southwest—Mt. Everest, the world's tallest peak, lies there, on the border between Nepal and China (Tibet). Plains are mainly in the north and east, and basins and plateaus are scattered throughout the country.

Flowing from west to east across nearly two-thirds of the breadth of the country are the two greatest of China's many rivers, the Yangzi (which the Chinese actually call the Changjiang, literally "The Long River," and which Westerners often identify as the "Yangtze" or "Yangtse"), and the Huanghe (lit., Yellow River). The Yangzi truly is a long river: at 3,500 miles, it is the world's third longest. The Yellow River, at 3,000 miles, is not far behind. Both rivers originate in the mountains of the western province of Qinghai, and at one point near their source they lie less than 100 miles apart. But it is hard to imagine two great rivers more unalike. The Yangzi swiftly flows eastward through South-Central China, passing through regions with fertile soil and well-developed agriculture. More than one-quarter of the entire country's cultivated land lies within the Yangzi River basin. The Yangzi annually carries an impressive 3.7 million cubic feet of water into the ocean, and it forms an important east-west transport artery. The Yellow River, in contrast, slowly flows through North China, carrying only 5% as much water, and for much of its distance it is not navigable except by rafts or very shallow-draft vessels. The Yellow River is well named since it is loaded with muddy, fertile sediment that it carries to its lower reaches and to the sea, a stupendous billion-and-a-half tons each year. A cup of turbid water scooped up from the river looks like coffee, and no wonder since it contains about

60 times as much silt as a cup from the Mississippi River. Most of this sediment comes from the Loess Plateau (which includes all or part of the provinces of Gansu, Shaanxi, Shanxi, and Hebei), a region where the sparse vegetation leaves the soil—a yellowish, fine, fertile loam called "loess"—vulnerable to erosion. About 400 million tons of the silt carried by the Yellow River are deposited as the river slowly winds it way across the broad and flat North China Plain. Consequently, if left untouched the riverbed would grow higher and higher, in some places at a rate of about 4 inches a year. To prevent flooding, for more than two millennia the river has been confined within dikes for much of its distance. As long as the dikes hold, the river cannot flood, but historically as the riverbed rose between the dikes, they had to be raised, and raised, and raised again. Today giant dredges wage a constant battle to keep the riverbed from building up. Along much of the North China Plain, the Yellow River flows 10 to 12 feet, and in some spots more than 30 feet, above the surrounding plain. Looking up at the dikes elicits an uneasy sensation: up there is a river, flowing some three stories high in the sky!

Political Geography

China is divided into 22 provinces (including the island of Taiwan, over which the People's Republic claims sovereignty but which is independent, an issue discussed later in this chapter), five so-called autonomous regions (mostly areas on China's borders and the homelands of minority peoples), and four municipalities (Beijing, Shanghai, Chongqing, and Tianjin—cities that also encompass several towns as well as considerable rural territory and are roughly equivalent to provinces). China also claims a number of uninhabited islets and reefs in the South China Sea, the southernmost of which lies just a few miles off the coast of Borneo.

The so-called autonomous regions are not really autonomous, although they come in for special treatment. To win the allegiance of the minority peoples living in these regions, the government has generally followed an enlightened policy of encouraging minority culture (language, music, etc.) and offering exemptions from or relaxation of unpopular policies (such as the one-child-per-family policy, discussed in Chapter 7). In return, the state demands absolute and total allegiance of the minorities, as it does of all people of China. Cultural differences are accepted, even encouraged, but the slightest hint of *political* divergence is ruthlessly suppressed. To appreciate why the Chinese government is extraordinarily sensitive to its borderlands, and to understand why it seems obsessed with the question of loyalty and national unity, we must plunge into the questions of who are the people of China and what has been their history, the subjects of the balance of this chapter.

PEOPLE

Cultural Geography

If you were to draw an imaginary line roughly equidistant between the Yangzi and the Yellow rivers, you would be tracing one of the most important dividing lines in Chinese culture. On one side of the line lies North China, traditionally credited with being the cradle of Chinese civilization and the political heart of the country—a dry, dusty, conservative region in which people sustain themselves on wheat noodles. On the other side lies South China, a wet, verdant, dynamic region where people feed on white rice. Sometimes these stereotypes—for that is what they are, of course—are expanded to include physique and even moral fiber. In the 1930s, Lin Yutang, a noted interpreter of Chinese culture, described the northern Chinese as "acclimatized to simple thinking and hard living, tall and stalwart, hale, hearty and humorous, onion-eating and fun-loving, children of nature." He dismissed people living on the southeast coast, south of the Yangzi, as "inured to ease and culture and sophistication, mentally developed but physically retrograde, loving their poetry and their comforts, sleek undergrown men and slim neurasthenic women, fed on birds'-nest soup and lotus seeds, shrewd in business . . . and cowardly in war, ready to roll on the ground and cry for mamma before the lifted fist descends."[4] There are probably some Chinese today who still believe in outrageous caricatures of this sort, but in fact throughout their history the Chinese have been a mobile people and have shared their genes freely so that there is no more innate difference between a farmer on the North China Plain and a carpenter in Guangzhou than there is between a New England schoolteacher and a Georgia truck driver.

Nonetheless, just as New England differs from Georgia, North China differs from South China in geography, history, and culture. The Chinese are sensitive to these differences and for most people they comprise an important component of personal identity. However, very broad differences, such as those between North and South China, in most instances count for less than more specific distinctions that mark one province from another, one area from another, and one city, town, or county from another. To this day, traditional culture—in dialect (see Chapter 3), music (Chapter 4), food (Chapter 5), housing (Chapter 6), and the like—varies from area to area. Even particular occupations and professions have traditionally been linked to particular localities. For instance, in the last two dynasties, businessmen from the province of Shanxi and its neighbor Shaanxi were found throughout the country running pawnshops and banks and engaged in inter-provincial trade.

A small indication of the sense of localism and local pride that is characteristic of China is revealed on the cover of a book published in Italy in 1999. There, on the cover, is inscribed the title, in Italian, *The Chinese of Milan.* The title is also given in Chinese, but it is a different title: *The Wenzhou People of Milan.* Presumably the Chinese title was written by a Chinese resident of Milan, someone who (without the publisher's knowledge?) could not contain his or her hometown pride. Today, businesspeople from the city of Wenzhou and its environs, in the province of Zhejiang, have to some extent taken the place once occupied by successful Shanxi merchants. Wenzhou has become exceptionally dynamic and prosperous within the past 20 or 30 years, and many of its residents have emigrated to elsewhere in China, or abroad to places like Paris and Milan, where they have established small, successful businesses.

The source of the strength and endurance of localism lies deep within Chinese culture, especially in something known as *guanxi.* Life in a Chinese milieu is unimaginable without the cultivation of personal connections or networks of relationships, which the Chinese call "guanxi." For example, in getting a job, good connections are helpful, and sometimes essential. Does the prospective employee have any guanxi with the prospective employer? If, for instance, it turns out that the applicant's uncle was a high school classmate of the employer's supervisor, a useful connection has been identified. Perhaps the uncle will contact the supervisor, to talk of old times and to mention the applicant. Depending on a host of circumstances—including any obligations the supervisor may owe the uncle—the phone call could be decisive.

Obviously, the closer people are related, the denser and stronger their mutual ties. Kin relationships are usually the strongest and most central, naturally, but other relationships built up by attending the same school (and particularly by being in the same year or class), by working together, by doing business together, and the like are all important sources of guanxi. Ties of these sorts are what links people from the same area, or in other words, what gives them a rich network of guanxi.

Of course, local pride can easily become local prejudice. In Shanghai for most of the twentieth century the people who collected the night soil and did other undesirable jobs were mostly *Jiangbeiren,* literally "people from north of the [Yangzi] River." The residents of Shanghai, many of whom themselves were recent arrivals in the city, tended to look upon these people from the counties just north of the river as at best uncouth bumpkins, and at worst as knavish rascals, unfit for decent, polite company, or good jobs.

To this day for many people "Jiangbeiren" remains a derogatory term, occupying much the same space that the word "Okies" once did in the United States.

Yet, localism of this sort is not exclusive, that is to say, it does not preclude other, higher loyalties, and in particular it does not conflict with a sense of nationalism, or at least it does not take priority over a sense of nationalism. People who have a strong sense of local identity are also ardently patriotic. There is not today, nor historically has there been, any serious sentiment for breaking up the country. Even when China was in fact disunited, as it was during the 40-odd years between the fall of the empire in 1911 and the founding of the People's Republic in 1949, almost without exception people fervently believed the disunity to be a horrible aberration. The warlords who carved up China among themselves during those years and fought war after war for control of land and resources, and who ran provincial regimes that in many instances were virtually independent of the national government, all claimed they were really nationalists.

There is an important caveat to this general, powerful sense of nationalism and unity: ethnic divisions in some regions run so deep as to call into question China's continued unity within its present borders.

Nationality and Ethnicity

China is a multi-ethnic society in which the government officially recognizes 56 "nationalities," or ethnicities: the majority, known as the Han, comprise 92% of the country's population; the remaining 55 groups—which includes Zhuang (at around 16 million, the most numerous minority), Uygurs (a Turkish-speaking people), Mongols, Tibetans, and others—are officially termed "national minorities." In this book, when we speak of "Chinese" we are speaking of the Han, unless specifically mentioned otherwise. When one thinks of "Chinese" it is usually of the Han; it is they who inhabit the historical heartland of China, speak the Chinese language, and follow the customs discussed in these pages.

As we have noted, the homelands of many of the national minorities are located along China's borders. Historically, many of these areas were controlled or ruled by China only at times, off and on; frequently the control was tenuous, more a matter of influence than direct rule. Even in recent decades, on the eve of the Communist revolution of 1949, some of these domains were, realistically speaking, beyond the reach of the Chinese authorities. The government today asserts that these areas, such as Tibet, have "always" been part of China, but that is political rhetoric, not historical fact.

Furthermore, several of the national minorities are today a people divided. Part of their population resides in territory within China, and are Chinese citizens, while just across the border, in an independent country, reside the rest. This is true of, among others, the Kazaks, Kirgiz, Koreans, Mongols, Tajiks, and Uzbeks. Although within the past century, the border regions where these particular people live have been relatively stable, territorial disputes elsewhere along its borders have led China to war with India (in 1962), the Soviet Union (in 1969), and Vietnam (in 1978).

Historically, relations between the Han and minority peoples have been complicated and variable. Over the centuries, as the Han population grew, its people spread outward into areas they considered the frontier, coming into contact with non-Chinese peoples, and in many instances driving them into the hills and mountains or entirely displacing them. Sometimes assimilation was the order of the day, with native peoples absorbed into the Han population, and occasionally it was the other way around, with the Han absorbed into the native population. In some places, assimilation continues to this day. The Manchus, to take a notable example, have become virtually indistinguishable from the Han, speaking the same language and following the same customs and ways of life. In some instances, there has been a degree of "disassimilation" whereby individuals who have considered their families Han for generations have found it expedient to "discover" their roots, and be officially recognized as members of a national minority, and in this way take advantage of various "affirmative action" policies.

When Han and non-Han peoples have met, the encounter at times has been violent. In recent centuries, Han and Chinese-speaking Muslims in the northwest and southwest have lived in close proximity, carried out business together, and at times intermarried, but from time to time they have also been at each other's throats, with clashes sometimes growing into full-scale rebellion and civil war.

Generally the Han looked upon other people as barbarians (the word "barbarian" appeared in Chinese documents more than two millennia ago, and was used again and again until modern times), and treated them with disdain, if not outright contempt. The Communist government has condemned this as "Great Han chauvinism," a charge that the authorities level with a certain amount of cynicism inasmuch as they themselves are guilty of lording it over the national minorities. In minority areas, some cadres (functionaries and officials in the Communist Party, in the government, or in government-run enterprises) and a few high-ranking officials are members of national minorities, but most, including the vast majority of top leaders, are Han sent in from the outside.

Over the centuries, non-Han peoples have sometimes lorded it over the

Han. Throughout the past two millennia or more, China was frequently invaded, particularly by people from the north and west, and parts of the country, and sometimes the entire country, were defeated and occupied for centuries on end, for example, by the Mongols (thirteenth to fourteenth centuries) and the Manchus (seventeenth to twentieth centuries). However, even when China was militarily defeated and occupied, its culture proved triumphant. If the invaders stayed long, they typically adopted Chinese political institutions, ruled through Chinese bureaucrats, followed Chinese imperial rituals, and otherwise became sinified to one degree or another. But they also left their imprint on Chinese customs and culture, in such diverse areas as clothing (see Chapter 5) and architecture (Chapter 6).

HISTORY

In navigating the more than 3,000 years of Chinese history, with its twists and turns and convolutions, travelers would do well to pay particular attention to the most important landmarks: the crucial and defining moments that fundamentally shaped culture and civilization in China. This is different from the usual route followed by historians, which is to recite the stories of the individual dynasties (or ruling houses), one after the other, like a train whizzing along the tracks: clickety-clack, one dynasty; clickety-clack, the next dynasty; clickety-clack, still the next. In our journey, we will not ignore the dynasties, for they were important. Indeed, the identification of the country with the reigning dynasty was usually remarkably strong, so strong that often Chinese called their country not Zhongguo (China) but by the name of the dynasty in power. But we will stress broader trends that crossed political divides.

Chinese history so far has had five defining moments: (1) the Bronze Age, seventeenth century B.C. to sixth century B.C. (writing, wheeled carts, spread of sedentary agriculture); (2) the Age of Philosophers and Warriors, fifth century B.C. to second century B.C. (iron, peasant armies, flowering of philosophy, introduction of a unified, imperial state); (3) the Age of Cultural Exchange, seventh century A.D. to tenth century (Buddhism, spread of the Chinese world, rule by civil servants); (4) the Age of Art and Commerce, eleventh century to fourteenth century (widespread rice cultivation, economic expansion, landscape painting, popular literature and drama); and (5) the Transition to Modernity, nineteenth century to today (population explosion, confrontation and accommodation with the Western world, fall of the imperial system, mass politics and mass culture).

The Bronze Age and Before: The Origins of Chinese Civilization

For many centuries the Chinese had a good idea of their origins, related in a creation myth concerning one Pangu, the first (almost human) being, who spent 18,000 years chiseling out the universe from chaos. When he died, the vermin on his body became the human race. This myth evidently dates to the fourth century A.D.; before then, what the Chinese thought about their origins is unclear.

In any case, the people of China have spent less time thinking about their origins than they have about their history. And for them history became particularly interesting and important with the so-called four Sage Kings: the Yellow Emperor (who by legend ruled around 4000 B.C.), Yao, Shun, and Yu, each of whom ruled in succession and each of whom is credited with inventions indispensable to civilization. The Yellow Emperor, for example, was believed to have invented the wheel, and Yu is remembered, as we have seen, for taming the waters.

Also as we have seen, Yu is credited with founding what the Chinese have long considered to be their first dynasty, the Xia. To this day, most Western scholars are unsure if there really was such a thing as the Xia dynasty, and some still dismiss both it and the four Sage Kings as nothing more than myths. But archaeological digs in recent years have uncovered the remains of what may be palaces dating from the time of the Xia, and if and when additional evidence is brought to light, it may well turn out that the Xia dynasty was more of a historical reality and less of a myth than has been supposed.

While scholars have been quick to dismiss the Xia, they readily accepted as reality that Chinese civilization was conceived, born, and reared through infancy exclusively on the plains of North China, something also accepted as an article of faith among the Chinese for as far back as can be determined. But here too recent archaeological discoveries suggest a fundamental rethinking is in order, for there is now evidence of at least one other advanced culture in what is now China, in Sichuan province, dating to around 1300 B.C., and thus contemporaneous with the Shang, China's second dynasty. Almost nothing is known of this culture—archaeologists have yet to discover its name, but merely call it "Sanxingdui," from the site where it was found. We do not yet know in detail how this nameless culture interacted with the Shang nor how it contributed to Chinese civilization. Its people, who possibly did not speak Chinese, seem to have been illiterate, although evidently they traded with the Chinese-speaking Shang. Despite this commerce, the Shang apparently took pains to clearly distinguish themselves from these and other peoples with whom they came into contact. An effort to draw distinct lines between Chinese and outsiders has become an enduring hallmark of Chinese culture.

The Age of Philosophers and Warriors

By the fifth century B.C., if not before, the Chinese were predominantly a sedentary, agricultural people, but were in frequent contact with nomadic pastoralists and forest dwellers to the north. For more than two millennia, right down into the twentieth century, various northern peoples and the Chinese were locked in intermittent warfare, with China sometimes successfully securing its northern borders and extending its power well into Mongolia and Central Asia, and sometimes with the northerners invading and occupying parts or all of China.

The Hundred Schools of Philosophy

During the later years of the so-called Spring and Autumn period (770–476 B.C.) and the Warring States period (475–221 B.C.), the Chinese constructed great walls to separate themselves from the pastoralists, as well as intermittent walls between the various Chinese states, which were nominally all part of the successor to the Shang, the Zhou dynasty, but in fact were at war with one another. Perhaps paradoxically, during these years of crisis, with China disunited and suffering from endemic warfare, culture flourished. This era—roughly from the sixth through the third centuries B.C.—has been aptly named the time of the "hundred schools" (meaning many) of philosophy, for there arose in the midst of the unremitting violence an extraordinary efflorescence of wisdom contained within a host of philosophies associated with a number of great thinkers, including Confucius (see Chapter 2).

Dawn of the Imperial Era

In the year 221 B.C. the Warring States period came to an end with the victory of the state of Qin (once romanized as "Chin" and likely the source of our word "China"), which defeated all its rivals and united the country into a single, strong, centralized state. Traditionally, the victory of the Qin is considered the start of the imperial era in China, which lasted all the way down to 1911. To put these two millennia from 221 B.C. to A.D. 1911 under the single rubric of "imperial" is justified because running through this great span of time was a common political thread, so to speak, a notion of how government should be organized and should relate to society.

The ideal, sometimes realized in practice and sometimes not, can be summarized with two words: *centralization* and *meritocracy*. The government was highly centralized, with ministries and bureaus in the capital city—not unlike most state structures today—and the country divided into provinces, each ruled by a governor, and the provinces divided into counties, each governed by a magistrate. The most important governmental officials were appointed; in other words, China was ruled by a bureaucratic civil service. A hereditary aristocracy existed, but it was usually of secondary, even minor, importance, and priests and organized religion likewise rarely played an important, legitimate role in government.

Until around the tenth century A.D. most officials were selected on the basis of recommendation, but beginning as early as the Han dynasty (206 B.C.–A.D. 220) civil service examinations were used to determine job assignments. In the following centuries, examinations increasingly became the preferred method of recruitment, and by the Song dynasty (960–1279) they had become the primary entrée to official position (see Chapter 2). This civil service system proved to be exceedingly effective and durable: it survived all challenges, inspired Western imitations, and remained in place until it was finally abolished in 1905 in a fit of "modernization."

The Age of Cultural Exchange

Like a giant seesaw, Chinese culture has on the one side a tendency toward exclusivity and chauvinism, which we have noted, but on the other side it has an opposite tendency, a proclivity for a ready acceptance of, and often a fascination with, the new, the foreign, and the strange. At various points in history, one or the other of these contradictory tendencies was ascendant; much of the time, the two balanced each other, albeit precariously. The tension between them has been more of a source of strength than weakness for it has facilitated the adaptation and assimilation of cultural influences that people found useful, interesting, and congenial and the rejection of those they found otherwise.

Rise and Decline of Buddhism

Before modern times and the arrival of Westernization, the most profound borrowing from foreign culture occurred from the sixth century to the middle of the ninth century when China eagerly welcomed from India, Central Asia, and as far away as Persia a rich panoply of objects and ideas ranging from food and clothing to music and dance and aesthetics and religion, above all the Buddhist religion. By the seventh century China truly had become the center of the Buddhist world. During this age, China's neighbors, especially Japan, Korea, and Vietnam, also hungered for Buddhism, and pilgrims flocked to China to learn more of the religion and to collect its sacred texts. As they returned home, the pilgrims carried back not just Buddhism but also a vast array of other elements of Chinese culture: art, architecture, philosophy, language, clothing, and a myriad of others, including Confucianism, which flourished for centuries in Korea—in many ways Korea became more Confucian than China—and to a lesser extent in Japan and Vietnam. To see the material remains of Chinese culture in this age, it is best to go not to China but to places like Nara in Japan, where several magnificent wooden temples patterned after those in Tang-dynasty China (618–907) are preserved (all those in China disappeared long ago).

Thus, aside from its importance as a religion (discussed in Chapter 2), Buddhism was of momentous significance as a vehicle for cultural transmission, both *to* China and *from* China to Japan, Korea, and Vietnam.

In China itself, although Buddhism left an imprint on a great many aspects of culture, it failed to exert a fundamental, long-lasting influence on government. Many Chinese objected to Buddhism all along, to its foreignness (for instance, good Buddhists practiced cremation, an abhorrent custom in the eyes of many Chinese) and to its economic impact (for instance, Buddhist monasteries, which numbered in the thousands and housed perhaps 2 million monks and nuns, paid no taxes). And, for good measure, critics could point to the usurpation of Empress Wu, who after the death of her husband, the emperor, in 649 became infatuated with a Buddhist monk, squandered a vast sum of money on monasteries, and put Buddhist tenets into practice by outlawing the slaughter of animals and fishing. All this might have been forgivable, but Wu had herself crowned empress in 690, the only time in Chinese history a woman ruled in her own right, an unspeakable violation of cultural norms and something that the Chinese made sure never happened again.

When Empress Wu was deposed in a coup in 705, the Tang dynasty was restored, and then went on to survive for another two eventful centuries, eventually succumbing to a variety of ills. Several of the later Tang emperors were ineffectual, the army was increasingly staffed and led by non-Chinese mercenaries of suspect loyalty, fiscal insolvency and mismanagement contributed to governmental weakness and an inability to deal with economic crisis, the state became incapable of enforcing its policies in the face of separatist tendencies, revolts broke out, and in the end the dynasty crumbled in 907. Half a century of disunity ensued, with the country divided among several short-lived competing regimes, until in 960 a powerful general reunited the country and established a new dynasty, the Song.

The Dynastic Cycle

In broad outline, this series of events describes what historians have called the "dynastic cycle." Throughout the imperial era, vigorous men, often of relatively humble origins, rebelled against a moribund dynasty, founded a new dynasty, and quickly consolidated their rule and instituted reforms. Succeeding generations of emperors made government effective and efficient, secured peace and prosperity, and promoted the arts and culture. But after several generations, or centuries in the case of some dynasties, vigor ebbed away: the army became flabby and unable to deal effectively with domestic and foreign challenges, the economy weakened, the people began to question the legitimacy of the dynasty (what the Chinese called "the mandate of heaven"), and government became corrupt, with irresolute emperors unable or unwilling to prevent ambitious sycophants or palace eunuchs from insinuating themselves in high positions. The eunuchs in particular were excoriated by the elite—in the seventeenth century the noted scholar and official, Huang Zongxi, declared that "for thousands of years everyone has known that eunuchs are like poison and wild beasts"—because they, as a group, were poorly educated, if not illiterate, came from nondescript families, and possessed only one virtue, which was loyalty to the emperor, or at least they were loyal so long as it served their purposes. When eunuchs acquired power it was usually a sign that bad times lay ahead.

The Age of Art and Commerce

Cultural and Economic Strength

From around the eleventh century, China entered into an unprecedented era of cultural renaissance and economic growth. For several centuries, in the midst of material plenty that far outstripped medieval Europe, the country enjoyed a flowering of both high culture among the elite and popular culture among the common people.

This multifaceted efflorescence involved, among other things, the development of a bookish aestheticism as the elite turned its back on the physicality of the earlier Age of Cultural Exchange. While games and physical contests always remained popular among the lower classes, educated people set the tone of the era by virtually abandoning sports such as polo, hunting, and riding, all of which were perceived as part of the "barbarian" culture that had been so welcome during the seventh and eighth centuries. This worked a lasting influence on Chinese culture: physical education disappeared, not to be reintroduced until the twentieth century.

Learned people turned their attention chiefly to literature, calligraphy, garden design, collecting books and works of art, and painting. Many of the emperors of the Song dynasty were avid patrons of painting, and a few were fine artists in their own right.

At the opposite end of the social scale, especially in the cities, there was an explosive growth in the audience for popular culture. A veritable middle class of shopkeepers, artisans, clerks, shop assistants, and servants arose and clamored for entertainment, which was available in abundance. Many shops and restaurants were open 24 hours a day and offered a remarkably rich variety of food and other goods. Books catering to popular tastes were abundant—woodblock printing had been invented in the eighth century, and moveable print in the eleventh century, 400 years before Europe—and popular performing arts, especially the opera, thrived (see Chapters 3 and 4).

The burgeoning market for culture was the outgrowth of a commercial revolution that saw a greatly expanded number of people with money in their purse. Some statistics suggest the dimensions of the economic upsurge. In 1078, cast iron production was around 125,000 tons, six times greater than in 900. This represented a per capita rate of production not reached by Europe until 1700. In 1050, the production of ceramic ware, much of which was of very high quality, was about five times greater than in 900. The most revealing statistics of all concern the minting of coins. In the year 804, 135,000 strings of copper coins were issued. (Round copper coins with a square hole in the middle, called "cash" by Westerners, were the usual medium for daily purchases. A thousand coins were considered a "string," whether they were actually strung together or not.) In the year 1000, 1.35 million strings were minted, a tenfold increase over 804. And in 1073, no less than 6 million strings were minted. This suggests a gigantic expansion of trade, and not only domestic trade.

Foreign trade too reached unprecedented levels. China's seaports, which were incomparably bigger and busier than those in Europe, were jammed with large merchant ships filled with cargo of every description. These ships, later called "junks" by Westerners (from a Javanese word), sported four or more masts, and were up to 400 feet long—five times bigger than Columbus's flagship, the *Santa Maria* (80 ft). Navigation was greatly aided by the compass, another Chinese invention, which ocean-going ships began to use around the tenth or eleventh century.

At the foundation of the economic expansion was an agricultural upsurge, connected especially with the widespread adoption of cotton and rice, which freed labor from the land and provided abundant food and raw materials. From about the eleventh century, cotton was cultivated in more and more areas, and over the following centuries it became by far the most important fiber (see Chapter 5). Also, around the eleventh century began one of the greatest events in the history of East Asia: the intensive cultivation of rice on a wide scale. Early ripening varieties of rice were introduced from Southeast Asia, which in some Chinese locales permitted two harvests per year. Even where this was not possible, improvement in plant stock and in cultivation techniques substantially increased yields.

Political and Military Weakness

Strangely, China's great wealth did not translate into military might. On the contrary, during this era the country faced frequent political crises and endemic military weakness. Despite the development of military technology (by the twelfth century, China's armies were equipped with cannons, rockets, grenades, etc.), the Song state preferred not to fight but to pit one nomadic people against another whenever it could, and when it could not, then to buy them off with lavish payments of silk and silver. For a while, this policy worked, but only barely. Throughout the Song dynasty, northernmost China was never under the control of the Chinese, and in 1126 a northern people called the Jurchen pushed southward to a point roughly midway between the Yellow River and the Yangzi River, capturing the emperor in the bargain. Much of the emperor's court, his government, and many of his subjects fled south of the Yangzi. China's center of gravity shifted with them: in the eighth century, 60% of China's population, which was then around 50 million, lived in North China; by the eleventh century, the ratio had reversed, and now 60% of the population, which had doubled to 100 million, lived in the south, in the rice-growing Yangzi River Valley. This ratio—40% in the north, and 60% in the south—still holds today.

In 1234 the Jurchen were expelled from North China by a people whose homeland was still farther north, the Mongols. Over the years, the Mongols—outstanding horsemen and experts at mobile warfare—had gradually moved south, and by 1279 they had smashed the Song and conquered all of China. Breaking with the Chinese tradition of generally naming dynasties after a region, the Mongols gave their new dynasty the imposing name of Yuan ("First" or "Primary"). The two succeeding dynasties, the Ming ("Bright") (1368–1644) and the Qing ("Pure") (1644–1911), adopted this new practice of selecting names that supposedly characterized their virtue.

Under the nearly century-long rule (1279–1368) of the Mongols, literature and art continued to thrive but the economy suffered from inflation caused by overprinting of paper money and by a pandemic of plague in the middle of the fourteenth century that reduced the population to around 60 million. Making the situation worse, the Yuan government levied rapacious taxes and subjected the Chinese to racial discrimination by, for instance, reserving for them the most severe punishments. Pushed to the wall, the people rose in revolt, which the Mongols, riven by internal disputes, were unable to resist effectively.

The long Ming dynasty that followed began with a half-century of economic reconstruction and military expansion into Mongolia, Central Asia, and Southeast Asia. However, the campaigns in the north, designed to contain and push back the former Mongol occupiers, began to meet with defeat within a few decades and came to a halt by the middle of the fifteenth century. Thereafter, the policy shifted to defense, including the rebuilding, strengthening, and extending of the Great Wall across North China to keep out the Mongols (see Chapter 6). At the same time, a second cultural renaissance began to flower, involving a multitude of economic, intellectual, and social developments. Although domestic commerce and international trade reached levels not even attained during the Song dynasty, an increasing number of farming households lost their land to rich landlords, and became their tenants or were thrown off the land. In a replay of the dynastic cycle, the government raised taxes to crushing levels in order to support a large, but weak and indisciplined mercenary army, and palace eunuchs took advantage of ineffective emperors and spreading corruption to seize lucrative government posts. When the emperor Taichang died in 1620 it was even rumored that he had been poisoned by the eunuchs. In response to these and other grave developments, toward the end of the sixteenth century a series of crises erupted. Demonstrations and riots broke out in cities, popular insurrections exploded in the countryside, and a struggle between the eunuchs and a group of concerned civil servants and intellectuals tore the government apart.

In 1644 the last Ming emperor, abandoned by everyone, committed suicide as a rebel army broke into Beijing. Within a month descendants of the Jurchen, now calling themselves Manchus, poured into China, routed the rebels, defeated the remnants of the Ming forces (a nearly four-decade-long struggle), and proclaimed a new dynasty, the Qing. Through the seventeenth century, China prospered under the Manchus, who closely followed the governmental structure of the preceding Ming dynasty and who as time passed became increasingly sinicized. Trade and agriculture thrived, and through diplomacy and warfare, the government expanded its control into Mongolia, Central Asia, and Tibet. By the middle of the eighteenth century China reached a size that it had never before, nor since, attained. It was simply the world's largest and richest country.

However, also by the middle of the eighteenth century troubling signs began to appear. Population at the beginning of the dynasty was around 125 million. By 1750 it had grown to 145 million (comparable to the population of all of Europe), and then it began to balloon, reaching over 350 million by around 1810 and 425 million by 1850. The problem was that the economy at this time was not expanding apace, and thus living standards began to fall and life became precarious.

By the beginning of the nineteenth century, the Qing was slipping into the classic pattern of dynastic decline. The economy was entering a protracted depression, marked in particular by an unfavorable balance of trade from around 1825, related in some measure to the importation of opium, as we shall see. The government was growing increasingly inept and corrupt, with more and more official positions going not to those who had scored highest in the civil service examinations but to those who could pay the most, for positions were being sold. Several populist rebellions broke out, which the army, having grown weak and inept, suppressed only with the greatest of difficulty. The largest, the Taiping ("Great Peace") Rebellion (1851–64), which espoused a primitive sort of communism and whose leader proclaimed himself "the younger brother of Christ," nearly succeeded. It was put down after 13 years of fierce fighting, during which much of the country was devastated and millions upon millions of lives were lost—this was probably the bloodiest civil war in human history.

While China was on decline from the middle of the eighteenth century, Europe in the eighteenth and nineteenth centuries was on the rise. This was the time of the industrial revolution in Europe, a time when the European powers, and later the United States, were seeking sources of raw materials and markets for their products. It was moreover an age marked by imperialist rivalries among the European powers, later joined by the United States and still later by Japan, for raw materials and markets.

The Transition to Modernity

Crisis in the Traditional Order

At three o'clock in the morning on September 14, 1792, an English gentleman, carried aloft on a palanquin (sedan chair), careened through the pitch-black streets of Jehol, a city in Manchuria where the emperor spent each summer. The gentleman was Lord Macartney and he was on his way to an audience with the emperor, Qianlong (1711–99). Macartney had been dispatched by King George III of England to establish diplomatic relations with China and initiate greatly expanded trade. However, negotiations were hampered at every turn by a fundamental disagreement over protocol, ritual, and the nature of interstate relations. The Chinese insisted that they were "the only civilization under heaven" and that the British, as "barbarians," could only be accommodated within the traditional tribute system whereby outside states signified their inferior status by presenting gifts to the imperial court and following an elaborate ritual that symbolized China's superiority. Macartney did in fact come loaded with gifts—interesting examples of British manufactures—but he definitely rejected the notion that Britain should accept an inferior position. The mission ultimately failed.

A letter from Emperor Qianlong to King George reveals China's understanding of its unique place in the world:

> We, by the grace of heaven, Emperor, instruct the King of England to take note of our charge. . . .
>
> As to what you have requested in your message, O King, namely to be allowed to send one of your subjects to reside in the Celestial Empire [China] to look after your country's trade, this does not conform to the Celestial Empire's ceremonial system, and definitely cannot be done. . . . The Celestial Empire, ruling all within the four seas, simply concentrates on carrying out the affairs of government properly, and does not value rare and precious things. Now you, O King, have presented various objects to the throne, and mindful to your loyalty . . . , we have specifically ordered the Department of Foreign Tribute to receive them. . . . Nevertheless we have never valued ingenious articles, nor do we have the slightest need of your country's manufactures. . . . You, O King, should simply act in conformity with our wishes by strengthening your loyalty and swearing perpetual obedience so as to ensure that your country may share the blessings of peace.[5]

If only Qianlong could have foreseen what would come to pass within half a century. The British would return, not as emissaries respectfully requesting diplomatic and commercial relations on the basis of equality, but as warriors out to impose their will on China. Toward the middle of the nineteenth century, Britain had the military might to kick open the door, and that is precisely what it proceeded to do. For years the British East India Company had been importing opium from India into China, in complete contravention of Chinese law. For the British, the trade was immensely profitable; for the Chinese, it was a scourge: not only did it weaken the nation by turning its people into abject addicts, it also weakened the economy because the Chinese paid for the opium by shipping out huge amounts of silver. The Chinese attempt to stop the trade by burning stocks of British-owned opium led to war, which ended in 1842 with China's defeat. The Chinese government was forced to sign the Treaty of Nanjing, first of the so-called unequal treaties. According to this document, and a subsequent agreement signed in the following year, China ceded Hong Kong to Britain (China did not recover it until 1997), and accepted other humiliating conditions. The success of gunboat diplomacy, as it came to be known, emboldened other Western powers to follow suit. One after the other, the foreign powers exacted concessions from China by the threat of force or the actual use of force when threats failed.

The weakness of their country in the face of Western imperialism came as a profound shock to the elite of China. Ideas about what should be done varied, but over the next 75 years the remedies proposed became increasingly radical. At first, diehard reactionaries rejected any thought that China needed to undergo fundamental reform, much less that it had anything to learn from the West. But, facing one humiliating defeat after another, it became clear to a group of progressives, known as the Self-Strengtheners, that what China needed was to acquire the physical accouterments that seemed to be the key to Western power while reinvigorating what they thought to be China's cultural strengths. Under the formula "Chinese learning as the base, Western learning for practical use," the Self-Strengtheners built arsenals, established institutes to translate Western works on technology and science, and conscripted and trained armies that, they hoped, could defeat the foreign powers on the battlefield.

The Self-Strengthening Movement played a crucial role in launching modern industry and in promoting Western technology and science. But it failed miserably in stemming the tide of Western encroachment. In part this was because the imperial government, inept and corrupt as it was, threw up obstacles almost every step of the way. It also failed because advanced, Western technology could not be easily separated from the ideology and social institutions that surrounded it. Thus, the effort to graft modern technology to an age-old, unreformed social system was probably doomed from the start.

The list of China's humiliations grew longer and longer as the foreign powers one after the other defeated China in several wars, and "carved up the melon" that was China. The growing crisis caused an increasing number of intellectuals to move beyond the formula offered by the Self-Strengtheners and to promote basic institutional reform, including constitutional monarchy. In the very last years of the nineteenth century a number of dramatic reforms in education, law, technology, and other crucial areas were announced, but the reforms remained largely on paper, as cultural and political conservatives throttled any attempt at fundamental change.

At about the same time, a popular antiforeign movement was beginning to rage across North China. In the summer of 1900 the Boxers, as they came to be known, marched from eastern China into Beijing, along the way attacking Christian communities and symbols of imperialism. The Boxers, so named because they were adept at traditional martial arts (including the "boxing" seen in popular kung-fu movies), followed various rituals that they thought made them invulnerable to swords and bullets. The result was another crushing defeat for China. The foreign powers assembled an army, marched on Beijing, and smashed the Boxers.

The Qing dynasty limped along until 1911, when it finally fell, bringing to a close the 2,000-year-long imperial era. Although in its final years the dynasty implemented a number of reforms, it was a case of too little too late. The notion of constitutional monarchy continued to have its adherents, but the trend in political thought had shifted toward republicanism. The leading figure in the republican movement was Sun Yat-sen (1866–1925), who had been educated partly in Hawaii, got medical training in Hong Kong, and after years of agitation for a republican revolution, became China's first president in 1912. Sun, and those who thought like him, were inspired by notions of liberalism and democracy as found in the West. In any case, within six months Sun was ousted from office by the powerful militarist and reformer Yuan Shikai (1859–1916), and China was soon divided among a number of military figures who became known as warlords. The warlords fought among themselves for control, and plunged China into a nightmare of internal warfare, disunity, and vulnerability that did not really come to a close until the victory of the Communists in 1949.

Cultural Iconoclasm and Communism

The warlords in the end proved to be less of a threat to republican ideals in China than did a march to the left among influential thinkers that culminated in the formation of the Chinese Communist Party. The depredations of the warlords, and their utter failure to resist imperialism, convinced many Chinese that only a radical solution could save China. Some radicals remained enamored of Western-style democracy, but felt that salvation would come not principally through political action but rather through a sweeping reshaping of culture. Other radicals agreed that China's traditional culture was the source of its weakness, but felt that cultural reform had to go hand in hand with political revolution.

This political and intellectual ferment came to be known as the New Culture Movement. This movement, which began around 1915, gradually melded with the May Fourth Movement, which took its name from a demonstration staged on May 4, 1919, by students from Beijing University and other schools in the capital against the anti-Chinese provisions of the Versailles Treaty, which resolved issues left over from World War I. What most rankled the students was that although China had been a member of the victorious Allied powers (which included France, Great Britain, and the United States), the so-called German concessions in the province of Shandong, land and privileges that Germany had wrung from China via an unequal treaty in the ninenteenth century, were not returned to China, but handed to Japan. The spirit that animated iconoclastic youth of the May Fourth era combined a fervent nationalism with a struggle against what people perceived to be the "dead hand" of China's past. In an article published in *New Youth* magazine in 1919, Chen Duxiu (1879–1942), dean of Arts and Sciences at Beijing University and a leading figure in the New Culture Movement, declared:

> They accused this magazine on the grounds that it intended to destroy Confucianism, the code of rituals, the "national quintessence," chastity of women, traditional ethics . . . , traditional arts . . . , traditional religion (ghosts and gods), and ancient literature, as well as old-fashioned politics (privileges and government by men alone).
>
> All of these charges are conceded. But we plead not guilty. We have committed the alleged crimes only because we supported the two gentlemen, Mr. Democracy and Mr. Science. In order to advocate Mr. Democracy, we are obliged to oppose Confucianism, the codes of rituals, chastity of women, traditional ethics, and old-fashioned politics; in order to advocate Mr. Science, we have to oppose traditional arts and traditional religion; in order to advocate both Mr. Democracy and Mr. Science, we are compelled to oppose the cult of the "national quintessence" and ancient literature.[6]

Chen's reference to Mr. Democracy and Mr. Science had great meaning for radical thinkers. In their mind, what gave the West its wealth and strength, what made it so progressive, and what made it so different from traditional China were its democratic values and its science. The insurmountable problem for the May Fourth generation was that their scientism clashed with their nationalism. While the West seemed to be the model of modern, progressive, democratic, and scientific society, the Western powers also continued to exploit China. The West thus simultaneously attracted and repelled progressive Chinese thinkers. How could this dilemma be resolved?

To an increasing number of young radicals, the answer appeared in the quintessential nineteenth-century political philosophy of Marxism. And what brought Marxism to the fore was the October 1917 Communist revolution in Russia. The attraction of Russia was that it was a large, and by Western European standards, poor, and backward country, yet by violent revolution it had thrown off the yoke of the past, and had launched upon a great social experiment to—so it claimed—eradicate the exploitation of man by man, industrialize the economy, and lead mankind into a future of happiness and equality.

Moreover, as a political philosophy Marxism had great attraction since it purported to be "scientific"; indeed, the Communists proclaimed that theirs was a "scientific socialism." No matter that the "science" of Marxism specified that the Communist revolution would be led by the industrial workers and naturally would take place in the most advanced industrial nations of the world—a description that definitely did not fit China early in the twentieth century, when it had no more than 2 million industrial workers. With incredible contortions, later theorists twisted and distorted Marxism in order to "explain" why revolution had broken out in Russia and why it could succeed even in poor and backward China.

The Chinese Communist Party (CCP) was formally established in 1921 by a handful of young men led by Chen Duxiu, the professor at Beijing University, and closely advised by agents sent by Moscow. For the next few years, the CCP generally followed the line laid down by Moscow's advisors. In 1923 the CCP, at the behest of Moscow, entered into a "united front" with the Nationalist Party (Guomindang) of Sun Yat-sen for the purpose of jointly struggling to unify the country, remove the warlord scourge, and resist foreign imperialism. In 1926 the Nationalist army, supported by worker and peasant organizations led in many cases by the Communists, launched the Northern Expedition, a campaign that struck out from the southern province of Guangdong with the goal of defeating the warlord forces as the army marched northward. In April 1927, as the Nationalist army entered Shanghai, Chiang Kai-shek (1887–1975), who had emerged as Sun Yat-sen's successor after 1925, staged a bloody coup, expelling the Communists from the united front and rounding up and executing as many of them as could be found. Thereafter the CCP, again at Moscow's urging, staged several armed uprisings in a few towns and cities, all of which ended in disastrous defeat. The remnants of the Communist armed forces retreated to remote areas in the countryside, where the Nationalists could not easily dislodge them and where they could begin to organize the peasants for revolution.

The War with Japan and the Chinese Civil War

The Communist movement in China might well have withered and disappeared in the 1930s had it not been for a fortuitous development. In 1931, the Japanese army invaded and occupied Manchuria. Although the local warlord resisted, the national government, now headed by Chiang Kai-shek, did nothing. Chiang justified his inaction by arguing that the Japanese were a "disease of the skin," while the Communists were a "disease of the heart" and thus had to be eradicated first. This decision proved to be a drastic mistake. A wave of outrage swept across China as people of all walks of life demanded that the country be defended from the invading Japanese. The

Communists capitalized on this by making a patriotic appeal for a second united front and all-out resistance to the Japanese. Chiang, however, remained adamant, and launched several "extermination" campaigns against the Communist strongholds. The last of these campaigns nearly succeeded. In late 1934, the Nationalists had encircled the main Communist forces in the hills of the province of Jiangxi. In a desperate move, the Communists broke out of the trap and in a year-long 6,000-mile march, fled to Yan'an, a poor and remote spot in the northern province of Shaanxi. Of the 100,000 who left Jiangxi, only 6,000 or so arrived in Yan'an. This rout, which became known appropriately enough as the Long March, the Communists later portrayed as a decisive moment on the road to victory.

Mopping up the remnants of the Communists looked to be an easy job, but in 1937 the Japanese launched a full-scale invasion of China that completely changed the picture. Reluctantly, Chiang accepted a second united front with the Communists, but real cooperation between the two sides was rare and they often seemed to devote more energy to fighting each other than the Japanese. The war with Japan cost the Nationalists dearly. The government retreated to the interior province of Sichuan, where it was cut off from important sources of revenue and from the coastal cities, such as Shanghai, which were its main sources of political support. By the time the war ended in 1945, the Communists had built up a strong, disciplined army and controlled substantial territory, particularly in North China. But in the civil war that soon broke out the advantage still appeared to lie with the Nationalists, whose army was at least twice as large the CCP's. Yet, for all its strength on paper, the Nationalist army suffered from several debilities, not the least of which was that it imperfectly incorporated several warlord armies whose leaders Chiang had been unwilling or unable to replace. These warlord-led forces had nominally become part of the Nationalist army, but in fact Chiang exercised little control over them.

This may not have been a mortal flaw for the elite units loyal to Chiang were well trained and well equipped by the United States. However, as a strategist and tactician, Chiang was not the equal of the Communist generals, and time after time he was outmaneuvered and outfought. However, as is usually the case in civil wars, the decisive struggle took place not on the battlefield but on the political front. Here the Nationalists helped defeat themselves. As inflation began to rage across China, the Nationalist government fed the flames by printing money as fast as possible until it literally became worth not much more than the paper it was printed on. The hardest hit were those, such as schoolteachers and civil servants, who lived on fixed salaries. It was precisely this group of middle-class predominantly urban dwellers who, under other circumstances, would have been the backbone of public support for the Nationalists. Furthermore, corruption began to eat away at the Nationalist government, which further eroded public support and undermined the morale of honest officials.

Reeling from defeat after defeat, the Nationalists finally retreated to the island province of Taiwan in 1949, and on October 1 Mao Zedong (1893–1976), the chairman and one of the founders of the CCP, standing on the rostrum above the Gate of Heavenly Peace at the head of Tiananmen Square, declared the establishment of the People's Republic of China (PRC). To this day the CCP considers the civil war unfinished because Taiwan remains independent and beyond its control. Reunifying the country by "returning Taiwan to the motherland"—by force if necessary—remains a paramount goal. In the half century since the Nationalists fled the mainland, however, the situation has become much more complicated. Taiwan has developed into a democracy, and the Nationalist's monopoly on power there has been broken; in 2000 Taiwan freely elected a president from an opposition party. Moreover, in the more than 50 years that Taiwan has been separated from the mainland, its people have lived a very different life from their erstwhile compatriots on the mainland. Even in 1949 there were important differences arising from the fact that Taiwan had been a colony of Japan from 1895 to 1945, as a result of the first Sino-Japanese War (1894–95), which ended with China ceding the island to Japan. Recent surveys show that an increasing number of people on Taiwan consider themselves to be "Taiwanese" rather than "Chinese," or "Taiwanese first, and Chinese second."

Land Reform, Collectivization, and the Great Leap Forward

In the first decade of its existence, the PRC followed the usual pattern of Communist revolutions by collectivizing the farmland and nationalizing the factories and other property of capitalists. In the countryside, in the so-called Land Reform (1949–52) the property of landlords was confiscated and re-distributed to "poor peasants," and thereafter land was collectivized step by step, culminating in 1958 in the formation of super-collectives known as "people's communes." The communes quickly turned out to be a disaster. In effect, all the output created by the thousands of people living in a com-mune was lumped together and then doled out on the basis of "need" or "work points" (see Chapter 6). In such a system, incentives almost evaporated as it became hard to see any correlation between the amount of work one did and the amount of pay one received. Output fell so drastically that famine broke out in 1959, resulting in 20 to 40 million deaths, and forcing the government to scale back the size of the communes. Collectivized agriculture continued until 1978, when, as part of a sweeping reform, the so-called responsibility system was introduced, which turned control of farmland back to individual households, in effect reintroducing private agriculture to China.

The commune movement coincided with another ill-conceived program, the Great Leap Forward. In 1958, under the slogan "more, better, quicker, cheaper," the government set out to mobilize the entire country to achieve rapid industrialization, symbolized by the declared goal of surpassing Britain in industrial production within 15 years. In the drive to increase production at all costs, quantity triumphed over quality. State-run factories, which did not have to be profitable, competed to acquire as many raw materials as possible, regardless of the cost, and then to churn out as much finished product as possible, regardless of the quality. Overall, the effect of the Great Leap Forward was to increase inefficiencies and imbalances and to reward profligate waste.

For all that, the rationale behind the commune movement and the Great Leap Forward made sense: if China were to develop, it would have to do so by pulling itself up by its own bootstraps. There was no alternative to self-reliance simply because China was isolated internationally. The enmity of the United States was a given, because of China's Communist ideology, because China and the United States fought a bitter war in Korea (1950–53), and because China "leaned to one side," as Mao Zedong put it—that is to say it supported the Soviet Union in the Cold War with the United States. The United States for its part did all it could to isolate and "contain" China, by refusing official diplomatic recognition, by prohibiting trade, by—in the Chinese view—interfering in China's internal affairs by protecting Taiwan, and even by making it illegal for Americans to travel to China. By 1958 China was becoming even more isolated as fundamental disagreements with the Soviet Union began to surface over such issues as "peaceful coexistence" with the capitalist world. In 1960 the rupture became total, with the Soviet Union withdrawing its advisors from China and China condemning the Soviets as "revisionists" and "social imperialists." Thereafter China found its friends and allies wherever it could among a handful of small and poor countries that could make no contribution whatsoever to China's development needs. In the Cultural Revolution decade (1966–76), China's "greatest friend" became tiny Albania, Europe's poorest country and an international pariah because of its paranoid totalitarianism. Even that faintly ludicrous relationship did not last, and China and Albania ended up hurling epithets at one another.

If the economic rationale behind what is often called the Maoist model of development made sense, the execution generally failed and thus the results fell short of what the leadership had expected. Nonetheless, the achievements of the PRC in its first 30 years are still impressive. Overall, and despite the setbacks of the Great Leap Forward, between 1949 and 1978 the economy grew at an annual rate of around 6%, diseases such as smallpox and diphtheria that had been prevalent in 1949 were eradicated, at least in the cities, and life expectancy increased from 39 years to 64 years. Even the simple joys of life were not left behind: beer production increased from 7,000 tons in 1949 to 400,000 tons in 1978.

Class Struggle and the Cultural Revolution

Following a rigid, and in many ways artificial, system the Communists after 1949 assigned everyone a class status (*shenfen*), a status that in most cases individuals not only bore for life and could not escape, but also a status that branded a family from generation to generation. Class was, following Marxist theory, supposedly based on objective, material criteria: principally whether one owned land or other property and how one made one's living (whether as an employee or an employer). Moreover, and most importantly, it was on the basis of one's class status that one was judged a member of "the people" or a member of the "exploiting classes" (and was thus by definition an enemy of "the people"). Whether one was placed in one of the classes that was considered a part of "the people," or on the other side of the dividing line, among the enemies, had a profound effect on one's life and the life of one's children (and grandchildren, in many cases). A typical result of being born into a family with a "bad class background" was recalled by a senior middle school student in 1964:

> One student was very famous in our school because of his grades. He was said to be the best student [School] Number 28 had produced in recent memory. He was also a veteran YCL [Young Communist League] member and had been on the school YCL committee. He was very active in school politics and was outstanding in sports. Of course his class background was very bad, but he had long seemed to have overcome it. When this student was not able to gain entrance to any university [presumably because of his "bad" class background], it caused something of an uproar among students of the school. Those of bad class background, and even some of middle class background, were stunned and went around saying to each other, "If he can't make it, what chance have I?"[7]

As this anecdote reveals, as a rule no matter how exemplary and revolutionary one's behavior, one was locked into one's class status forever. Furthermore, although class status was based on objective criteria, this is not to say that it was necessarily reasonable or fair. "Landlords" (the worst class background), for instance, were defined as those who owned farmland but rented it to tenants and did not work it themselves. This class, then, could include those who by Chinese standards owned large tracts of land and lived relatively comfortably, as well as poor, old widows who owned a scrap of land that brought in barely enough rent to keep them fed.

While the initial assignment of people to classes could at least be justified by citing Marxist-Leninist dogma (the "exploiters" owned property, and lived off the goods produced by the labor of the property-less working class), how could one justify continuing to apply class labels after the material basis of classes had disappeared? How could the state condemn a person as, for instance, a "landlord" when that person no longer owned any land? How could classes in fact continue to exist once virtually all productive private property had been expropriated? By the mid-1960s, Mao Zedong had become concerned almost to the point of obsession that people in China, including some of his closest comrades in arms, were reaching the wrong answer to these questions, that they were beginning to think that class no longer mattered, that they were forgetting class struggle. Mao came to believe that if this trend went unchecked, there was the danger of "capitalist restoration" in China. Since, from Mao's perspective, the biggest "capitalist roaders" were not only inside the CCP, but occupied the very highest positions there, the only way to root them out was to attack them from outside the Party. This in brief was the genesis of the Great Proletarian Cultural Revolution (1966–76), a chaotic, confusing, violent upsurge that, at least during its heyday in 1966–68, tore the country apart.

The Cultural Revolution

Mao's shock troops were the Red Guards, youth all the way down to middle school students, who organized themselves into bands that competed with each other, sometimes violently, to "drag out the handful" in the CCP that were "following the capitalist road" and to "smash the remnants of the decadent old society," all with the blessing of Chairman Mao. The suffering and destruction at the hands of the Red Guards was appalling. Yue Daiyun, a professor of Chinese literature at Beijing University, recalls an encounter with the Red Guards, a very mild incident when compared to the beatings— and worse—endured by many:

Late one night [in August 1966] a group of seven or eight young people, none of whom I recognized, pounded on our door. Demanding that we open every glass bookcase, they strewed the contents about the room. The most valuable set of books in our library was the *Buddhist Canon,* only four copies of which remained in the country. . . . The

students announced that all such books were superstitious . . . and confiscated one volume from each boxed set, declaring that these would
be thoroughly investigated. . . . When the search party demanded to
see our records, I reluctantly brought out my precious stack of classical
music. . . . The Red Guards methodically shattered every disc with a
large rock, then, satisfied with their revolutionary action, left the house.
Numbly I pick up the useless pieces, piled them in a dustpan, and
carried them out to the trash heap.[8]

By 1968 the Red Guards had succeeded in driving out those top leaders
in the CCP who opposed Mao. Many leaders were hauled before mass rallies,
where they were beaten, abused, and humiliated. Liu Shaoqi (1898?–1969),
the head of state of the PRC (1959–68) and thought to be Mao's successor
before the start of the Cultural Revolution, was villified as "the No. 1 Party
person in authority taking the capitalist road," then thrown into prison,
where he died, allegedly because he was denied medicine for his diabetes.
Thousands of people, big and small, in and out of the Party, were killed, or,
like Lao She (1899–1966), a renowned author beloved for his humor and
sympathy for the poor and downtrodden, committed suicide.

The Red Guards succeeded in wreaking havoc throughout the country.
To resurrect some semblance of balance and stability, Mao called on the
army to round up the Red Guards and other urban youth—14 million in
total—and send them out into the countryside to "make revolution" by
working the land. From that point until Mao's death in 1976, the CCP was
reconstructed and many of those who had been purged were brought back
in.

The Post-Mao Reform

In 1978, Deng Xiaoping (1904–97), one of the top Party leaders who had
been purged during the Cultural Revolution but was later rehabilitated to
become the most powerful figure in China, launched a sweeping reform
movement that reached into all corners of society. The object of the reform
was to modernize China and bring it wealth and power, essentially the same
goals as the Maoist program, but by radically different means. Under Deng
and his successor Jiang Zemin, the farms have been decollectivized, more
and more state-owned industries are being privatized, and individual initia-
tive and private enterprise have been encouraged—as Deng proclaimed, "To
get rich is glorious." Moreover, under a so-called open-door policy, foreign
investment (usually in the form of joint ventures with state-owned Chinese
enterprises) has exploded, growing from virtually nothing in 1978 to an
estimated $640 billion in 2000. Under the reform, the economy has boomed,

although the benefits have not been evenly distributed and the rising tide of prosperity has left many people behind. At the same time, class struggle, the defining feature of Maoism, has essentially disappeared from the Party's rhetoric. The economic good times and the end of the worst abuses of class struggle, together with a strident nationalism, seem to have become the basis for the legitimacy of the rule of the CCP. As such, one cannot help but wonder about the stability of the government once an economic downturn appears, as it inevitably must.

The foundation of the reform can be summed up in one word: pragmatism. As Deng Xiaoping put it, "It doesn't matter if the cat is black or white as long as it catches mice." The pragmatism and openness, however, have strict limits, particularly when it comes to politics. When the economic reform began, many people inside China and out hoped that political reform would develop apace, and in particular that democracy would somehow emerge. In fact, political reform has taken place; many counties now have elections for local-level leaders, and the legal system has grown more sophisticated and open, so much so that people have sued government bureaus and often won. Furthermore, the political atmosphere is incomparably freer than it was 20 years ago, and it is quite common for people to criticize the government openly. But democracy is impossible since the CCP has made it abundantly clear that it, and it alone, must continue to rule China. As Deng once declared, the authorities must resist "any tendency inside or outside the Party which weakens or opposes the Party's leadership."[9]

The insecurity of the CCP and its absolute intolerance of any organized opposition was amply displayed in 1989. In the spring of that year, university students, especially in Beijing, staged massive demonstrations in support of democracy. In a highly symbolic move, demonstrators occupied Tiananmen Square in the center of Beijing, and several launched a hunger strike. Most of the demonstrators did not have a clear idea of what they wanted. None said they wanted to overthrow the CCP, and all said they wanted democracy, but few were able to articulate what they meant by that. At first, the government attempted to persuade the students to disband; Zhao Ziyang (b. 1919), then general secretary of the CCP and second in power only to Deng Xiaoping, personally went into Tiananmen Square to plead with the demonstrators. And Li Peng, in an equally extraordinary move, agreed to meet with several student leaders. At the interview, which was filmed, Li made no effort to hide the disgust on his face as the students rudely lectured him: the arrogant berating the arrogant.

The pleading and willingness to talk did no good, and the government then raised the stakes by imposing martial law. But still the students refused to disperse. Then, at last, the army was called in, and on the night of June

4 it moved to clear Tiananmen Square, shooting and crushing demonstrators in the streets near the square beneath tank tracks, killing and wounding hundreds in the process. Before the bloodshed, the people of China, who watched the democracy movement unfold, as well as the tens of millions around the world who also saw it on television, probably wondered if the authorities would really order the army to shoot unarmed students and civilians. After June 4, all doubt was dispelled. No one could any longer doubt that the CCP was capable of unleashing deadly force against anyone it perceived as a threat to its rule. At the same time, since 1989 the government has remained committed to Deng Xiaoping's policy of openness and reform, so that China has led Asia and much of the rest of the world in economic growth over the last decade.

As for the democracy movement, it has withered since the Tiananmen incident. Its leaders are in jail or in exile, and although occasionally there are people who, for instance, have tried to organize opposition political parties, they are quickly thrown into prison. Today, the Chinese people are absorbed not in fighting for what, at least for now, appears impossible, namely, democracy, but in struggling to achieve what is possible, namely a better and richer material life.

NOTES

1. This anecdote was related by Hoyt Tillman in a personal communication.

2. Throughout this book, all monetary values are in U.S. dollars.

3. *Beijing Scene* 6, no. 8 (Dec. 3–9, 1999), http://www.beijingscene.com (June 5, 2000).

4. Lin Yutang, *My Country and My People* (New York: John Day, 1935), p. 18.

5. Quoted in Alain Peyrefitte, *The Immobile Empire* (New York: Alfred A. Knopf, 1992), pp. 289–92.

6. Quoted in Chow Tse-tsung, *The May Fourth Movement: Intellectual Revolution in Modern China* (Stanford, CA: Stanford University Press, 1960), p. 59.

7. Quoted in Stanley Rosen, *Red Guard Factionalism and the Cultural Revolution in Guangzhou (Canton)* (Boulder, CO: Westview Press, 1982), p. 89.

8. Yue Daiyun and Carolyn Wakeman, *To the Storm: The Odyssey of a Revolutionary Chinese Woman* (Berkeley: University of California Press, 1985), pp. 167–68.

9. *Dagong bao* (Jan. 27, 1981).

2

Thought and Religion

TO SEPARATE Chinese philosophy and ways of thought in their broadest sense as general beliefs, concepts, and attitudes, from Chinese religion, is difficult. When an outsider, watching rituals and observances that certainly appear religious, asks Chinese practitioners, "What religion do these observances belong to?" a common reply, often given with a puzzled expression on the face, is "Why, these are just Chinese ways of doing things." Part of the reason for this answer stems from a fluidity of thinking, a proclivity for eclectically accepting—or rejecting—ideas and notions without feeling that systems of thought or belief must be accepted in toto, to the exclusion of competing or contradictory ideas. In this way, the sum total of a person's beliefs and concepts can be, and usually is, made up of disparate pieces taken from here and there. It is misleading to label such a bundle of beliefs and concepts with a single word such as, for instance, "Buddhist."

Another reason for this answer is that certain beliefs and observances are accepted as a matter of course, so that they are not conceived of as belonging to a special category called "religion." For a great many people, to be "Chinese" is to speak the Chinese language, to live in China (or have one's ancestral home in China), and to "act Chinese," which would include, among other things, worshiping or venerating one's ancestors.

Of course, some Chinese strongly identify with a system of belief, such as communism, or religion, such as Islam, that expects or demands exclusivity. Such people are not necessarily any less "Chinese" for this, and the Communists indeed for the past two decades have spoken of "socialism with Chinese characteristics." What the Communists mean by this is unclear—probably no more than "socialism" (that is, communism) as practiced in

China, or more specifically, the policies and programs of the Chinese Communist Party. The CCP would dearly like people to believe these policies and programs are a reflection of Chinese culture, or that they are somehow imbued with the essence of Chinese culture. This argument represents a fundamental shift from the line of the CCP during the Maoist years, when it was often said that China was, in Mao's words, "poor and blank." Mao could not have been more wrong: instead of being "blank," China was filled with a profound traditional culture that resisted the machinations of the Communists at every turn. The Communists today are no less wrong in thinking that their ideology is somehow "Chinese."

THOUGHT

On February 2, 1974, the front page of virtually all major newspapers of almost all major cities in the world provided exactly what readers expected: news of current events, perhaps a human interest item or two, and possibly a weather report. *People's Daily*, the official newspaper of the Chinese Communist Party, however, splashed across its front page the headline "Continue the Struggle for Criticizing Lin Biao and Confucius to the End."

An article on struggling to criticize Lin Biao might be expected. After all, Lin Biao, the erstwhile number two man in the Communist Party, had apparently plotted to assassinate China's paramount leader, Mao Zedong (but in the attempt had lost his own life). But what sense could there be in criticizing Confucius, a philosopher who had been dead for almost 2,500 years?

In fact, by early 1974 a huge campaign to criticize Confucius had been underway for about half a year. The criticizing was carried out all across society: in lectures, posters, writings, songs, plays, even in comics. Try to imagine something comparable in the United States: a massive movement to repudiate Plato, with messages criticizing the ancient Greek philosopher plastered on billboards, with critical articles in every newspaper and magazine, with television specials on his evils, with songs condemning Plato on every radio station, and so forth. As if such a development in the United States were not surrealistic enough, imagine that a decade later the situation were entirely and completely reversed: Plato is once again a cultural hero, with the president reminding the people of the country that "we all should learn from Plato."

What would be surrealistic in the United States is precisely what happened in China. Within less than a decade Confucius was thoroughly rehabilitated. In 1989 Jiang Zemin himself, the president of China, praised Confucius as "one of China's great thinkers" and declared that the people of China "must thoroughly study his fine ideals and carry them into the future."

How can what happened in China be understood? Much of the answer lies in the fact that in 1974 the Communists were using Confucius as a symbol of the old society they wished to eradicate. They were also evidently using him as a surrogate for someone high up in the Party who was still powerful and could not be attacked openly, a technique they often employed. People thought the target might be Zhou Enlai (1898–1976), China's prime minister, who sat on the Party's Political Bureau for 48 years—a record— but never vied for ultimate leadership and instead faithfully served the Party and its top leader. Confucius too, as we shall see, did not seek to be a ruler but rather to find and faithfully serve a worthy king. In any case, the campaign would have made no sense unless contemporary Chinese felt that Confucius was relevant to life today, that his ideas, and those of other ancient thinkers, still had the power—for good or ill—to shape society. The past is very much a part of China's present; in no other society does history loom so large.

The Origins of Chinese Thought and Philosophy

Confucius (551–479 B.C.) lived in a time of crisis. In the face of endemic warfare and a sustained assault on traditional notions of propriety and social organization, society was undergoing a protracted, fundamental transformation of customs, manners, economics, and political organization. As often happens in such times, a yearning for stability, peace, and harmony led people to reflect on some of the fundamental questions of human existence. This, the era of the "Hundred Schools" of philosophy from the sixth through the third centuries B.C., roughly coincided with the golden age of Greek philosophy, when men like Plato (429–347 B.C.) and Aristotle (384–321 B.C.) laid the foundations for the basic ways of thought in Western civilization.

In China during this era, the proponents of various philosophies and ways of thinking ranged from the Legalists, who favored strict application of the law, and whose greatest thinker Han Feizi (ca. 280–233 B.C.) declared that "punishments should be severe and definite so that the people will fear them"; to logicians such as Gongsun Long (4th–3rd century B.C.), who is remembered for such rarified arguments as "a white horse is not a horse"; to the so-called Naturalists, such as Zou Yan (ca. 305–240 B.C.), who speculated about the laws of the universe and who is sometimes credited with writing China's first book on geography (now lost); to "realistic" Confucians such as Xunzi (ca. 298–238 B.C.), who tried to reconcile Legalism and Confucianism and declared that human nature is intrinsically bad; to Sun Wu (ca. 5th century B.C.), who is credited with writing *Sunzi's Art of War*, a text on the conduct and principles of warfare. All these schools of thought and thinkers, as well as many others, left an imprint on Chinese thinking. To take one example, Sun Wu's text has been read all through Chinese history, and was extolled by Mao Zedong for helping the Communists win victory in 1949.

Ultimately, after many centuries, two schools emerged dominant in China: Confucianism and Daoism. Although very different in most respects, these two were also complementary. Confucianism was fundamentally conservative: Confucius the philosopher considered himself not an innovator but a transmitter of traditional values and practices. But there was another aspect of Confucius as well. While he espoused traditional institutions and values, Confucius gave them his own interpretations. Chinese thinkers throughout the ages tended to look toward the past as a golden age, as a time that was somehow purer than the present, as a font of ideas and traditions that remain only to be discovered, understood, and applied in order to achieve the best possible society. At the same time, respect for tradition rarely degenerated into a rigid attempt to prevent reinterpretation of the past. Rather, the wisdom of past generations tended to be considered a set of principles to be absorbed, interpreted, and applied in order to solve life's contemporary problems. Thus, Confucianism as it evolved was fundamentally a practical philosophy, a guide to living. This too reflects the fact that Confucius, and the people who came after him and strove to apply his teachings, were practical people. Confucius sought to become an advisor to a wise ruler in order to put into practice his ideas for reforming society. This sort of connection between philosophy and practicality, especially in the sense that learned men should mold society and serve it by leading government, has been an enduring feature of Chinese thought.

If one were to distill the essence of Confucianism, one might say it is a guide to harmonious and stable human relationships. Confucius emphasized that in life each person has a role, or several roles, to perform. As he put it, "Let the ruler act as a ruler should, the minister as a minister, the father as a father, and the son as a son." In other words, each role in life entails norms or social expectations to which individual behavior should conform. Furthermore, life's roles are hierarchically organized. Thus, in the Confucian scheme men are superior to women, parents to children, and rulers to subjects. However, while human relations are hierarchical, they are also reciprocal. The obligation of men is to cherish and protect women, of parents to love their children, of rulers to teach and enrich their subjects.

How are people to know what is expected of them in each of their roles? The answer for Confucians down through the ages has been clear: education. Confucius himself was mainly an educator. For much of his life he devoted

himself to instructing a group of disciples, teaching them by setting an example, but also by applying the Socratic method of dialogue. The *Analects*,
a text assembled by Confucius's followers after his death, consists almost
entirely of questions put to the philosopher by his disciples and his answers
to them. The overwhelming majority of the passages in the *Analects* begin
with the words "The Master said," which are followed by Confucius's ex-
position of his precepts. The very first words in the *Analects* indicate the
centrality of learning: "The Master said, 'Is it not a pleasure to learn with
constant perseverance and application?' "

The implications of the simple notion that proper behavior is something
to be learned and cultivated are profound. First, education and learning
become of paramount importance. Throughout its history, China has been
unsurpassed by any other nation in its devotion to learning. Second, per-
fectibility is within the grasp of everyone. If one learns how one ought to act
in society, that is, to follow one's duties (Confucius called this *yi*, righteous-
ness); and if one learns the rules of propriety (*li*), that is, the rules of conduct
and ceremonies laid down in the ancient records; and finally, if one becomes
imbued with what is the core Confucian virtue, *ren* (benevolence, or human-
heartedness), that is, consideration for others, and acts in accordance with
what one has learned, then one will become what Confucius called a *junzi*,
a "superior man." Third, Chinese society has generally accepted that it is
men of learning, "superior men" in the Confucian scheme, who must lead
society. Thus throughout the 2,000-year history of the Chinese empire the
hereditary nobility, the priesthood, and the military—groups that governed
many other traditional societies—were relatively weak. Instead, the state usually was governed by a bureaucracy of officials selected on the basis of merit.
As a rule merit was determined by examination. At least in theory, almost
any man (but not women), no matter how humble his origins, could sit for
the examinations and, if he passed them, might rise to the very highest
stations in society. This social mobility—or at least, possibility of social mobility—greatly contributed to social stability. The main feature distinguishing the Chinese bureaucracy from a modern civil service was that in the
former the examinations required an incredibly thorough, detailed, and intimate knowledge of ancient texts, mainly the so-called Confucian classics.
To prepare for the examinations required years of single-minded study, including memorization of a prodigious quantity of textual material. Passing
the imperial examinations did not necessarily guarantee an official post, but
it did confer great status and authority. Western scholars of China have called
this class of men who passed the examinations "scholar-officials."

Complementing and in many ways balancing Confucianism was Daoism,
a philosophy that emphasizes nature and escape from rigid, rule-bound so-

ciety. *Dao* (literally "the way," or "the road") referred to something that is difficult to put one's finger on, something rather mystic. "The Dao that can be described in words is not the eternal Dao; the name that can be named is not the eternal name. The unnamable is the beginning of heaven and earth; the namable is the mother of all things. . . . The Dao is eternal, nameless." The words are from the *Laozi*, also known as the *Daodejing* (The classic of the way and the virtue), a text whose provenance is as cloudy as its contents: it is thought to be a collection from several sources (its authors and compilers are unknown) around the time of Confucius, and it purports to contain the words of Laozi (lit., the Old Master), a person about whom nothing is known with certainty, if indeed he existed at all.

Daoism advocated individual freedom and attunement to nature. As the *Laozi* explains, "The more restrictions and prohibitions there are in the world, the poorer the people will be. . . . The more laws that are promulgated, the more thieves and bandits there will be." In the eyes of the Daoists, laws, rules, regulations—the essence of government—are established to regularize human relations, establish uniformity, and suppress difference. The problem with this is that it goes against nature. The *Zhuangzi*, a text probably compiled in the third century A.D. of materials from various periods and purporting to be the words of the philosopher Zhuangzi (ca. third century B.C.), recounts a story of what can happen when nature is ignored: "Long ago, when a seabird alighted outside the capital of Lu, the marquis went out to welcome it, gave it wine in the temple, had . . . music played to entertain it, and had a steer slaughtered to feed it. But the bird was confused and too timid to eat or drink. In three days it was dead. This was because the bird was treated as one would treat oneself, not as a bird. . . . Water is life to fish but death to man. Being differently constituted, their likes and dislikes must necessarily differ." The Daoist ideal, then, is near anarchy in the sense of no government. People should avoid conventional social obligations, follow their inclinations, and pursue a quiet, simple, and spontaneous life close to nature. With such a prescription for life, what need is there for government?

From time to time, various rulers found Daoism congenial, but since rulers are usually concerned with acquiring and wielding power, not with throwing it away, Daoism never found much application in government. It did, however, have a great influence on art and literature, and on popular or folk religion.

Since Confucianism and Daoism offered fundamentally different answers to questions about human nature, the ideal form of government, and so on, at first glance they might seem to be totally incompatible. However, they also shared connections and commonalities that made it possible to weave them together into patterns of thought that sustained elite society—and deeply influenced all levels of Chinese society—for over two millennia. This intermeshing of disparate and often antithetical ideas and notions, this propensity to hold ideas that may be contradictory, is a fundamental characteristic of Chinese thinking.

Patterns of Thought: Continuity and Change

In his *Short History of Chinese Philosophy*, published in 1948, Feng Youlan devotes more than half of his discussion, 216 pages, to the period from the Warring States (from 475 B.C.) to the founding of the Han dynasty (206 B.C.)—that is to say, the first 600 or so years of Chinese philosophy. The remaining 1,700 or so years he covers in only 125 pages. It would seem that not much of significance occurred in the nearly two millennia after the Hundred Schools!

In truth, Feng was perfectly justified in the weight he assigned to the Hundred Schools. This is not to say that important new currents of thought were absent from Chinese society, but rather that the variety and vibrance of the Hundred Schools was not equaled in later ages. Except for the heyday of Buddhism, beginning around the sixth century, it is only in the past 150 years that anything resembling the earlier sweeping and penetrating questioning of man and society has occurred. This may be because it is only since the middle of the nineteenth century that China has encountered a crisis comparable to that of the Warring States age.

In the realm of thought, what came after the Hundred Schools was not stagnation, but stability. For most of the 2,000-year-long imperial period, there seemed to be general agreement about how human relations should be conducted, or at least sufficient agreement so that intelligent people saw little need to come up with fundamentally new concepts of man and society. The stability in patterns of thought was normally enough to permit the assimilation of sweeping social, economic, and technological changes without the undermining of confidence in what people believed.

It is true that by the seventh or eighth century, Confucianism was in danger of losing its vitality and hence its ability to meet the challenge of Buddhism and Daoism. But around that time, scholars began to rejuvenate Confucianism, a movement most closely associated with the philosopher Zhu Xi (1130–1200), which reached its high point toward the end of the Song dynasty and then went on to become perhaps the most influential mode of thought among the elite right to the end of the imperial era. This rejuvenated Confucianism, called by Western scholars "Neo-Confucianism," recognized that part of the appeal of Buddhism and Daoism lay in their sweeping explanations of nature and the universe and also in their answer to the human need for spirituality. It sought to counter this by borrowing heavily from both Buddhism and Daoism. From Daoism, it borrowed a cosmology (theories of the nature of the universe), especially the notions of *yin* and *yang*, two primordial cosmic forces, constantly opposing and at the same time complementing each other. It also drew heavily on the sixth-century B.C. *Book of Changes* (Yijing), the most translated and talked about classical Chinese text in the West, a work originally used for divination, which was built around the concept of yin-yang dualism. From Buddhism, it borrowed the notion that humans should strive to achieve Buddhahood (or enlightenment), except that it substituted the idea of sagehood. The difference was that to achieve enlightenment in Buddhism it was necessary to seek spiritual self-cultivation outside of society and the material world, while in Neo-Confucianism sagehood was something to be sought in this world, by serving one's family and one's country.

The development of Neo-Confucianism illustrates the tendency in Chinese thought to balance antithetical elements, to search for commonalities, and to take the middle path whenever possible. Overall, ways of thinking in China have been remarkably syncretic (combining and fusing different and disparate elements). Thus, it has often been said, with a bit of exaggeration, that throughout history the typical Chinese gentleman was a Confucian during the day (in his dealings with society), and a Daoist in the evening (in his inner life). Combining opposites in this way, which has been at the core of Chinese thought, is symbolized by the concepts of yin and yang, the negative and positive principles of universal life. Yin is identified with the female, negative, dark, passive, destructive, and so on; yang with the male, positive, bright, active, constructive, and so forth. Dualistic, yin-and-yang thinking has found its way into virtually all aspects of formal thought (religion, science, medicine, philosophy, etc.) as well as popular thinking.

What has been lacking in Chinese thought, according to many scholars, is a tradition of individualism and democracy. Some even argue that not only does China lack such a tradition, but that Chinese values positively run counter to individualism and democracy. Arguments of this sort, which draw implicit or explicit comparisons with the West—and, incidentally, usually portray Chinese thought as somehow deficient—tend to exaggerate the role that individualism and democracy have played in Western history and to underplay their place in China. Rhapsodizing over the "age-old history of Western democracy" is possible only so long as certain inconvenient facts, such as that slavery was legal in the United States less than 150 years ago, are forgotten; extolling the "centuries-long centrality of individualism in Anglo-Saxon culture" is possible only by ignoring such facts as that the word "individualism" did not even exist in the English language until the year

1827. As for China, for a concrete and magnificent illustration of individualism go to the city of Xi'an, where, in a huge excavation, covered over with a roof to make it into a museum, there is an army of thousands of full-size terra-cotta warriors, buried in the tomb of the emperor of the Qin dynasty, who died in 210 B.C. The head of each warrior was painstakingly crafted so that no one warrior looks like any other; each is completely distinctive: over 7,000 individuals. Or, for a textual reference to individualism, turn to a description of the philosopher Yang Zhu, who lived around the time of Confucius. Mencius (371?–289 B.C.), the most important Confucian philosopher after Confucius himself, reproachingly said, "The principle of Yang was 'Each one for himself.' Though he might have benefited the whole world by plucking out a single hair, he would not have done it." Or, for an economic reference, so to speak, consider that where market economies exist, today and historically, Chinese entrepreneurs, including the simplest peddlers, have thrived. In short, when looking at what individualism means concretely, it is difficult to argue that Chinese are less individualistic than others.

Democracy too is not alien to China. The list of ideas and institutions conducive to democracy is a long one. To name just a few: First, the Hundred Schools' philosopher Mozi (ca. 479–381 B.C.) argued for an impartial love, in contradistinction to the hierarchy of obligations and authority that was fundamental to Confucianism, and for an ethics in which everyone would "enjoy equally and suffer equally." Second, in the imperial era, villages were essentially self-governing. Residents built and ran their own temples and schools, organized crop-watching societies (to prevent theft of crops in the field), constructed and maintained irrigation works, and, except when it was time to pay their taxes, otherwise lived their lives in minimal contact with the government. Third, voluntary associations, from merchant guilds to secret societies (anti-government, clandestine political, religious, and gangster associations), were found everywhere in the country before 1949. Fourth, the rule of law, usually thought to be a crucial if not essential component of democracy, for most of history was stronger in China than in the West. During much of the imperial period, the county magistrate was required to follow strict procedures in conducting trials—to gather evidence and to render judgments based on sophisticated, detailed, codified law. Although punishments could be severe, it was common for sentences to be commuted. In any event, death sentences had to be referred to higher courts and go through an elaborate review procedure. Compared to Europe before the eighteenth century, or the People's Republic after 1949, the legal system for most of the imperial period was impartial, lenient, and effective. Fifth, the republic established in China in 1911 really was a republic, however imperfect it may have been. It had elections, and a parliament, and contending political parties. Sixth, modern China had a remarkably vibrant and free press, beginning with the daily *Shenbao*, established in Shanghai in 1872. Some of the best journals published superb investigative reports and did not hesitate to criticize the government. Finally, Taiwan today is by any measure a democracy, a very young democracy to be sure, but nonetheless one that is vigorous and genuine. And Taiwan does not seem to have become any less Chinese for it. Thus, the conclusion is clear: the explanation of why the People's Republic is not a democracy is not to be found in some flaw in Chinese culture or national character but in the nature of the Communist political institutions.

RELIGION

In a table on "the Principal Religions of the World" in a recent almanac, an explanatory note mentions that "statistics of the world's religions are only very rough approximations. . . . The compiling of statistics is further complicated by the fact that in China one may be at the same time a Confucian, a Taoist [Daoist], and a Buddhist."[1] The compilers of the table might have added "and a Muslim, or a Christian," or a follower of practically any other religion as well. One of the enduring features of religion in China has been that a great many people are perfectly comfortable in following more than one faith. "In 'prayer' meetings to ward off a raging cholera epidemic . . . during World War II," recounts anthropologist Francis L.K. Hsu, "I saw included at many an altar the images of not only the numerous Chinese deities but also of Jesus Christ and Mohammed as well."[2] That is not to say that sectarianism does not exist in China. However, the most powerful tendency in religion in China is inclusivity not exclusivity.

The old notion that China has three religions—Confucianism, Daoism, and Buddhism—or, as is usually said today, that it has five religions—the aforementioned three plus Islam and Christianity—does not accurately describe the situation on the ground. In the first place, it is difficult to call Confucianism a religion since it lacks a clergy and is little concerned with spirits and deities. Furthermore, there is a huge universe of so-called popular or folk religion, a rich and diverse amalgam of beliefs and practices that do not neatly fit within the boundaries of Confucianism, or Daoism, or Buddhism.

Today most Chinese probably consider themselves non-religious. Nonetheless, a great many of these "non-religious" people participate in observances and ceremonies—for example, ancestor veneration or traditional festivals—that may be considered religious. Furthermore, especially for people in the countryside, participating in or at least supporting festivals and observances that are ostensibly religious is an accepted part of community life. For instance, in many villages collections are taken up to fund one religious festival or another, and all families are expected to contribute—and almost all in fact do so. This is not a matter of belief. No one is required to "believe" in any of the gods that are being honored, but every family is expected to support community solidarity.

From the late nineteenth century to the middle of the twentieth century, when Chinese here and there began to convert to Christianity, community solidarity came under assault. Christian villagers often condemned traditional religious celebrations as heathen, and sometimes refused to participate. Their fellow villagers considered this refusal not a question of belief, since everyone was free to believe or not to believe in whatever they wished, but a question of refusing to support the community and honor the obligations incumbent on all of its members.

The Christian assault on community solidarity was never of great significance simply because Christians were not found in most villages. But the assault from another source—the state—has had a great impact. The official ideology of the People's Republic holds, in the famous (or, depending on your point of view, infamous) words of Karl Marx and Friedrich Engels, that religion is "the opiate of the people." Nonetheless, religious freedom has been enshrined in Chinese law from the beginning of the People's Republic, but with a crucial proviso: religion may be practiced only with the approval of the government. As the government has explained it, "the state protects legitimate religious activities, but no one may use religion to carry out counterrevolutionary activities or activities that disrupt public order . . . [and] no religious affairs may be controlled by any foreign power."[3] Of course, what constitutes "legitimate" religious activity and what disrupts "public order" are decided by the government. In essence, policy on religion seems to be premised on the notion that any religious activity that can be controlled by the state may be useful to the state, and thus essentially "official" religion is to be permitted and perhaps even to be encouraged to some extent. On the other hand, any religious activity that cannot be controlled by the state may be a threat to the state, and hence such activity must be suppressed. Thus, the state recognizes five established, organized religions—Daoism, Buddhism, Islam, and Catholic and Protestant Christianity—and condemns the rich tradition of folk religion, which has no unified dogma, no nationwide organization, no full-time clergy, as "superstition." The state's distrust of popular, unregulated religion long predates the Communist period. Chinese history is peppered with the rise and fall of sects, big and small, many of which violently attacked the state, the cornerstone of orthodoxy. Thus the imperial state, like the PRC, tended to view unorthodox religion as threatening. Aside from this, many thinkers during the imperial period were genuinely concerned about the potential for charlatans to manipulate the ignorant. Finally, modern China's struggle against China's past led to condemnation of "primitive" religious practices. In 1928 the Nationalist government promulgated a law on "Preserving and Abandoning Gods and Shrines" that described many traditional practices and beliefs as "an obstacle to progress" and claimed that China was becoming "the laughing stock of the scientific world" because of its superstitions.[4]

The five officially recognized religions in the PRC are in effect arms of the government: they are subject to the control of the Religious Affairs Bureau, a national government bureau, with agencies in the various provinces and localities. Protestant churches, for instance, are managed by the Three-Self Patriotic Movement, and Catholic churches by the Chinese Catholic Patriotic Association. The Roman Catholic Church, which the state considers "controlled by a foreign power" (the Vatican), is outlawed. Yet, on the whole the government of the People's Republic has not considered religion per se a major issue. In the 1950s there was an initial crackdown in which most Buddhist monks and Daoist priests were returned to secular life, foreign missionaries were expelled (often after being accused of spying), and a great many temples, shrines, and churches were closed or converted into secular uses (such as storehouses). But in taking these steps, the Communists were concerned not so much with stamping out doctrine or theology as with undermining loyalty to institutions other than the state and Party.

During 1966 and 1967, the first two years of the Cultural Revolution, the Red Guards launched a violent assault on the "Four Olds" (old ideas, culture, customs, and habits) and destroyed temples and shrines, religious statues, and ancestral tablets in people's homes. In most places, public religious activity and observances of popular, communal festivals became impossible. Religion went underground, but fear of discovery, which could lead to violent, even fatal, attacks, undoubtedly caused many people to shun any religious observance, no matter how private. After 1978, in line with the political and economic reforms launched under Deng Xiaoping, public religious observances once again became possible, as long as they remained within strictly defined limits. A number of temples and churches have been renovated, and, especially in recent years, the state seems to pay minimal attention to religious observances even outside the officially sanctioned religious bodies so long as they remain low key. On the other hand, what is tolerated in one place may be punished in another, and what is possible at one time may land the practitioner in jail in another. Such is the capriciousness of governance in the PRC.

Buddhism

Buddhism has exercised a profound influence on China, an influence that extends far beyond religion, into art, philosophy, literature, popular thought, and countless other aspects of culture.

Buddhism originated in India in the fifth century B.C., as an outgrowth of Hinduism. At the age of 29, the prince Sakyamuni left home and spent the next six years seeking enlightenment. It was not until one day when he was sitting under a bodhi tree in meditation that he suddenly attained enlightenment. As the Buddha ("enlightened one"), he spent the next 45 years expounding his teaching, after which he entered nirvana. The essence of his teaching was that life is suffering, that suffering arises from desires, and that salvation is thus to be found in the annihilation of desire. All sentient beings (creatures with consciousness and feelings, essentially every living thing but plants) are trapped in a cycle of constant rebirth; whether one is reborn as a higher or lower creature is determined by one's karma, which is one's good or bad deeds accumulated in this and previous lifetimes. To escape the cycle, one must surrender worldly pleasures and build up good karma. Only in doing so will one enter nirvana, the heavenly paradise where there is no rebirth. Ideas about how to build up good karma varied from denomination to denomination: through meditation, or faith, or doing good works, or reciting the Buddhist scriptures (sutras), and so on.

Although it is difficult to say when Buddhism first appeared in China, it is clear that by about the second century A.D. it had established a toehold. From the fifth century, a time of disorder in China, Buddhism began to enjoy a great upsurge, and won countless adherents from all walks of life, from humble laborers to aristocrats to the emperor himself. Buddhism had entered an age of great influence, and as it did so Confucianism appeared to go into eclipse: powerful Buddhist temples and monasteries proliferated, provided some of the most influential advisors to the imperial court, accumulated vast estates that paid little or no taxes, enrolled tens of thousands of monks and nuns, enserfed entire families, schooled children, and published volume after volume of didactic tracts. By the beginning of the ninth century, Buddhism reached its zenith in China. Thereafter a nativist reaction, which called for a turn away from "foreign" things, began to whittle away support for Buddhism at the imperial court and in society at large. This culminated in the middle of the ninth century in an imperial decree proscribing foreign religion. Nearly 5,000 monasteries were closed and nearly 300,000 monks and nuns were defrocked. While this certainly delivered a severe blow to Buddhism, it by no means destroyed the religion. Rather, Buddhism thereafter became more of a religion, competing with others on equal ground for adherents, and less of a political and economic force.

Portraying Buddhism as "foreign" was a half-truth. As Buddhism spread in China, it was refashioned and reshaped by pre-existing Chinese ideas, interests, and values. Although Buddhism did not include the idea of a supreme being or God, for instance, its various denominations and sects offered worshipers plenty of deities, especially bodhisattvas, compassionate figures who had renounced or postponed their own salvation in order to help free mankind from the cycle of constant rebirth. The most beloved bodhisattva by far has been Guanyin. In India, Guanyin had been portrayed as a male, but in China by around the eleventh or twelfth century, somehow he got transformed into a female. As a gracious, motherly deity, the Chinese version of Guanyin is in many ways reminiscent of Mary, the mother of Christ, as portrayed by Christians; indeed Guanyin was sometimes represented holding an infant. The popular devotion to Guanyin as the "Goddess of Mercy," who comforted the suffering and blessed women with children, reflected the enduring popularity of mother figures in Chinese religion. Although female deities are not numerous, they are adored. On the other hand, the elitist Chinese penchant for keeping women in their place also contributed to the sinification of Buddhism as, for example, when Indian Buddhist texts were translated into Chinese. The original Indian phrase "Husband supports wife" became "The husband controls his wife," and "The wife comforts the husband" became "The wife reveres her husband."[5]

By the Song dynasty, Buddhism had considerably recovered from the suppression of the ninth century. In the sense of doctrinal vibrancy, however, it steadily declined through the end of the imperial period. Only two of the earlier schools of Buddhism—Chan (better known in the West by its Japanese name, Zen) and Pure Land—survived as viable teachings. Chan, an indigenous Chinese form of Buddhism, stresses meditation and sudden enlightenment. The Pure Land school, on the other hand, holds that arduous self-discipline and meditation are unnecessary; all that is required for salvation is faith and devotion. But the prevailing trend in Chinese Buddhism was toward syncretism, mutual borrowing of doctrines and practices, and proliferation of countless forms of popular devotion.

After the revolution of 1911 and the establishment of the republic, there were various attempts to organize Buddhist clergy on a national scale and to revivify and elevate doctrine. In large measure this was part of the general movement to resist Western and Japanese dominance, and in particular a reaction against Christian missions. However, in the face of the general march toward the left in Chinese thought and society in the first 50 years of the twentieth century, this revivalism accomplished little. After the establishment

Figure 2.1. Worshipers at the Dabei (Great Mercy) Temple, in Tianjin, on the first day of the Spring Festival (Chinese New Year's Day; see Chapter 8), 1998. The burning of sticks of incense, which many worshipers are holding, is not only a part of Buddhist rituals but also of ancestor worship and most other commemorative rituals. *Courtesy of Thomas DuBois.*

of the People's Republic in 1949, government policy on Buddhism, as in so many other areas, fluctuated between political supervision and heavy-handed suppression. Although the reforms introduced in 1978 have led to the re-opening and renovation of many temples, worshipers generally remain the elderly (especially women) and novices appear to lack dedication and discipline. There is little evidence of a revival of intellectual and cultural vitality.

A form of Buddhism known as Lamaism and practiced in Tibet and in Inner Mongolia must be considered quite separate from Buddhism in the core of China. Before 1949, Tibet was essentially a theocratic state, where the Buddhist church exercised both religious and secular authority and in many respects dominated society. For a decade after the Communist revolution, the dominance of the Buddhist church continued. In 1959 the Chinese army invaded Tibet, the Dalai Lama fled to India, and thereafter the Chinese government took steps to revolutionize the "feudal" institutions of Tibet. This, in turn, stimulated a nationalist reaction, led by dissident monks. Martial law has been proclaimed several times and monks have been jailed and beaten, and some have been executed. Tension between the Han-dominated state and ethnic Tibetans is always present; confrontation is always near.

Daoism

Daoism as a religion is quite unlike Daoism as a philosophy. The latter, as we have seen, advocates acceptance of nature. As a religion, however, Daoism came to involve a search for ways to overcome nature, especially a search for superhuman (and thus supernatural) powers through following complex rituals. Many Daoists sought immortality through the use of magic, herbs and minerals, breath control, and special diets. While this sort of alchemy has often caused Daoism to be dismissed as superstition, the search for magical elixirs and formulas led believers to explore various sciences and to make important contributions to medicine, chemistry, and astronomy.

Daoism, a native Chinese religion, generally views human desire as positive and life as something to be enjoyed. In this it stands opposite Buddhism. It is similar to Buddhism, however, in the sense that it has an institutionalized church with canonical texts, a clerical hierarchy, liturgies, and a pantheon of gods. The Daoist gods are very much like the officials of the imperial era, hierarchically organized, each with specific duties and powers. The Otherworld in fact is nearly a mirror image of this world, and is organized and run like this world (or like this world was in imperial times), with the gods as officials who can be promoted and rewarded, or demoted and penalized, according to their performance. Many Buddhists too have a similar concept of the Otherworld as somewhere rather like this world. Early Buddhists in China believed that the Western Paradise, as they called heaven, was a place in which one was reborn as an infant, and then grew up, got married, worked, and, in the end, died.

For its institutional foundation, Daoism owes most to the so-called Heavenly Master Sect led by one Zhang Daoling, around A.D. 150 in the province of Sichuan. An indefatigable organizer, Zhang founded a series of vibrant dioceses, each with an imposing temple. The management of the dioceses was remarkably open, even democratic, and women occupied several leading positions, in contrast to later centuries. As part of its celebration of life, the Heavenly Master Sect rituals apparently included various group sexual practices. With the Chinese emphasis on yin and yang, the use of sex to promote harmony and health, which was particularly identified with Daoism, played some role in Chinese culture, despite the prudish disapproval of Confucians. Today, presumably, Daoism is completely devoid of such practices.

Daoism is an immensely practical religion, in the sense that the job of Daoist priests is to exorcise demons and in other ways protect the well-being of those who seek their help. Rituals are colorful and entertaining, which goes far in explaining why Daoist temples are frequently crowded with tourists. The Daoists are masters of pomp and are particularly good at incorporating marches and music in their rituals (see Figure 4.3). That Daoist temples are often located on scenic mountaintops also helps draw tourists. Yet, as a faith Daoism appears to be far less popular than Buddhism, Christianity, or Islam. Today only a few hundred Daoist temples are open to the public, compared to thousands of Buddhist temples.

Folk Religion

Folk religion, or popular religion as it is sometimes called, refers to a uniquely Chinese conglomeration of practices and beliefs that have no unified theology, no full-time clergy, no structured organization. In fact, there is not even a Chinese term for what scholars call folk religion. The precise content of folk religion defies summing up in a few words. At best, we can say that it consists of an amalgamation of diverse elements—ancestor veneration, local cults, popular Buddhism, popular Daoism, Confucianism, and others— that varies somewhat from place to place. An article in *People's Daily* in 1979, repeating the official line, spelled out the so-called feudal superstitions of folk religion as "sorceries, magic potions and drugs, divination and fortune-telling, getting rid of calamities and praying for rain, praying for sons and daughters, controlling demons, healing sickness, practicing physiognomy and palm reading, practicing geomancy [*fengshui*] and other activities."[6] But folk religion involves more than this. Its basic ideas reflect and incorporate beliefs and values that pervade Chinese culture as a whole. In this sense, folk religion is truly a native, Chinese religion.

The core of folk religion lies in ancestor worship and cults of local deities. "Ancestor worship" is often a misnomer because in many families honoring ancestors is less a matter of religious practice than an expression of deep respect. Many households, especially in the countryside, set aside a small table on which are displayed photographs of deceased family members, but also frequently photographs and memorabilia of important public figures, such as Mao Zedong and Deng Xiaoping. Traditional observances that extend beyond the immediate family have resurged since 1978, especially in rural areas. In many villages and towns, lineages (people of the same surname who trace their descent from a common ancestor) have reopened or built anew lineage halls in which are displayed tablets bearing the names of important ancestors and in which genealogies are stored and ceremonies are held. For instance, in the village of Xiaochuan (population 3,310 in 1992), where 95% of the male residents are surnamed Kong and claim descent from

Confucius (whose surname was Kong), the Kong lineage hall was rebuilt in 1992 and today serves as the site of an annual celebration of Confucius's birthday, involving a number of elaborate ceremonies including preparation of sacrificial food, a procession through the village to the hall, and prayers to the ancestors.[7]

While in China the family may be the primary focus of an individual's loyalty, sentiment, and responsibilities, solidarity with social groups outside the family and lineage, in particular the community, have also been crucial. In villages and other close-knit communities, cooperation among members of the community are often essential for everyday life. In such an environment, acceptance of and participation in local religious traditions can be important symbolic reaffirmations of community solidarity.

In rural China from the mid-1950s to the early 1980s, when land and other productive assets were collectivized, community solidarity was guaranteed by the collective form of production. There were countervailing tendencies, of course, and competition between families for power and whatever wealth was distributed to individual members of the collective. However, all members of the collective had to work together and "going it alone" was impossible. Once collective production was abandoned, starting around 1979, and farmland and other assets were distributed to individuals or families, for solidarity to survive required a new approach. More often than not, the "new" approach was a revival of traditional community religious practices, in particular observances and ceremonies surrounding local deities.

Local deities in the popular religious tradition are said to have once been men and women who acquired extraordinary powers—quelling demons, making rain, healing disease, and so on—which they now exercise on behalf of those who entreat them. Thus, rather than being omnipotent gods, or even gods with wide-ranging powers, most deities occupy a niche: the Stove God, the Earth God, the Gate God, the City God, the God of War, and so on. A few of the most powerful, especially the Buddha and the Goddess of Mercy (Guanyin), are usually thought to be omniscient or nearly so. Recently, some people consider Mao Zedong to occupy the same lofty pantheon with the Buddha and Guanyin. Some taxi drivers, for instance, put a medallion with his picture in their cabs (in the same way and for the same purpose that Catholics may put a St. Christopher medal in their cars) and some farmers post his portrait on the living room wall, in the same way that their forefathers in the late imperial era posted paper prints of the gods (see Figure 2.2). The deification of Mao makes perfect sense: In life, in the fantastic cult of personality built up around him during the Cultural Revolution, he was portrayed as almost god-like in his power and prescience; in death, it is easy to believe his spirit continues to wield extraordinary power.

Figure 2.2. A devotional poster of Mao Zedong in the style of traditional portraits of the gods, hanging in the living room of a home in rural Henan (1998). The inscription reads "Heaven's beloved son; Eternally providing protection." *Courtesy of Thomas DuBois.*

For most people, the relation between themselves and the deities is remarkably practical. People have needs and desires and the deities can grant wishes. In return, supplicants are expected to pay back a deity who grants a wish. The worshiper approaches a deity (represented by a statue or a picture), usually in a shrine or at a festival, lights one or many sticks of incense, mentally makes a request and also makes a vow to repay the god if the request is granted, bows or prostrates before the deity, and, finally, puts the incense in a burner in front of the altar. If the request is granted, then the vow is carried out—most common are burning paper money for the god, or presenting sacrifices of food, alcohol, or cigarettes. If the wish is not granted, there is no question of carrying out the vow, and the worshiper typically feels entirely free to approach another god with the same request.

Practicality is also the essence of spirit healing. In many villages are found people, both men and women, who are thought to have healing powers. These healers have no special training nor are they otherwise distinctive from their fellow villagers. Techniques of healing vary from practitioner to practitioner. Some exorcise evil spirits who are thought to cause illness, others direct their patients to repent and admit their misdeeds, and a few give their patients herbs. There are still places in China where access to modern medicine is difficult. Yet even where modern medical treatment is readily available, some villagers still resort to spirit healing. Many do so because they have first turned to modern medicine, but have not been cured. Others pursue both modern medical treatment and spirit healing simultaneously. Apparently, many people who go to spirit healers do not quite believe in the efficacy of healers, but think it is worth a try.[8]

Christianity

The roots of Christianity in China can be traced back to the sixth and seventh centuries when Persian merchants along the Silk Road, which stretched from Central Asia to northwest China, brought with them a variant of Christianity known as Nestorianism. In the seventh century, the imperial court permitted the construction of Christian churches, but in the mid-ninth century, as part of the sweeping proscription of foreign religion, Nestorianism was outlawed. Although in subsequent centuries pockets of Nestorianism were found here and there, by the fifteenth century it had disappeared from China. Occasionally Roman Catholic missionaries made the long trip to China, but these were rare events that again seem to have ended by the fifteenth century.

In the sixteenth century, a handful of Catholic Jesuit missionaries arrived in China. Although the Jesuits established several missions directed at the common people and managed to win a number of converts, their focus was on the imperial court itself. The Jesuits hoped that by going to the very top of society and winning the support of, if not converting, the emperor, Christianity would then spread to all of China, from the top down. While this strategy had been remarkably successful in the Counter-Reformation in Europe, where the elite were already Christians and where the problem for the Jesuits was to convince wavering aristocrats not to convert to Protestantism, it was much more problematic in China. The Jesuits were welcomed by several of the emperors, but it was more for their knowledge of astronomy, mathematics, and other subjects than for their religion.

It was not until the mid-nineteenth century that a large number of Christian missionaries arrived and began to score notable success in proselytization. The boon, and the bane, of Christianity was that it was inevitably associated with Western imperialism. Foreign missionaries were protected by the unequal treaties and foreign military might, which undoubtedly facilitated their work. Some converts, known as "rice Christians," took advantage of this "foreign connection" by calling for foreign assistance in disputes with their non-Christian neighbors. Thus in the eyes of many Chinese, the missionaries and the converts looked to be an arm of the foreign encroachment. Despite the good work done by many missionaries (in running hospitals and clinics, schools for the children—including girls—of the common people, etc.), Christianity has had to struggle with the legacy of imperialism.

The policy of the PRC with respect to Christianity, then, appears to be more a case of asserting native Chinese control than resisting a foreign religion per se. Since the beginning of the reform era, there has been an impressive revival of Christianity. The official Chinese Catholic church claims 4 million members; the underground Roman Catholic Church claims no less than 10 million.[9] But official policy remains that religion in China must be controlled by Chinese. Regulations on foreign missionaries promulgated in 1994 state that "foreigners cannot set up religious organizations or offices, or run religious places or schools. Foreign religious people must not cultivate religious disciples among Chinese citizens nor appoint religious clergy."[10] Nonetheless, there is evidence of a great deal of clandestine, and not so clandestine, religious activity in contravention of state policy. For instance, two Roman Catholic bishops quite openly run a diocese in the province of Sichuan.[11]

Islam

Islam was brought to China around the seventh century by Persian and Arab merchants. Initially, Muslims dwelt apart from Chinese and retained their distinctive, and distinctively foreign, way of life. But as time passed, through intermarriage, assimilation, and proselytization Muslim Chinese communities began to arise. Once this happened—by the fourteenth century—one could speak of "Chinese Muslims" and not merely "Muslims in China."

The government of the PRC classifies most Chinese Muslims as "Hui," one of the 55 official minority nationalities. The rationale for this labeling is questionable. It is a catchall category that includes people who would otherwise be classified as Han except that they happen to be Muslim. Unlike other minority nationalities, the Hui are not attached to any particular territory, although they form a sizable majority in Ningxia (officially, Ningxia Hui Autonomous Region) in the northwest, and a very sizable minority in the provinces of Gansu (also in the northwest) and Yunnan (in the south). Yet they can be found almost everywhere in the country, particularly in the largest cities. Chinese who are Christians remain Han, as do Buddhists. But people who speak Chinese, who have lived for generations in the core of China, and who in many cases are not observant of any religion and share most values and ways of life with their Han neighbors, can still be classified as Hui. It must be kept in mind that the official classification of "minority nationalities" is precisely that: official. It does not necessarily reflect objective criteria or accord with how people identify themselves. During an interview, when asked, "Are there ethnic minorities in Yunnan who are Muslim?" the head of the Islamic Association in that southern province replied "No, Yunnan Muslims are all Han. . . . But there are Muslims among ten national minorities in China."[12] This statement reflects a common feeling that people who speak Chinese, and look like and live like Han, are Han, even if they are also Muslim. The government does not see things this way, and insists that such people are a "minority nationality," namely the Hui. Many Han share this view, and consider that anyone who is a Muslim cannot be a Han.

"Hui" and "Muslim" are by no means synonymous. As the head of the Yunnan Islamic Association stated, there are Muslims among ten ethnic groups or national minorities. The most numerous predominantly Muslim non-Han peoples are the Uygurs, at around 6 million, whose homeland is the far western province of Xinjiang (or, officially, the Xinjiang Uygur Autonomous Region). Other predominantly Muslim minorities—such as Kazaks, Kirgiz, and Uzbeks—also reside mostly in Xinjiang.

Relations between the Chinese state and followers of Islam have usually been difficult. To varying degrees, Muslims have tended to look westward, toward the center of the Muslim world, for their cultural affiliation rather than eastward, toward China. Recent centuries have been peppered with outbreaks of violent resistance to rule by the Chinese state. Most of the clashes involved Hui in Gansu and Yunnan, people who were living in close proximity to Han or interspersed with Han communities. Relations between the Han and peoples of Xinjiang were, until recently, not of great importance to the authorities since Xinjiang was on the far periphery, distant from large Han settlements. But that has changed in recent decades, and demonstrations, sometimes violent, which the authorities condemn as "terrorism," have occurred from time to time. The authorities have responded vigorously, and have executed many. The trials that precede these executions are closed, and in any event the outside world has not yet become as interested in the crisis in Xinjiang as that in, say, Tibet. Not a great deal is known about the motivations of the so-called terrorists: what role is played by nationalism, by Islam, and by perceived injustices suffered at the hands of Han Chinese remains an open question.

NOTES

1. *Almanac of World Facts* (New York: Rand McNally, 1997), p. 25.
2. Francis L.K. Hsu, *Americans and Chinese: Passage to Difference* (Honolulu: University of Hawaii Press, 1981), p. 255.

3. Xinhua News Agency (April 18, 1982).

4. *China New Analysis*, no. 1440 (Aug. 1, 1991): pp. 5–6; Clarence Day, *Chinese Peasant Cults: Being a Study of Chinese Paper Gods* (Shanghai: Kelly and Walsh, 1940), pp. 190ff.

5. Arthur F. Wright, *Buddhism in Chinese History* (Stanford, CA: Stanford University Press, 1959), p. 37.

6. Quoted in Peter Barry, "A Resurgence of Feudal Superstitious Practices in China," *Ching Feng*, no. 23 (1980).

7. On the Kong hall in Xiaochuan, see Jun Jing, *The Temple of Memories: History, Power, and Morality in a Chinese Village* (Stanford, CA: Stanford University Press, 1996).

8. On the worship of deities and spirit healing, see Thomas DuBois, "The Sacred World of Cang County: Religious Belief, Organization, and Practice in Rural North China during the Late Nineteenth and Twentieth Centuries" (Ph.D. dissertation, UCLA, 2001).

9. *China News Digest*, Global News, no. GL98–067 (May 15, 1997).

10. James D. Seymour and Eugen Wehrli, eds., "Regulating Foreign Missionaries," in *Religion in China. Chinese Sociology and Anthropology* 26, no. 3 (spring 1994): p. 96.

11. *China News Digest*, Global News, no. GL98–057 (April 22, 1998).

12. Quoted in Donald E. MacInnis, *Religion in China Today: Policy and Practice* (Maryknoll, NY: Orbis, 1989), p. 226.

3

Literature and Art

IN 1898 OR 1899, a physician was called to the household of Wang Yirong, a noted scholar in Beijing, to treat a member of the family ill with malaria. The physician prescribed a medicine containing "decayed tortoise shell." When the medicine was brought back from the pharmacy, Wang examined it closely. To his astonishment, he found inscribed on the tortoise shells ancient Chinese characters. These, in fact, turned out to be the earliest record of Chinese writing, dating back some 3,000 years. (Later archaeological discoveries have uncovered still earlier examples, 3,500 years old.) The inscriptions—most are simple questions such as whether it will rain or not—had been made by diviners, who had heated the shells (the scapula of oxen and sheep were also used), causing them to crack. The diviners then interpreted the cracks to ascertain an "answer."

What is fascinating about these oracle bone inscriptions, as they are called, is that anyone today who is literate in Chinese can, with a bit of instruction, recognize in them the precursors of contemporary Chinese characters. In other words, one can immediately discern a direct connection between written Chinese of today and written Chinese of more than 3,000 years ago. The oracle bone character for "heaven," for instance, 兲, is today written as 天. The character for "field," inscribed on oracle bones as 田, is today virtually identical, 田.

Chinese characters, as is well known, are ideograms (rather like pictographs), and are not an alphabet. Although characters may appear to be made up of random lines, they actually consist of a number of "strokes" that can only appear in a definite pattern. The problem for the learner is that the number of patterns is huge and the arrangement of the patterns is almost infinite. Virtually all characters have an intrinsic meaning: for instance, 山 (*shan*) means "mountain," and 好 (*hao*; consisting of two elements that can stand alone as separate characters—女 meaning "woman," and 子 meaning "child") means "good." However, when confronted with an unfamiliar character, it is nearly impossible to be certain of its meaning. The same is true of its pronunciation. The majority of characters have a "phonetic" element that hints at the pronunciation, but it is sometimes difficult to identify what part of the character is the "phonetic," and in any case the fit between the "phonetic" and the actual pronunciation is often imperfect: one can guess at the pronunciation, but one is apt to be wrong much of the time. In this respect, Chinese is by no means unique. In any language, when encountering an unknown written word, one can do no more than guess at the meaning. However, alphabetical languages have the great advantage that the pronunciation of words is more or less apparent.

The question of pronunciation takes us into the realm of *spoken* language. It is generally accepted by scholars that Chinese consists of seven major dialect groups, most of which are mutually unintelligible. About 70% of the population (mostly in North and West China) speak some form of the Mandarin dialect. It is the Beijing version of Mandarin, with some modifications, that has been designated by the government (in 1955) as the national language, *putonghua* ("common language").

Chinese is not particularly rich in sounds: Mandarin has about 420 syllables compared to about 1,200 in English. On the other hand, Chinese is a tonal language. Mandarin has four tones; thus each syllable (with some exceptions) can be pronounced four different ways, yielding almost 1,700 distinctive "sounds," more than in English. It has often been said that Chinese is monosyllabic, meaning that the vast majority of words are one syllable in length. If this were true, then with only 420 syllables (or, including the tones, 1,700 vocables) spoken Chinese would have so many homophones (that is, words of the same sound) that it would be incredibly confusing. In actuality, speakers of Chinese communicate with no more confusion and with no less precision than do the speakers of any other language. This is because most Chinese words—if by a "word" we mean a single unit of meaning—actually consist of two syllables, and some of more than two. While it is true that each character is but one syllable, it is a mistake to equate characters (written symbols) with words. Most words are written with two characters. For example, *xuexiao*, "school," is written 學校, which is composed of two characters, *xue* 學, and *xiao* 校. Historically, it would appear that Chinese once was monosyllabic, but over time, many distinct syllables became homophonous, threatening utter confusion. This led to the creation of new, polysyllabic words by combining existing monosyllabic words.

Hence, in the example of xuexiao, the first character (xue) as an independent word meant (and still means) "study," and the second (xiao) meant a "corral."

Given the complexity of written Chinese, it is not surprising that attempts have been made at simplification. In 1956 the government replaced a few hundred characters with simplified versions. This was at best an exceedingly modest reform. The simplified characters represent only a fraction of the 6,000 or so characters that a well-educated person would know, and furthermore the simplification amounts merely to reducing the number of strokes in this handful of characters, making them somewhat easier to learn and a bit faster to write. In 1958 the government began to adopt the *pinyin* system of romanization (i.e., using 26 Latin letters for writing Chinese). This too was a very modest reform, intended merely to supplement the characters—mainly as an aid to children learning to read and to promote the spread of putonghua—and not to replace them. While in principle it may be possible to throw out the characters and rely entirely on an alphabet, there is no serious demand for such a radical step. Eliminating the characters would have a profound—and unfortunate—influence on Chinese culture. It would gravely weaken the tie with the past: unable to read characters, people would be cut off from all that was written in the past. To transcribe ancient and classical texts with an alphabet would simply not work: classical Chinese vocabulary was much different from spoken Chinese today; thus to read classical Chinese rendered in a phonetic alphabet would require nothing less than learning a new language. Eliminating the characters would also weaken China's cultural cohesiveness. Written Chinese is essentially unconnected with dialect; thus, no matter what dialect one speaks, one reads and writes with the same characters (with some exceptions) used by every other literate Chinese. If Chinese were written in a phonetic alphabet, however, mutual unintelligibility would seem inevitable. Finally, discarding the characters would be a great aesthetic loss. There is an intimate connection between the writing of Chinese characters and Chinese painting in particular and other arts in general. Calligraphy, as we shall see later in this chapter, is perhaps the greatest of the arts of China.

LITERATURE

Traditional Literature

Traditional Chinese literature can be likened to two trees growing side by side. Down at the base, the trunks of the trees are separate and easily distinguishable. But up above, the branches intermingle and twist and turn so that it becomes difficult to tell one tree from the other. One of the trees of Chinese literature is serious writing; the other is pleasureful writing. At least, this is how Confucian gentlemen of days gone by divided literature. They considered novels and dramas "little arts, unworthy to enter the Hall of Great Literature,"[1] while they thought poetry was the greatest of the literary arts, perhaps because the earliest writing that can be considered literature (the *Book of Songs*, ca. 1000 B.C. to 600 B.C.) was poetry. Given the Confucians' adoration of ancient things, they cherished the *Book of Songs* (they even credited Confucius with editing it); it was valued because writing good poetry demands great concentration, sensitivity, and mental discipline—all beloved of Confucian scholars; and, finally, it was appreciated because it could, and often did, become rigidly formulaic (with prescribed meter, rhyme, etc.)— and slavish rigidity was often characteristic of Confucians. Poetry could be entirely pleasureful, but it could also perform a very serious role: traditionally, poems served as vehicles of political critique as well as ways of expressing the poet's dreams and ambitions.

The delight in the formulaic is also evident in the Chinese classical canon. For 2,000 years education in China was subject to the overwhelming influence of a handful of texts. Intellectual attainment was effectively measured by how thoroughly a person had gained familiarity with these texts—even to the point of memorizing entire books. The selection of what was included in the classical canon differed somewhat from dynasty to dynasty. The oldest enumeration specified the Five Classics, all dating from around the time of Confucius or earlier. From the Song dynasty to the end of the imperial period, the so-called Four Books favored by the philosopher Zhu Xi (1130–1200), who led a revival of Confucianism, became the mainstay of classical learning. These four works—the *Analects*, the *Mencius*, the *Great Learning*, and the *Doctrine of the Mean*—were all vehicles for conveying the aim of Confucianism: "to teach and influence people to be good."[2]

In this respect, traditional Chinese literature, from the great classics of "serious" literature to novels and other popular forms of entertainment, was marked by a common tendency: didacticism. This is only a tendency, and not all traditional literature expounded an obvious lesson or moral platitude, but most did. Indeed, the more popular forms of literature, including those that are most entertaining, are often the most moralistic and preachy. In short, the notion of art for art's sake was not widely accepted in China. Thus when the Communists proclaimed that literature must be a political weapon, their approach, although not the specifics of their message, was very much in line with traditional notions. Mao Zedong declared in 1942 that "all culture, all literature and art belong to definite classes and are geared to definite political lines. There is in fact no such thing as art for art's sake."[3]

In addition to didacticism, another central feature of Chinese writing is that almost every genre began as a popular form of literature, and was later adopted and developed by the elite. This is most certainly true of poetry. For instance, about half of the 300 some poems in the *Book of Songs* (*Shijing*) are songs of the common people, on love, courtship, and daily life. It is also true of the novel, which sprang from the folklore passed on in storytelling. Public storytellers are recorded in the Tang dynasty (618–907), although they must have had ancient roots. Down to modern times, storytellers have found receptive audiences of all ages on street corners, in teahouses, and in village lanes. Many of China's great novels, such as the *Water Margin* and the *Three Kingdoms*, in a sense were compilations of romantic cycles made popular by storytellers. Perhaps because novels rose out of storytelling, their focus was on action rather than ideas, and the bulk of the most popular fiction, from traditional times to today, is full of exciting action.

Drama also has been heavily influenced by the traditions of storytelling and action. Traditional Chinese drama—often called Chinese opera—is quite unlike unadorned spoken drama, such as in Shakespearean plays; simple spoken drama essentially did not exist until the May Fourth period. Instead, Chinese drama—which entered its golden age during the Yuan dynasty (1279–1368) and is still performed today—is a remarkably rich and diverse form of entertainment, combining instrumental music, singing, dancing, acrobatics, mime, sword play, and so on. Chapter 4 explores the performative aspects (music, dance, etc.) of traditional opera or drama. Here, we can note that the themes and plots are typically traditional and usually involve dramatic historical incidents concerning great or villainous emperors, kings, ministers, and generals. However, plays about such eternal subjects as loyalty among friends and love and romance are also popular. What is essential to all operas, no matter what the theme, is that the audience be amply entertained. With a clash of gongs punctuating spectacular leaps and bounds, with arias sung with gusto, with comic sketches involving clever mime, and with all the rest, it is hard to imagine anyone in the audience getting bored.

Chinese drama is rich and diverse in another sense also: it encompasses a plethora of local, divergent styles. Generally speaking, drama can be divided into northern and southern styles, based on language and other particularities. In Beijing opera, the most widespread and popular of all the styles of Chinese drama, traditionally men perform female roles, while in the southern, Shaoxing opera women often play all parts, including male roles. This connection with locality, and the use of local dialects in dialogue and lyrics, is perhaps a key to the long, historical durability and popularity of the dramatic arts. As the spoken language changed over time, dialogue and lyrics in traditional drama also changed. This distinguishes Chinese drama from, say, Shakespeare's plays. Because Shakespeare committed his plays to paper, the great beauty of his language has been preserved; but, on the other hand, modern audiences have a difficult time understanding Elizabethan English. In some ways, then, it may be fortunate that the transmission of Chinese drama has been mostly oral, for this has permitted the changes and adjustments necessary to keep the dialogue and lyrics understandable. In this respect, all other genres of Chinese literature—poetry, essays, novels, and other fiction—have been at a disadvantage. Presumably, in the earliest period—a millennium or more before the rise of traditional drama—the written language fairly closely followed the spoken language, but as time passed, writing and speech increasingly diverged. In part, this divergence grew out of the nature of written Chinese—that is, the fact that it is not alphabetic. An alphabetic system of transcription, it might be argued, is more flexible and adaptable than an ideographic system based on characters. But if true, this is only a matter of degree. The separation between the spoken and written languages was much more a result of the influence of the scholar-official class. Men of this class not only cherished the ancient texts, but loved to display their erudition, to demonstrate that in their own writing they could imitate the ancients. Furthermore, cherishing the ancient classics went hand in hand with disdaining popular literature, especially folk literature in the vernacular. Thus by the opening of the twentieth century there was a immense gulf separating refined, high literature and the spoken language. In modern parlance, high literature simply did not speak to the common people.

From a Literary Revolution to Revolutionary Literature

The New Culture Movement that arose around 1915 was a response to, among other things, the conviction that literature did not address the concerns of modern people and had become hackneyed and ossified, if not dead. Much of the problem, in the eyes of the iconoclasts, was that the classical literary writing style (*wenyan*) was far removed from the vernacular and difficult, if not impossible, to understand without extensive schooling. In 1917, Hu Shi (1891–1962), who had recently obtained his doctorate in philosophy from Columbia University in New York, proposed the use of *baihua* ("plain speech," the vernacular language) for serious writing. Previously the vernacular had been mostly confined to "frivolous" literature—including most of the great novels and dramas.

The shift from the classical language to the vernacular involved not only style and diction, but also *content*. It was on this issue—content—that the proponents of the vernacular style quickly began to diverge. On one side stood the liberals, represented by Hu Shi and others, who wished to eschew politics while concentrating on reforming China's culture and society. On the other side were the radical iconoclasts, who increasingly sought to turn literature into a revolutionary weapon: they wanted not merely a literary revolution but revolutionary literature. The history of Chinese literature from that point to today has been rewritten by the Communists to make it seem that literature developed in a linear fashion, sweeping away all that was old and "feudal." To construct history in this way, the Communists have often focused on Lu Xun (1881–1936), who is generally recognized as twentieth-century China's greatest writer. Lu Xun, said to be China's first practitioner of the modern short story, is best known for his biting, and oftentimes bitter, satirical stories of Chinese society. He never joined the Communist Party, but was canonized by the Party after his death. According to a popular history that reflects the Party's position, Lu Xun "drew strength from the Communist Party's support. In the darkest days of reactionary rule, he held aloft the banner of revolutionary literature. . . . He wrote biting critical essays, trenchantly condemning the rule of the Kuomintang [the Nationalist party], and extolling the achievements of the Soviet Union."[4]

The truth about Lu Xun, and about the history of Chinese literature in the twentieth century, is somewhat more complicated. In the first place, many thoughtful writers—not just political reactionaries—resisted throwing out the classical writing style: the traditionalist Gu Hongming (1857–1928) declared, "More bread and jam were consumed than roast turkey throughout the world; yet . . . should [we] all eat 'only' bread and jam?"[5] Still more resisted turning themselves into tools of the revolution: Liang Shiqiu (1902–87) in 1928 wrote, "The creation of literature cannot undergo any form of coercion. . . . A writer accepts orders from no one, only the orders of his own heart; a writer has no mission except that of his own heart's demand for truth, goodness, and beauty."[6] The greatest resistance, however, came from the reading public. Most readers, of course, had absolutely no objection to baihua; after all, the vernacular had always been the vehicle for popular literature. However, as in most times and places, few Chinese readers in the twentieth century demanded political tracts thinly disguised as fiction; what they wanted was entertainment. Before 1949, when the reader had plenty of choices, the best-selling fiction by far consisted of lowbrow stories and novels, such as that produced by the so-called Mandarin Ducks and Butterflies school, which grew up in Shanghai, China's largest and most modern city. In the 1910s, it was unusual for a highbrow book or magazine to reach a circulation of 50,000; popular literature, however, could sell several times that figure; the most popular titles sold over a million. In comparison, the circulation of even the best-selling revolutionary fiction was infinitesimal.

Literature in the People's Republic

From Liberation (1949) to the Cultural Revolution (1966)

Following the establishment of the People's Republic in 1949, a strange phenomenon emerged: with the victory of the political revolution, the literary revolution came to an end. Striking new literary forms, exploration of new social relationships, of unfamiliar ideas and notions—in short, subjectivity—became increasingly difficult, even impossible. Instead, "revolutionary literature" emerged victorious. But "revolutionary literature" was stultifyingly formulaic. It was a political tool, to be created by writers but according to the blueprint drawn by the Party. Acceptable themes were set by the Party, and likewise the Party dictated the "targets" of literature—the intended audience as well as the subject to be "struggled" against. The Party could never be the target, because the Party could never be wrong. Individual leaders could be wrong, but not until the Party declared them wrong.

The result was a mechanical didacticism and heroes who were paper cutouts, always "Tall, Big, and Perfect" (the literal meaning of the name of the protagonist—Gao Daquan—in the novel *Golden Highway* [1972], by Hao Ran). Still, many authors, even those who willingly accepted their role as "tools of the revolution," had a difficult time avoiding subjectivism and adjusting to the new environment. The easiest solution was to adapt traditional forms to contemporary themes. For instance, storytellers continued their craft as in the past, but dropped such traditional topics as love between young scholars and beautiful maidens in favor of such themes as the battle between poor, honest peasants and rich, avaricious landlords.

The Cultural Revolution Decade (1966–1976)

In a sense, the Cultural Revolution decade may have been a relief to creative writers since, with pitifully few exceptions, it became impossible to publish anything new. All artistic, literary, and cultural periodicals ceased publication. Even old works—in many instances, *especially* old works—by bona fide revolutionary authors were condemned as "anti-revolutionary" or "feudal"; Western works were dismissed as "bourgeois" and "yellow," and disappeared from bookstore shelves. By far the most circulated work was the so-called little red book—*Quotations from Chairman Mao*—a pocket-sized, red-plastic-covered handbook containing brief quotations from Mao Zedong's works, of which perhaps a hundred million were issued. But the little red book was in no way literature, nor was it even a political tract. Instead, it was treated as a quasi-religious tome, which people pored over and memorized and cited on every possible occasion. As for drama, nothing was performed but the eight Revolutionary Model operas that had been personally approved by Jiang Qing, Mao's wife. These plays have been described as "feeble Punch and Judy shows, where the only 'revolutionary' daring is to maneuver on stage, to languorous . . . music, platoons of the People's Liberation Army complete with banners and wooden rifles."[7] It is ironic that a movement called the Cultural Revolution should have been a cultural wasteland.

The Reform Era (post–1978)

In late 1978, as part of his reform program, Deng Xiaoping proclaimed that henceforth the authorities would "let a hundred flowers bloom, let a hundred schools of thought contend," in other words, they would, within limits that have never become perfectly clear, throw open the doors of culture that had been hermetically sealed during the Cultural Revolution. Authors responded with a veritable orgy of writings. In the first years, writers were by and large cautious about probing the limits of the "hundred flowers" policy. The initial major development in fiction was so-called Scar literature, which focused on the wounds of the Cultural Revolution, but did not probe deeply and instead generally satisfied itself with putting the blame squarely on the shoulders of the Gang of Four (Jiang Qing and three of her associates who had "risen like helicopters" during the Cultural Revolution). This was followed, in the 1980s, by a much more exciting development: Root-seeking literature. Root-seeking authors—Ah Cheng, Jia Pingwa, Han Shaogong, Li Hangyu, Mo Yan, and others—reveled in ancient (or at least, traditional) Chinese philosophy and myth; they aimed at discovering the "authentic" source of Chinese culture, which they thought to be hidden deep, deep in the past, and deep, deep in the countryside. What they found, and wrote about, were mixtures of light and dark, of new and old, of the uplifting and the sordid. Mo Yan (b. 1956) in his well-known novel *Red Sorghum* (1986) declares the Chinese countryside to be "unquestionably the most beautiful and the most repulsive, the most other-worldly and the most mundane, the most sacred and the most profane, the most heroic and the most contemptible, the most hard-drinking and the most romantic place on earth."[8]

Root-seeking literature was part of a sweeping "cultural fever," as the Chinese called it: a national fascination—expressed in writing, film, song, and other cultural forms—with uncovering and celebrating China's essence. At the same time, during the 1980s there was a countervailing "fascination with things Western," including a rage for Western books in translation. These translations (or reissues of old translations) included many of the classics of Western literature (such as Shakespeare), as well works by famous modernist authors (Heinrich Heine, Henrik Ibsen, James Joyce, and so on) and "postmoderns" (such as Kurt Vonnegut and Jorge Luis Borges). Collectively, Western works have had an impact on Chinese readers that goes beyond the introducing of new terms and literary themes. The more profound of Western writings have introduced new ways of looking at the world, raised readers' consciousness, and generated intense cultural debates.

According to the author Han Shi, who wrote a book (in Chinese) entitled *The Eighties: Thirty-three Books That Changed China* (1992), the most influential Western works in the 1980s included Alvin Toffler's *The Third Wave*, Sigmund Freud's *The Interpretation of Dreams*, Max Weber's *The Protestant Ethic and the Spirit of Capitalism*, D.H. Lawrence's *Lady Chatterley's Lover*, Simone de Beauvoir's *The Second Sex*, Jean-Paul Sartre's *Being and Nothingness*, Havelock Ellis's *The Pyschology of Sex*, and Richard Nixon's *1989, Victory without War*. Together, these books suggest a philosophical, as well as psychological, preoccupation with identity (personal, cultural, and national), morality, romance, sexuality, politics, and economic change. These issues continue to preoccupy Chinese intellectuals.

For all the power and popularity of this "cultural fever," it is too utopian for some writers. A group of so-called Experimental novelists, including Ge Fei, Yu Hua, Can Xue, and Su Tong, have rejected the literary establishment, stretching the limits of taste with depictions of sadism and cannibalism, exposing the dark side of contemporary China without the high-minded concern for human dignity, social justice, and national development characteristic of Scar literature and Root-seeking literature. Can Xue's novella *Yellow Mud Street* (1989) captures the dark Experimentalist theme of hopelessness:

> In the attics of the small dark huts, the citizens drowsed. They drove away the flies with lazy motions of their flyswatters. Sometimes they would raise the swatters high and yell at the rats crawling toward the table, "I haven't died yet!" Occasionally the loudspeaker on the street started up, shaking the air and shattering their eardrums. . . . Though they listened attentively, they could understand nothing.[9]

The image and tone are reminiscent of the words of Lu Xun:

> Imagine an iron house having not a single window . . . , with all its inmates sound asleep and about to die of suffocation. Dying in their sleep, they won't feel the pain of death. Now if you raise a shout to wake up a few of the lighter sleepers, making these unfortunate few suffer the agony of irrevocable death, do you really think you are doing them a good turn?[10]

A fundamental difference between the Experimental novels of authors like Can Xue (b. 1953) and the stories of Lu Xun is that the latter held out hope while the former are unremittingly depressing and pessimistic.

Experimental novels have their counterpart in Experimental poetry, a highly controversial subject. From roughly 1979 to 1984, so-called Misty poetry reveled in illogic, erroneous grammar, and deliberate density and obscurity. This infuriated both mainstream poets and the authorities, who, because they could not quite understand what was being written, could not be certain it was not subversive, even "anti-Party." In any event, the Misty poets came under attack for their supposed nihilism. It may be hard to deny that the Misty poets were nihilistic. The best-known single line of Misty poetry is from Bei Dao (b. 1949): "I don't believe." In 1983–84, the Communist Party launched an "anti-spiritual pollution campaign" that vehemently criticized Misty poetry, Experimental novels, "Western trash," and all other manifestations of uncontrolled culture that the Party found threatening. The campaign marked a transition from Misty poetry to various forms of avant-garde writing collectively known as "poetry of the newborn generation." This transition was not necessarily caused by poets buckling under to the dictates of the state, but by writers—including many young poets—moving into all sorts of vibrant, new directions, most of which were no less subjective and controversial than Misty poetry. This flowering of vital, diverse forms of poetry has included "Stream of consciousness," with its emphasis on the emotional world of the individual, "Stream of life," which uses colloquial language to portray the lives of everyday people, "Root-seeking poetry," and about a hundred others. The novels, stories, and plays of Gao Xingjiang (b. 1940), who was awarded the Nobel Prize in literature in 2000, the first Chinese to win that accolade, were part of this avant-garde movement. Gao's plays of the 1980s have been described as examples of theater of the absurd, and his work in general, in the words of a publisher's blurb, as beacons that "illuminate the gritty realities of life, death, sex, loneliness, and exile." It was this kind of writing that got Gao in trouble with the Chinese authorities in the 1980s and caused his work to be condemned as "spiritual pollution." The announcement in 2000 that Gao, who left China for France in 1987 and later became a French citizen, had received the Nobel Prize was met with a few derisive comments, but mostly silence, from the Chinese authorities. In any case, Gao has not been published in China since the late 1980s, and he is by no means well known there.

By around 1990 a major shift in culture was underway, a shift from the "new era" of the 1980s to the "post-new era" of the 1990s—an age of commercialism, satire, and self-mockery. By almost any measure, by the 1990s China's print culture was vigorous and vibrant. In 1978, only 186 newspapers and 930 journal and magazine titles were published in the entire country. In 1995 those figures had skyrocketed to 2,202 newspapers and 8,135 journals and magazines—many of them produced by private commercial publishers. In 1978, only about 15,000 book titles were published; in 1995, well over 100,000 appeared, ranging from orthodox political tracts to pulp fiction to pornography.[11] This explosion of publications has made it difficult for the state to resist what it considers "harmful" cultural influences. The authorities can (and sometimes do) still censor or ban "objectionable" literary and artistic works, and punish errant writers, artists, and publishers. But it now seems clear that public demand, not the government, carries the greatest weight in the creative world.

Indicative of the shift toward mass, popular literature is the popularity of the author Wang Shuo (b. 1958). Wang—who has written 20 or so novels—is more than an author: he is a phenomenon, a pop superstar. His characters, the by-products of China's market economy, ridicule intellectuals, officials, and polite society, while they spend their time drinking, gambling, bragging, and seducing women. Wang freely admits that his work "has no moral principles"; but in truth his novels seem to have a purpose: to assail the pretentiousness and hypocrisy of orthodox society. As Wang has said, intellectuals are guilty of "doing too many bad things in China."[12]

From this sort of literature it is just a short step to writing that is totally commercial. A good example is the best-selling novel *The Abandoned Capital* (1993) by Jia Pingwa (b. 1953). The plot revolves around the aimless escapades of a jaded writer against a background of urban vice and corruption. Jia cleverly sprinkled the book with blank spaces, suggesting that he had self-censored particularly salacious passages, and also mocking modern-day editors who, for instance, excised obscene passages from recent editions of the sixteenth-century novel *Jinpingmei* (The plum in the golden vase), replacing them with editorial notes such as "fifty characters have been deleted here." In any event, there remain plenty of sexually explicit passages in *The Abandonded Capital*. The government denounced the book as "cluttered with pornographic and sexual references" and banned it within months of its publication—but not before it had sold at least half a million copies. The success of *The Abandoned Capital* demonstrates how the dynamics of the marketplace have frustrated literary censors. According to government figures, during a major crackdown in 1991–92, more than 30 million illegal books and magazines, including some 200,000 works of "pornography," were seized. Yet the tide of threatening works could not be stemmed.[13]

Not all popular literature is "cheap trash." Martial arts fiction, which has affinities with traditional action novels and which was very popular before the Communist takeover in 1949, staged a comeback in the 1980s and 1990s, and now, according to one authority, "enjoys a broader readership and exerts greater influence than any other literary genre in Chinese literature."[14] The most noted writer of martial arts fiction may be Jin Yong (b. 1924), a resident of Hong Kong. One of his classics, *The Flying Fox of Snowy Mountain*, has undergone 12 editions since it was first published in 1959, and has also been made into a television series and a movie.[15] Another of his many novels—*The Hero with Two Falcons* (1958)—has sold close to a million copies.[16]

Finally, since the 1980s ancient philosophical works such as the *Analects*, the *Daodejing*, and the *Book of Changes* have attracted many readers. The reason seems to be the "fever" for the revival of China's cultural traditions and "national spirit" that has swept the land. Even more popular are the four famous novels from the Ming-Qing period: *Water Margin*, with its themes of sworn brotherhood, loyalty, ambition, and righteous revenge; *Romance of the Three Kingdoms*, similarly full of courageous action; *Journey to the West*, a colorful adventure story and Buddhist allegory; and the *Dream of the Red Chamber*, a microcosm of traditional Chinese culture, and generally considered to be China's greatest traditional novel.

ART

Tradition and Transformation

Economy and Excess

Two threads run through Chinese art, stretching over four millennia and encompassing an incredibly rich variety (in techniques, media, purposes, and practitioners). The threads are economy and its opposite, excess—the *yin* and *yang* of Chinese art. Much of Chinese art, from its very earliest stirrings, is highly elaborate, heavily decorated, and vigorously, even gaudily colored. Take a typical bronze ritual vessel from the late Shang dynasty (ca. 1300 B.C.) (Figure 3.1). It is hard to find a square inch free of decoration. Examples of highly decorated objects and works of art, long separated in time from the Shang dynasty, could be multiplied again and again. Such art is complemented by works that reflect a quite opposite taste, works that are remarkably restrained, spare, and efficient.

An outstanding example of the latter is the landscape (Figure 3.2), a hanging scroll in ink on paper, by the great Ni Zan (1301–74). To eyes unfamiliar with Chinese aesthetics, Ni's work may appear to be more of an outline than a completed painting. Large expanses—the water in the lake, the sky, and so on—are blank. One would probably search in vain for a traditional Western oil painting with similarly large blank spaces on the canvas. Just why Ni Zan left these empty spaces is an interesting question. It certainly was not be-

Figure 3.1. Bronze *you*, a ceremonial millet wine bucket used in rituals, from the Shang dynasty (ca. 12th century B.C.). *© Copyright The British Museum.*

cause he was insufficiently skilled to delineate water and sky. Rather—if we try to read Ni's mind for a moment—it was because, applying the notion of economy, there was no need to elaborate the water, the sky, and so on. No need because Ni's object in this painting, we surmise, was to draw the viewer's attention to the relationship between the man-made, rustic pavilion in the painting and nature (represented by the mountains, the trees, etc.). To include in the painting all possible detail would have given it verisimilitude but at the cost of robbing it of its sense of spontaneity. Presumably, then, Ni had good reason to leave areas of his painting empty. Emptiness is, in fact, a central component of Chinese aesthetics. If the painting were completely full, it would be overfull—the crucial separate elements depicted would run together and lose their force and focus. Lest this seem too abstract and rarefied, consider the example of music. Music is not continuous sound; rather it consists of sounds (notes) divided by silence (rests); or, more precisely, we might say that music consists of sounds *linked* by silence. Or consider the example of writing. Imagine a book printed with no spaces between the words. Every reader would declare: "I can't read this book. I've got to have spaces between the words!" The empty spaces, in short, are essential.

Figure 3.2. *River Pavilion and Distant Mountains,* by Ni Zan (1301–74), an ink-on-paper hanging scroll (32 in. × 13¼ in.). *From the collection of the Tang family on loan to the Asian Art Museum.*

Linking the Word with the Image

In the painting by Ni Zan, the empty space that is the lake links the pavilion with the mountains on the distant shore. But what precisely does Ni want to show about the relationship of man and nature? Is the viewer witnessing forlornness—after all, no human being inhabits the picture—or is the painting telling an entirely different story? In this instance, the viewer need have no doubt for Ni has written an inscription on the painting, and the inscription fills in the details, so to speak. Inscriptions, often poems, are an integral part of most Chinese paintings in the traditional style. Typically, they contain the name of the artist, some words about the subject of the painting, and perhaps a few words apropos to the production of the painting (when, where, and why it was executed, etc.). Occasionally, a painting will contain inscriptions added by different hands: perhaps a friend of the artist who is moved by the painting's beauty or whimsy, or later owners. If the style of the calligraphy of the inscription and the wording suit and complement the painting, then the inscription can be said to become part of the painting and add to its beauty.

One also sees on most traditional paintings the vermillion imprint of seals (or chops). Traditionally, seals in China performed much the same function as in the premodern Western world; that is, they were affixed by authorities to authenticate documents. They are still used this way in China. Moreover, in traditional China, seals were also used in combination with, or more often in lieu of, signatures. The painting *Wang Xizhi Watching Geese*, a horizontal hand scroll that would be laid on a desk and unrolled bit by bit, by the celebrated Qian Xuan (1235–1301), has been liberally stamped with seals of all sorts and styles (Figure 3.3). The seals together with the various inscriptions, or colophons as they are often called, provide a marvelously vivid history of the painting. Studying the inscriptions and the seals, we begin to discover the many hands through which the painting passed over the centuries, and to get a hint, or more than a hint, of the feelings and reactions this work of art elicited in those who gazed at it in distant times. Thus is forged a link between us and not just the artist, but also others—however lofty they may have been—who, like us, enjoyed this masterpiece. Furthermore, seals themselves, as in Qian's painting, can be works of art. To produce a magnificent seal requires great skill in both carving and calligraphy. Styling of a seal—it may be big or small, or in between; it may be square, rectangular, round, or oval; it may use one or another of an almost limitless variety of calligraphic styles, from ancient and imposing scripts to ones that are simple and humble, almost crude—leaves ample room for artistic expression.

The connection between word and image in traditional Chinese art, particularly in painting, is made unbreakable by the cement of calligraphy. In traditional times, the two classical fine arts were typically spoken of together, almost as if they were one: *shu-hua*, calligraphy and painting. These sister arts use essentially the same tools—brushes and ink (or ink and color)—and the same ground—paper or silk—and the same techniques. According to Zhao Mengfu (1254–1322), a renowned painter, calligrapher, poet, and

Figure 3.3. *Wang Xizhi Watching Geese*, a hand scroll (36½ in. × 9³⁄₁₆ in.) in ink, color, and gold on paper, by Qian Xuan (1235–1301). *All rights reserved. The Metropolitan Museum of Art.*

scholar, "Rocks are like the *feibo* style of writing [with hollow lines in the strokes], and trees are like the *chuan* style of writing [with relatively even and twisted strokes]. The method of painting lies yet in the 'eight fundamental strokes' of writing. If there is one who can understand this, he will realize that the secret of calligraphy is really the same."[17]

The essence of calligraphy and traditional painting is rhythm: to produce a character, just as to produce an image, the brush must be moved with the right speed at the right time—here smoothly and evenly, there with a quick twist—and must be pushed down toward the surface or raised from it at just the right place at the right moment. Since Chinese paper and silk are absorbent, usually more absorbent than the paper and canvas typically used in the West for watercolor and oils, if the calligrapher/painter hesitates and stops the brush at the wrong moment, the ink begins to spread, and the stroke is ruined. Furthermore, the artist gets only one chance: a line cannot be erased or overwritten in order to improve or correct it. In this respect traditional Chinese painting differs fundamentally from Western oil painting, where because the oil paints tend to be opaque and are often applied thickly to a relatively nonabsorbent canvas, the painter can apply paint on top of paint, to achieve interesting effects, to be sure, but also to paint over mistakes and even to redo an entire, unsatisfactory composition.

The intimate relationship between image and word infuses popular folk arts as well. For instance, in paper cutting, which by the seventh century was immensely popular during folk festivals and celebrations, and which remains very popular today (see Figure 8.3), auspicious characters are commonly an integral part of the work. As in times past, calligraphy can be found everywhere in contemporary China. It graces private homes, shops, restaurants, and office buildings, in addition to old temples, monasteries, and palaces. It is engraved on metal, wood, and stone, and even the face of rocks and mountains.

Symbolism

In all cultures, symbols possess remarkable power and evocativeness; many are capable of conjuring up the strongest emotions, sentiments, and passions. Consider the Christian cross, or the American flag, or the Nazi swastika. Symbols such as these, as we well know, are so very powerful that people are willing to die—and kill—for them. Other symbols, of course, incite much less passion. Yet all symbols are alike in the sense that they stimulate something deep in the human psyche. It is this quality that makes them such powerful markers of cultural identity: to distinguish a Chinese from a Spaniard, look no further than the symbols that stir their souls. It is also this quality that artists over the ages have exploited to move their audience.

The cultural specificity of symbolism is nowhere clearer than in objects that have entirely different meanings for different cultures. In the West, the bat, for instance, generally has unpleasant associations. In China, on the other hand, the bat symbolizes good luck and prosperity (probably because "bat" and "prosperity" are homophonous—both are pronounced *fu*). Similarly, in Western paintings the dragon has been depicted as a frightful breast—consider the many paintings on the subject of St. George slaying the dragon—while in China it has always connoted benevolence, power, longevity, prosperity, and the renewal of life. The dragon was long associated with the emperor.

A pun on the sound *yu* invests fish with the meaning of "abundance." Mandarin ducks signify conjugal affection; roosters, hens, and chicks symbolize family prosperity. The most prominent plant symbol in China, past and present, is the bamboo. It symbolizes the scholar—upright, strong, and resilient, yet gentle, graceful, and refined. The bamboo is sometimes grouped with the plum and the pine—the "Three Friends of Winter," so called because the bamboo and pine are evergreen and the plum is the first tree of the year to flower, often sending forth its delicate and beautiful flowers when the ground is still covered with snow.

Receptivity

In art, as in so many other areas of culture, the people of China have generally been an eager audience for what strikes them as exotic, interesting, and novel. Thus, historically connoisseurs and the public alike have provided a demand for foreign art, art outside the Chinese tradition, and Chinese artists in turn have tended to respond by incorporating, to varying extents, foreign techniques, materials, and sensibilities into their own work. At the same time, consumers of art have also demanded that which is familiar and traditional. The result has been a continual enrichment of Chinese art over the ages—old forms of art have been reproduced, passed on, and cherished generation after generation, while new layers of art have been successively added to the rich storehouse of Chinese aesthetics.

The first great period of outside influence coincided with the coming of Buddhism to China. The adoption of Buddhism from India entailed not only a new religious and philosophical outlook, but also a new artistic expression. This was most obvious in sculpture, an art that before Buddhism had been of relatively little importance in China. From the tradition of Indian sculpture, which itself had been strongly influenced by Persian and Hellenistic art, Chinese Buddhist sculptors borrowed a gentle, serene rhythm, evident in the almost undulating massing of the sculpted figure and in the superb representation of clinging drapery that forms wave-like folds about the body. The second great period of outside influence coincided with the arrival of the West. In the eighteenth century, the Jesuit painter Giuseppe Castiglione introduced Western naturalism to the emperor's court. However, the influence of Western art at this time remained strictly limited: although the paintings of many so-called court artists, employed by the emperor, began to reveal Western influences (in, for instance, perspective), the great bulk of Chinese art remained little affected by European currents.

It was not until early in the twentieth century that Western art began to exert a profound influence on China. In 1912, the first year of the republic, the Shanghai Fine Arts Institute was founded. The institute introduced drawing with pencils and charcoal, and watercolor and gouache, on nonabsorbent paper instead of ink and color washes on absorbent paper or silk. Along with these new materials came new techniques. Most notably, the students learned to render solid form in light and shade—characteristics of Western realism— as a counterpart to the technique in traditional Chinese painting that rendered form through modulations of the line. Under the leadership of the Shanghai Fine Arts Institute, the subject of works of art also was borrowed, notably drawing from life, including the nude. Traditionally, depicting the human body was little esteemed, and the nude had never been considered a suitable subject for fine arts. Instead, Chinese painters had preferred to depict, with a few swift brushstrokes, such creatures as mice and insects.

The introduction of drawing from life represented nothing less than a revolution. In traditional China, painting was usually done in the studio. The artist looked not at his subject, but instead tended to re-create paintings of the old masters or even to learn forms out of handbooks, such as the exceedingly popular *Mustard-Seed Garden Painting Manual* (Part I published in 1679, and Parts II and III in 1701). This habit—part of the same culture that led the civil service examinations to require rote memorization—was so deeply ingrained that when many painters began to turn out Western-style works they produced uncritical imitations. Originality and creativity were in short supply.

The rush to "learn from the West" constituted but one stream in the art of modern China. Traditional art continued to be produced and appreciated, and has endured to this day. *Guohua*, painting in the traditional Chinese style, has continued to develop and thrive. When thinking of guohua, the artist who comes immediately to mind is the great Qi Baishi (1863–1957), who had few rivals when it came to producing sparkling, happy, creative, whimsical, and thoroughly "Chinese" paintings (see Figure 3.4).

Popular traditional folk arts have also stood the test of time. In the 1930s and after, in the Communist-controlled areas, woodblock prints—an old, traditional form—and cartoons, both now with "suitable" subjects (the exploitation of poor peasants by landlords, etc.), were used to get the Communist message across. Cartoons were far from monopolized by the Communists, for in the twentieth century all over China they came to per-

Figure 3.4. *Oil Lamp and Rat*, by Qi Baishi (1863–1957), painted in 1947 when the artist was 84 years old. Qi used this subject in several paintings. The inscription reads "March 1947, Old Man Baishi." Literally, the date reads, "The third month of *ding hai*," ding hai being a year in the series of the ten Heavenly Stems and twelve Earthly Branches, which in the twentieth century works out to 1947 (see Chapter 8). *From* Qi Baishi zuopin ji *(Collected works of Qi Baishi) (Tianjin: People's Fine Art Publishing House, 1990).*

form many thoroughly familiar roles: in advertising, in political comment, and in comics. The tradition of telling stories with cartoonlike illustrations dates from the Han period, if not earlier, and for centuries Chinese children have pored over strip picture books of famous novels. For most people, reading serial picture books was their first taste of the popular classics of Chinese literature.

"Revolutionary" Culture and Counterculture: Art in the People's Republic

From the establishment of the People's Republic in late 1949 until the start of the Cultural Revolution in 1966, art in China continued along the three lines of development that had characterized the first half of the twentieth century. The first line consisted of art in the Chinese tradition, the second of art closely patterned after the Western tradition, and the third of art that in various respects combined and mixed the two traditions. What changed most was the fact that Communists were now in power and hence in a position to dictate that "art must serve the revolution." Concretely this meant that the new government continued to cultivate traditional folk arts and also promoted Western-style works, but with the proviso that all works of art were to be vehicles of propaganda. "Socialist realism," a notion imported from the Soviet Union, became the ruling doctrine. According to this new orthodoxy, which was applied especially to oil paintings, acceptable subjects revolved around such themes as strong, determined, healthy workers and peasants forging ahead with production. And, as the name implies, techniques were to be strictly limited to "realism": abstractionism and non-representationism were steadfastly rejected. Guohua painters too had to accommodate the new order. Landscapes, flowers and birds, bamboo, and other subjects were to be replaced by a new preferred subject: the human figure, heroically "making revolution."

Some artists found ways around these strictures, by emphasizing the symbolic meaning of traditional motifs (for instance, the red of plum blossoms could be said to represent the Communist victory or the blood of martyrs), or by painting landscapes to illustrate one or another of Mao Zedong's poems, and so on. However, with the start of the Cultural Revolution in 1966, such resistance became impossible.

The Cultural Revolution

When it comes to art, the Cultural Revolution decade (1966–76) can be passed over quickly. Artistic creation, except for propaganda, essentially ceased. Art was no longer something to be produced by professionals trained in academies but by "the people": peasants and workers with no special artistic training (and often with no special aptitude either). The result was poster art, even though some of it was quite good (see Figure 3.5). Most professional artists, like other intellectuals, were sent to work on farms or in factories. Under the pretext of erasing the "Four Olds," rampaging Red Guards invaded artists' homes, studios, and museums and destroyed countless works of art, doing irreparable damage to their nation's cultural heritage.

Art from the Reform Era to Today

After 1978 and the launching of the reform movement, art followed much the same path as that trod by literature. In a rapid move away from the stultifying confines of socialist realism, artists experimented with a variety of

Figure 3.5. *Commune Fish Pond,* a so-called peasant painting, by amateur artist Dong Zhengyi, exhibited in Beijing in 1973 and reproduced as a popular poster. *Photograph provided by the author.*

forms and styles: some sought inspiration in models from the West, while others agonized over the issues of national and personal identity. Scar painters replicated the agenda of the authors of Scar literature: their works exposed the cruelty and abuses of power during the Cultural Revolution, but some also celebrated leading figures in the CCP who, it was thought, had exercised a restraining influence during the Cultural Revolution. Hagiographic portraits, especially of the late premier Zhou Enlai (d. 1976), were commonplace. Moreover, the style of much of Scar painting was little removed from the "poster art" of the Cultural Revolution. The "Native Soil" movement in art was a visual counterpart to the Root-seeking school in literature: its artists painted the countryside and made it almost exotic. But their style too tended to be derivative. The models in this case were traditional European styles, particularly the seventeenth-century Dutch school and the nineteenth-century French representational painters, but also French neo-classicism and modern American painters like Andrew Wyeth.

As in literature, reaction to the Scar and Native Soil agenda moved along several divergent paths, particularly in the direction of avant-gardism and— roughly in the opposite direction—of a revival of guohua. The event that marked the resurgence of traditional painting was a large exhibition, accompanied by an academic conference, held in Beijing in 1988. This exhibition eschewed the word "guohua" (literally, "national painting") in favor of "water and ink painting." This change in terminology marked a growing recognition that painting in China could no longer be rigidly divided between works in "the Chinese style" and those in "the Western style."[18]

Moving in a direction quite different from "water and ink" painters, a fringe group of dissidents known as the Stars drew on unconventional symbolism to convey their political, social, and cultural messages. This symbolism often has obscure, ambiguous meanings, and seems to echo the Misty poetry. For example, a painting by Huang Rui (b. 1952) even includes Bei Dao's inspirational poem, "Our Every Morning Sun." Other examples of their symbolism carry a perfectly clear political message. For example, a wooden mask sculpted by Wang Keping (b. 1949) and entitled *The Silent One* depicts a man with a cylinder stuffed in his mouth, like a huge cork. The Stars' first officially sanctioned show, in 1979, displayed 170 paintings, graphics, and sculptures, including some nudes, abstractions, and semi-abstractions, and drew at least 40,000 viewers. Whether people understood what the Stars were doing is unclear, although undoubtedly because of their provocative political stance they received widespread attention from foreign observers. By the early 1980s, the group began to dissolve, and in a pattern that would be repeated by many Chinese artists in the 1980s and 1990s, a number of its most accomplished members—including Wang Keping, Ma Desheng (b. 1952), Li Shuang (b. 1957), Huang Rui, and Ai Weiwei (b. 1957)—eventually left China for Europe, the United States, or other parts of Asia. Their reasons for emigrating varied, but in general they left less out of political motives than because of personal considerations and the fact that the market for their work was mainly outside China.[19]

In all, the Stars represented a critical breakthrough in Chinese art, facilitating, or at least presaging, the so-called New Wave movement of 1985. Like many other groups in the 1980s, the New Wave artists received nourishment from Western notions of art. Strongly influenced by Marcel Duchamp, their aim was to subvert traditional Chinese aesthetics. For some, this meant quite literally deconstructing their artistic productions. Huang Yongping (b. 1934), for instance, burned many of his works at exhibition sites in an attempt to "abandon art." Some New Wave artists—notably Gu Wenda (b. 1955), Zhang Peili (b. 1957), Zeng Fanzhi (b. 1964), and others—used embarrassing or otherwise discomforting images to dismay or disgust their audience. These images involved the depiction of voyeuristic intrusions, pain, bondage, degeneracy and decay—recalling, of course, the shock tactics of China's Experimentalist writers.

The year 1989 was a turning point in Chinese art, as it was in many other areas of life in China. In early February the prestigious China Art Gallery sponsored a "China/Avant-Garde" exhibit, in which nearly all of the major avant-garde artists of the decade participated. On the opening day, the artists

Tang Song and Xiao Lu fired shots at their own installation, creating chaos and temporarily closing the show. Although Tang and Xiao were arrested, they were released within three days, no doubt because they were both the offspring of high-level officials. This event highlighted the delicate issue of cadre privilege in Chinese society and also marked the abrupt end of official support for avant-garde art in post-Mao China.

The disillusion of many artists upon the closing of the show, compounded by the traumatic events at Tiananmen Square in the spring of 1989, gave birth to what has been termed "Cynical realism." This movement rejected the heroic idealism of the 1980s and instead adopted a "roguish" perspective on life—focusing on themes of dissipation, indifference, jadedness, and sarcasm. The "poster boy" of this sort of alienated art might well be Fang Lijun (b. 1963), whose unflattering portraits of himself and his friends reveal them to be bald, apelike men, in the midst of giant yawns. Liu Wei (b. 1956), a kindred spirit, has created a series of distorted images of family members and army officers, satirizing their self-important postures. Liu says that his portraits reveal "the helplessness and awkwardness of my family and of all Chinese people."[20] One is reminded of the literary work of Wang Shuo.

Another response to the events of 1989 was an explosion of enthusiasm for "Political Pop." This movement had already begun in the mid- and late 1980s, motivated by fondness for the pop art of Andy Warhol and others. In 1990 the artist Wang Guangyi (b. 1956) began his Great Criticism series, a humorous approach to political art. In this series, which coincided with the rise of "Mao fever" in China, Wang juxtaposed slogans of the Cultural Revolution with images and brand names of popular foreign consumer products, such as Coca-Cola and Canon cameras. At about the same time, Liu Dahong (b. 1962) produced his Four Seasons series, which shows Chairman Mao in the midst of scenes inspired by recent political developments as well as traditional religious motifs, myths, operas, popular tales, and folk customs. The inhabitants of these bizarre scenes range from comrades in arms and doting admirers to animals (both dead and alive), skeletons (alive), and a curious tourist. In 1992, Li Shan (b. 1944), famous for his use of pink and red paint to portray shockingly explicit sexual images, used echoes of this imagery to produce obviously androgynous portraits of Chairman Mao. Another Pop artist, Feng Mengbo (b. 1966), took characters from the Revolutionary Model operas of the Cultural Revolution period and showed them as video game figures.

Whatever the theme or message of Chinese art in the 1980s, at the center of artistic creation was oil painting. By the 1990s, however, this was no longer so. Performance art, mostly an underground genre during the 1980s, and large public art became increasingly prominent through the 1990s. A huge work of art—*Ice: Midland '96*—created for the reopening of a shopping center in January 1996 in the city of Zhengzhou combined both public art and performance art. Three artists—Wang Jin, Jiang Bo, and Guo Jinghan—created a "Great Wall" of ice, about 100 feet long, 8 feet high, and 3 feet thick. The wall contained nearly 300 items: merchandise that had been salvaged from the old shopping center, which had burned down the previous year; photographs of the fire; equipment used in putting out the fire; and so on. After the ceremony, people were encouraged to pull from the melting wall whatever they wanted, and take it away. About 100,000 people participated, surely some sort of record for a bit of performance art.[21]

Lithography, previously a marginal genre, also blossomed in the 1990s. Li Fan (b. 1966), an artist and teacher in the Chinese Academy of Art, is a leading exponent of color lithography. His works have been characterized as "urban archaeology," a struggle to capture historical moments in the rapidly changing urban landscape of Beijing. Li portrays the culturally hybrid nature of scenes in Beijing—the mixture of cars, buses, bicycles, Chinese and foreign restaurants, boutiques and bookstores, old buildings and new—with great accuracy, using thick lines and a flattening effect. The solid appearance of these scenes contradicts the fluid, unstable nature of urban life in Beijing and other cities today, where entire neighborhoods seem to disappear overnight to be replaced by shopping centers and high-rises.[22]

Finally, mixed media exploded onto the scene in the 1990s. Unlike oil painting and Chinese-style painting, which tended to be produced by artists who often had careers that can be traced back to the 1970s or even earlier, most of the artists using mixed media and "hybrid materials" began their careers in the mid-1980s or 1990s. This is true of most of the New Wave artists, including Xu Bing (b. 1955). Xu's most famous work is *Tianshu* (A heavenly book), a large installation consisting of page upon page of printed "text," some draped from the ceiling, some hung on the walls, some placed on the floor (Figure 3.6). The "text" is mostly composed of thousands of characters invented by Xu, that is to say, it consists of "words" of no meaning. This work—first exhibited in Beijing in 1988, and then later in Madison, Wisconsin, and elsewhere—calls into question the linkage between meaning and words, or between understanding and signs in general.

Installations with the theme of written texts, like Xu Bing's *Tianshu*, were especially popular in the 1990s. In some, entire rooms—walls, floors, ceilings—are covered with characters. And in others, the value of blank space in traditional Chinese painting has been turned on its head, with characters jammed into a work of art until there is almost no space between them. Paradoxically, this makes the little remaining blank space all the more precious.

Figure 3.6. Installation of *Tianshu (A Book from the Sky)*, by Xu Bing, at the Elvehjem Museum of Art, University of Wisconsin-Madison, November 30, 1991–January 19, 1992. *Photo courtesy Elvehjem Museum of Art.*

Obviously, some of the most imposing, vibrant, and creative works of art and of literature in contemporary China appear to be quite untraditional. Yet, at the same time many of them reflect a particularly Chinese aesthetic concern with the link between words and images. How words and images are handled may be new and experimental; but the ongoing concern itself with artfully connecting words and images reflects a long and brilliant tradition.

NOTES

1. Lin Yutang, *My Country and My People* (New York: John Day, 1935), p. 214.

2. Liu Wu-chi, *An Introduction to Chinese Literature* (Bloomington: Indiana University Press, 1966), p. 5.

3. Mao Tse-tung [Mao Zedong], "Talks at Yenan Forum on Art and Literature," *Selected Works of Mao Tse-tung*, vol. 3 (Peking: Foreign Languages Press, 1965), p. 86.

4. Tung Chi-ming, *An Outline History of China* (Peking: Foreign Languages Press, 1959), p. 385.

5. Ku Hung-ming [Gu Hongming], "Returned Students and Literary Revolution," *Millard's Review*, no. 11 (Aug. 16, 1919): pp. 432–38.

6. Liang Shiqiu, "Literature and Revolution," in Kirk A. Denton, ed., *Modern Chinese Literary Thought: Writings on Literature, 1893–1945* (Stanford, CA: Stanford University Press, 1996), pp. 310–11.

7. Simon Leys, *Chinese Shadows* (New York: Viking, 1977), p. 143.

8. Mo Yan, *Red Sorghum*, trans. Howard Goldblatt (New York: Viking, 1993), p. 4. I have slightly revised the translation.

9. Can Xue, *Old Floating Cloud*, trans. Ronald R. Janssen and Jian Zhang (Evanston, IL: Northwestern University Press, 1991), p. 51.

10. Lu Xun, "Preface to *Call to Arms*," *Lu Xun: Selected Works*, vol. 1, trans. Yang Xianyi and Gladys Yang (Beijing: Foreign Languages Press, 1980), p. 37.

11. *China News Analysis*, no. 1578 (Feb. 1, 1997); Judy Polumbaum, "New Chinese Literature," *Poets and Writers Magazine* (Jan./Feb. 1995).

12. Interview with Wang Shuo, in *Asiaweek* (Aug. 9, 1996).

13. Polumbaum, "New Chinese Literature," p. 31.

14. Cao Zhengwen, "Chinese Gallant Fiction," in Wu Dingbo and Patrick D. Murphy, eds., *Handbook of Chinese Popular Culture* (Westport, CT: Greenwood Press, 1994), p. 237.

15. The novel has been translated under the title *Fox Volant of the Snowy Mountain*.

16. Cao Zhengwen, "Chinese Gallant Fiction," p. 250.

17. Quoted in Lin Yutang, *My Country and My People*, p. 292. I have slightly amended Lin's translation.

18. Institute of Chinese Painting, *Zhongguo hua yanjiu* (Research on Chinese-style painting), vol. 6 (Nanjing: Jiangsu meishu chubanshe, 1990). "Water and ink" (*shui-mo*) was by no means a new term; what was new was the careful and conscious avoidance of the term *guohua* and the "separatism" it implies.

19. On the Stars, see Michael Sullivan, *Art and Artists of Twentieth-Century China* (Berkeley: University of California Press, 1996), pp. 221–24.

20. Quoted in Andrew Solomon, "Their Irony, Humor (and Art) Can Save China," *New York Times Magazine* (Dec. 19, 1993): p. 47.

21. Wang Jin, Jiang Bo, and Guo Jinghan, "Guanyu 'Bing: 96 zhongyuan' de

wenhua yuyi" (The cultural meaning of "Ice: Midland '96"), *Meishu yanjiu* (Art research), no. 3 (Aug. 1996).

22. Yin Shangxi, "Li Fan: Shicheng kaogu yu kongjian xushi" (Li Fan: Urban archaeology and the narrative of space), *Meishu yanjiu* (Art research), no. 3 (Aug. 1996): pp. 61–62.

4

Music and Dance

ALTHOUGH MUSIC and dance throughout Chinese history have served to give voice to the most basic human emotions—love, joy, sadness, and so on—they have also performed the crucial functions of regulating human relations and teaching the people. From the very beginnings of Chinese civilization, music or dance or both have been an indispensible part of ceremonies and celebrations, such as weddings and funerals, that symbolize and reaffirm the ties that bind people together. For most of Chinese history, when the vast majority of people were illiterate, the lessons of the past came not through the dry pages of history books but more often through the vibrant media of music and dance, especially in Chinese opera and musical drama.

EDIFICATION AND ENTERTAINMENT: MUSIC IN THEORY AND PRACTICE

The Role of Music

Throughout China's history, music has played a vital role in virtually all aspects of the life of the people, whether it be recreational, religious, social, or economic. From the improvised chants shouted by gangs of laborers to the poems studiously sung by scholars, from the attractive ditties sung by peddlers to advertise their wares to the suggestive love songs intoned by farmers on a summer's evening, from the soft and subtle music performed at Confucian temples to the raucous instrumental pieces that reverberate at popular dramas and operas, music in one form or another has permeated life in China.

Even today in many places when couples marry they do so to music. The bride is carried in a sedan chair or cart (or increasingly in a truck or car) from her father's house to the house of her future husband, accompanied by musicians—a sizable band with a variety of instruments if the father is wealthy, or just a few people with gongs and cymbals if the father is not so wealthy. And after death, music also comes in to play: funeral processions include hired musicians who raise a din with horns, drums, and cymbals. Naturally, over the centuries customs in music, as in other realms, have changed and some have disappeared entirely. Yet others have endured with remarkable fidelity, and still others, which once fell into disuse, have revived. Finally, in every age there have been important additions to Chinese music— new instruments, new genres, new techniques.

Clearly, music in China has been more than a diversion or entertainment. Confucius asked rhetorically, "Are bells and drums all that is meant by music?" In other words, it is not the sound of instruments alone that constitutes music. Just as in art and literature, music has its place in uplifting people. From this perspective, the essence of music is not pleasant sound, but transcendent, *ethical* power. From very ancient days—long before the time of Confucius—music was an integral element of ritual and an essential regulator of cosmic harmony and hence of harmony on earth. Since the universe was not formless and chaotic—or at least since people wanted to prevent the universe from falling into chaos—ritual music was strictly ordered and precise. Until the very end of the imperial period in 1911, music continued to be part of state ritual; so central was it that a fourth-century B.C. text declared that "government is modeled upon music."

Music in ritual extended beyond the state and elite society into the lives of the common people: music for worship, state service, work, and community and family celebrations, all of which entailed a rich panoply of instruments. But music also was, and remains, an entertainment and an art to express the emotions. The poems in the *Book of Songs* mostly consisted of folk songs, on themes of love and daily life. In later ages, poetry continued to be written to be accompanied by music or to be sung or chanted. Unfortunately, the melodies have been lost; what remains are the lyrics, the poems themselves.

The Structure and Sonic Quality of Traditional Music

Traditional Chinese music possesses its own distinctive rhythm, tone quality, beat, and embellishments. In each of these aspects it is quite unlike Western music. Much of what makes it distinctive has to do with the sound quality and playing style of Chinese musical instruments. Similarly, traditional Chinese singing tends to have an immediately recognizable sound quality, one that is different from Western voice production. Although Chinese singing style differs from region to region and genre to genre (for example, popular narrative singers in the north generally use a relaxed, natural voice, while singers from the southwest tend to produce a steady vibrato), in general it is noted for its high, thin, nasal quality. Not until the twentieth century did Western-style voice production, with its resonant tone, begin to influence singing in China.

The earliest Chinese music evidently followed a pentatonic (five-tone) scale and essentially it continues to do so today (although other scales are sometimes encountered). Since the earliest times, the Chinese state was preoccupied with absolute pitch and with "rediscovering" the so-called yellow bell (*huangzhong*) pitch, the fundamental pitch on which all other pitches are calculated. If the yellow bell was not properly set, it was believed, all of society would suffer: crops would fail, public disorder would arise, and the state itself would be threatened. However, as far as musical practice was concerned, this sort of thinking remained an intellectual exercise. When musical ensembles actually played, different instruments often followed different levels of temperament (temperament being the adjustment of the intervals of the scale by slightly varying the pitch), with the result that music had a somewhat "out of tune" flavor. Although in modern times ensembles and orchestras have "corrected" this by adopting an equal-tempered scale, the flexible, poly-temperamental phenomenon was a vibrant ingredient in traditional music.

Rhythm has been of secondary importance in Chinese music. Compared to the driving, dynamic, and complex rhythms of African and Indian music, for example, traditional Chinese music is mostly in simple duple meter (that is, two beats or a multiple of two beats per measure). Pride of place in Chinese music is given to melody and to timbre (or tonal quality). In the 1930s, the musicologist John Levis built an entire book around the notion that the Chinese language, with its tonal characteristics, forms the basis of Chinese music. If we think of melody as a line of tones, then Levis may have been right in saying that "the Chinese possess a language which employs the basic elements of melodic movement consciously in all the words of the language."[1] This is another way of saying that Chinese is a tonal language and sounds "sing song." In any case, melody stands at the forefront of Chinese music. Indeed, it is so important that all instruments in ensembles play the same melody, so that there is no harmony or counterpoint. This is the opposite of Western music, where harmony takes precedence over melody. If an instrumentalist in a Western string quartet fails to show up, the performance cannot go on because each instrument is absolutely essential to producing the harmony that is an integral part of the composition. In Chinese ensembles, on the other hand, instruments can be easily added or subtracted since harmony is not a consideration.

The soul of Chinese music lies in timbre, that quality of sound that distinguishes one type of instrument or voice from all others. It was around the eighth century B.C., or earlier, that the Chinese developed the "eight timbre" (*bayin*) system for classifying instruments, one of the earliest attempts in the world at such a classification. This ancient system categorized instruments according to the material from which they were made (or which gave them their distinctive sound): metal (for bronze bells), stone (for chimes), skin (for drums), gourds (for the mouth organ), bamboo (for flutes), wood (for percussive wooden beaters), silk (for the cords of stringed instruments), and earth (for clay ocarinas). The importance of the bayin system lies not in its accuracy as a way of classifying popular instruments in more recent centuries—it is not very accurate for that purpose—but rather in the importance it places on timbre. That importance lies in more than just the unique sound of the various instruments in each family, but also in the manipulation or coloring of sound. For instance, the very same note played on the *qin* zither can be given subtle coloration by fingering techniques: plucking the string inward produces a thinner sound, while plucking it outward yields a fuller sound. Chinese music down through the ages has inherited a love of timbre. It can be said that what Chinese music lacks in harmony it makes up for in timbral quality: the enjoyment of a tune lies not only in appreciation of its rhythm and melody, but also in its instrumentation, that is, in its delightfully unique sounds.

Traditional Instruments

Some of the most popular Chinese instruments are not entirely Chinese. This is true of the *erhu*, the most popular of several closely related two-stringed fiddles, which probably had its origins in Central Asia. By the fourteenth century, the erhu had become a popular instrument in Beijing opera and in other ensembles, and by the twentieth century it had also become a very popular solo instrument, which it remains today. The erhu is analogous to the violin, and performs roughly the same role in ensembles. Also like the violin, it is an excellent instrument for performers to demonstrate their virtuosity, or for amateurs to amuse themselves and friends with a lively tune. In modern times, inexpensively priced erhu have been readily available, and consequently almost anyone, no matter how tight his or her budget, can afford one. The player of the erhu need not fear the embarrassment once suffered by a Western violinist who forgot to bring his bow, for in the erhu the bow is "captured" between the two strings (Figure 4.1).

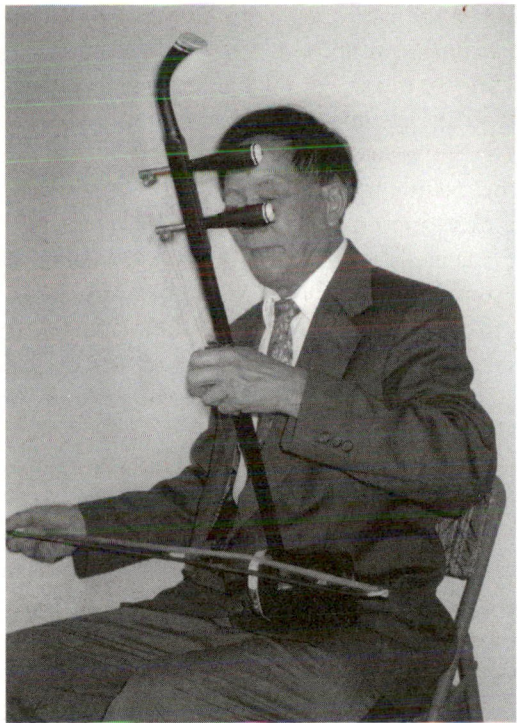

Figure 4.1. Performance on the *erhu. Photograph provided by the author.*

The *pipa*, a fretted four-stringed pear-shaped lute dating back to the Han dynasty, originally was probably also a foreign import, perhaps from as far away as the Middle East. Like the erhu, by the twentieth century the pipa had become an immensely popular solo instrument, while at the same time it has remained a popular instrument in ensembles. Just the look of the pipa alone suggests that this is an instrument that will keep the performer fully occupied—its body is covered with frets (29 in all), from the neck almost to the very bottom of the belly, where the strings are attached. Watching a pipa performance is a stirring experience: the fingers of both hands of the performer seem to fly up and down the instrument, from one fret and string to another with breathtaking speed (Figure 4.2).

The premier Chinese horn is the *suona*, which was introduced from Central Asia, or from India according to other accounts, around the sixteenth century. This double-reed instrument with a wooden body and a brass or copper horn boasts a particularly loud and shrill tone that slices through the air (Figure 4.3). This makes it especially suitable for attracting attention—

Figure 4.2. Kindergarteners learning to play the *pipa*, in suburban Beijing, 1998. *Courtesy of Ken Chamberlain.*

it is impossible to ignore its piercing tone—and indeed one of the early uses of the suona was to marshal and inspire the soldiery. The suona is still used in similar ways. For instance, during the communization movement of the late 1950s, pictorial magazines sometimes featured photographs of farmers marching to the fields behind one or two individuals blowing on suona. The suona has been an essential part of wedding and funeral processions, and in the theater it has also been a standard. In Beijing opera, for instance, the loud tones of the suona announce the arrival on stage of the emperor.

Instruments like the erhu, pipa, and suona, and many others may originally have been foreign, but over time they were developed and adapted so that they became a thoroughly integral part of Chinese musical culture. A number of other major Chinese instruments are still older—so old that their origins are lost in the distant past. Foremost among these is the qin (also known as the *guqin*), a long, seven-stringed zither that according to legend was invented by Fuxi, a mythical ruler who reigned ca. 3000 B.C. and by some accounts was the progenitor of the Chinese people. Archaeological evidence of the qin dates back to around the fourteenth or fifteenth century B.C. By the time of Confucius, the qin had become an elite instrument, a symbol of "correct" music, and an essential feature in ritual ceremonies. Over the centuries it remained the instrument of choice of scholars, many of whom had their portrait painted with a qin across their lap. Probably few of them played the instrument well if they played it at all. But that did not matter: the role of

Figure 4.3. A procession of members of a Daoist religious group, in Tianjin, on the occasion of the celebration of a popular deity, the Heavenly Empress, 1998. The four men at the front of the procession are playing *suona. Courtesy of Thomas DuBois.*

the qin in the portrait was to symbolize virtue and erudition. For such a symbolic role, the qin is the perfect instrument. It produces a soft, delicate sound (some people complain it is too quiet and have looked into ways of increasing its volume), it is unequaled by any other Chinese instrument in its timbral nuances (there are, for instance, 60 kinds of vibratos in qin fingering techniques), and it is relatively expensive (the body is covered with many layers of highly polished lacquer, sometimes mixed with gold dust).[2]

Another ancient instrument, a mouth organ called the *sheng*, managed to cross the divide between popular and elite instruments by becoming important in both aristocratic rituals and popular performances. The sheng—still popular today—consists of a circle of bamboo pipes, each with a reed fixed to its lower end, inserted into a bowl-like vessel (about the size of two hands cupped together) fashioned from a gourd (in ancient times), or (in later centuries) from wood, or (in modern times) from copper or brass. The sheng is the only Chinese instrument that regularly sounds more than one note at a time and so is particularly suited to solos.

It would take several more pages merely to list all the remaining traditional instruments, some of which can only be seen in old paintings and have not been heard for centuries, and others—for example, the *dizi*, a horizontal flute—that are still common today. A list of gongs alone would number at least 20 items. Suffice it to say that Chinese musical culture includes an extraordinarily large variety of instruments—horns and flutes; stringed instruments that are plucked, bowed, or struck; percussives (drums, gongs, cymbals, clappers, bells, etc.)—that together make for an extraordinarily rich diversity of sounds.

Music and Identity

Until modern times, the composers of traditional Chinese music were usually unknown and performers were virtually anonymous. In part, this was the result of a lack of satisfactory methods of transcribing notes. Over the centuries, there were several methods of notation, but these mostly showed such things as where the hands were to be placed on the instrument. There was no equivalent of the modern Western method of writing music. Instead, music was mostly learned by the "aural" method—the performer played by ear—and was handed down from performer to performer or from master to disciple. Since there was no authoritative musical score to which performers might refer, they were free not only to interpret a piece of music by adjusting its tempo, dynamics, and so on, but also to add, subtract, and rearrange material until they virtually became composers themselves. The anonymity of professional musicians was also a reflection of their low social status. Throughout much of the late imperial period, the law lumped professional musicians together with other so-called weed people—vagabonds, prostitutes, and the like. In cities and towns, musicians performed wherever they could find an audience: sometimes in theaters, but also on street corners, at temple fairs, in teahouses, in brothels. In the countryside, where villages were too small and too poor to support full-time resident musicians, performers had no choice but to roam from place to place, performing here and there for meager payment. Those few musicians who staffed the orchestras of aristocrats and the imperial court were considered no more than servants.

The introduction of Western music, modern ideas of entertainment, and modern means of communication during the twentieth century revolutionized this tradition. The spread of mass-circulation newspapers and glossy magazines, movies, radio, and the phonograph made possible the creation of a mass popular commercial culture. The public, at least in the big cities, could now read about and see pictures (stills or movies) of musicians and via radio or record could actually hear them perform. This facilitated widespread advertising, promotion, and "hype"—all essential ingredients of a "star" system. In addition, the New Culture Movement, which identified all that was old and characteristically Chinese as backward while all that was Western as progressive and modern, played a role. If the West adulated stars and treated them as cultural icons, then China, to be modern and progressive, needed to do the same.

One of the biggest celebrities from the 1910s to the 1950s was Mei Lanfang (1894–1961), who played female roles in Beijing opera. Wherever Mei performed, he drew wildly enthusiastic and adoring crowds. Mei was also probably the first Chinese entertainer to be celebrated abroad: he hobnobbed with Charlie Chaplin, by far the most popular American comic actor of the time, and received an honorary degree from the University of California. Mei's acclaim at home and abroad, while routine for Hollywood stars, was something entirely new to China. It was said that when Mei was engaged for an entire season he was paid, in gold, the astronomical equivalent of $20,000 a month—a sum that put him on par with the greatest of Hollywood stars.[3]

In the twentieth century, Western-influenced popular music, including jazz, which was the rage in the West from the 1920s, invaded urban China. In the big cities, especially Shanghai, nightclubs and bars sprang up, creating new venues for the performance of "new music." Western classical music also made its appearance, first in Shanghai, China's largest and most modern metropolis. A classical orchestra was formed in Shanghai early in the twentieth century, but at first it performed mostly for foreigners, and its musicians were nearly all foreigners (the first Chinese musicians were not hired until the 1930s).[4] The Shanghai National Conservatory of Music, the first Chinese institution for training classical musicians, was established in 1927. Although it offered a few courses in traditional Chinese music, overall in what it taught and in its methods, it was very much like a conservatory in any major European city. Not until 1965 was a conservatory—the Chinese Music Conservatory, in Beijing—established to train professionals in traditional Chinese music.

For most Chinese, enjoying Western-style music was not a simple matter of "worshiping the West," for, just as the Communists have proclaimed, foreign things could be made to serve China's needs. The public schools that began to proliferate in China early in the twentieth century taught new-style songs with patriotic, revolutionary themes current at the time: modernization, the struggle for national strength, women's liberation, and so on. These tunes, mostly marches, tended to be adapted from Japanese popular and military songs that had been largely borrowed from Western European or

American melodies. Public school music was thus a mix of Western music with Japanese overtones overlaid with Chinese themes—fusion music par excellence.

Nationalism also dictated the recovery of "authentic" Chinese music. From around the 1920s, a movement to collect folk songs and disseminate them beyond their locales gathered steam. Folk songs, which had always been popular in the countryside, now reached an entirely new level of popularity in the cities. The themes of Chinese folk songs were largely the same as the themes of folk songs everywhere: love, courtship, and heartbreak; odes to one's home region; harvest songs; and so on. However, as folk songs were extracted from their environment and revamped and sanitized into abstractions that supposedly represented "the music of the people," they often became something the villagers did not recognize as their own. At the most extreme, folk songs became crudely politicized. In the 1930s and 1940s, the Communists sought to transform folk songs into vehicles of propaganda by attaching new, political lyrics to the melodies. Imagine the reaction of villagers to old tunes now sung to lyrics such as "Chairman Mao's words are engraved on our hearts."

With the Communist victory in 1949, the music scene underwent an important change as the new state became a patron and promoter of music all across China, just as it did of literature and the arts. In many ways, musical culture flourished in the period from 1949 to the start of the Cultural Revolution in 1966. Professional performers were organized into state-sponsored unions, troupes, and orchestras, and many for the first time began to enjoy financial security and social status. Freed from their previously precarious existence, they were now able to develop their art, and the highly skilled solo performance, which had been emerging during the first few decades of the twentieth century, blossomed. At the same time, Beijing opera and other regional dramatic music prospered as did Western-style orchestral music. Some of the most interesting new orchestral music involved the combination of Western techniques and instruments with the tonality and style of traditional Chinese music. Most new arrangements, however, amounted to little more than adding a few traditional instruments to essentially Western orchestras.

As we have suggested, the communist state, like the imperial state of old, has looked upon music not merely or primarily as entertainment but as a tool. By fostering traditional Chinese music the new state was simultaneously furthering nationalism, and by promoting the music of other countries— both folk songs and Western-style orchestral music—it was demonstrating internationalism and solidarity with "the people" of the world. In all instances, what the state required was music with revolutionary themes. The titles of a few orchestral works composed during the 1950s clearly suggest the results: *The Long March Symphony* (referring to the Communists' "heroic" 6,000-mile retreat from Central China, 1934–35), Symphony no. 2 *The War of Resistance against Japan,* and the suite from the opera *Guerrillas of Honghu Lake.* Nonetheless, during the 1950s it was still possible to draft compositions without overt political themes—for instance, *Yellow Crane,* a symphony with a fairy-tale theme, performed by a Western orchestra with a bamboo flute (dizi). With the start of the Cultural Revolution, this freedom disappeared.

The meager musical diet during the 10 years of the Cultural Revolution (1966–76) consisted of the eight Revolutionary Model operas and the songs and local dramas that were spun off from them, plus songs with lyrics taken from Chairman Mao's quotations, such as the paean with the incredible but typical title of "The Revolutionary Struggle on the Ideological and Artistic Fronts Must Be Subordinate to the Political Struggle," and, finally, a few popular revolutionary tunes. The two most popular songs—popular in the sense that they were most frequently played—were "The East Is Red" and "Sailing the Seas Depends on the Helmsman" (the "helmsman" being, of course, Mao Zedong). In the late 1960s, the former virtually replaced China's official national anthem ("March of the Volunteers," a patriotic song composed during the Sino-Japanese War of 1937–45). Musically, the model operas—with titles like *The Red Lantern, Taking Tiger Mountain by Strategy,* and *The Red Detachment of Women*—incorporated many of the characteristics of traditional Beijing opera, but featured a Western-style orchestra with a mixture of Chinese and Western instruments along with a modified vocal style that was more songlike or Western sounding. In addition, Western ballet postures and movements were thrown in. Thematically, the model operas were limited to simplistic, unremittingly "revolutionary" plots with cardboard characters. Heroines and heroes were perfect and without blemish; villains were completely evil; "middle characters" were simply totally absent. With few exceptions, during the heyday of the Cultural Revolution all other music—including the masterpieces of the Western classical repertoire as well as popular traditional selections—was banned. In particular, the qin, associated as it was with the hated "feudal" overlords, was silenced.

For all their limitations and monotony, the Revolutionary Model dramas, with their synthesis of regional and Beijing opera styles and of Chinese and Western instrumental and voice styles, pointed the way toward a national contemporary style of opera, a style that at last might break free of the bonds of local and regional music. If development had continued along this path, a national style might well have emerged. However, with the end of the Cultural Revolution in 1976 and the beginning of the reform movement in 1978, most people wanted to have nothing to do with music that symbolized the "ten bad years" of the Cultural Revolution. Instead, freed from rigid constraints of the recent past, tastes moved in entirely new directions.

Pop and Rock: Music for Today?

Music in contemporary China seems to be following several paths simultaneously. In the 1980s, in the first few years of reform, traditional genres—regional opera, Beijing opera, folk songs, popular traditional instrumental pieces, and all the rest—burst forth once again and won enthusiastic audiences. But this warm reception was short-lived and many forms of traditional music are now facing a crisis. Audiences have decreased to such an extent that in several major cities regional opera is no longer performed. This waning enthusiasm is reflected in dwindling enrollment in traditional Chinese music courses at conservatories; students want to learn Western instruments and perform Western music.

What has replaced traditional music at the top of the "hit parade" is pop and rock. In the 1980s, pop from Taiwan and Hong Kong began to flood into China. A huge audience emerged for performers like the Taiwanese singer Deng Lijun (1953–95), also known as Teresa Teng, and, more recently, Wang Fei (b. 1969), also known as Faye Wong, who was born in Beijing and moved to Hong Kong at the age of 19, where she became a superstar. Teresa Teng was perhaps the first East Asian vocal superstar. With her sweet voice, clean-cut girl-next-door looks, and sincere delivery of light, romantic, pop songs, she appealed to people of all ages. Teresa first reached stardom in Japan in the 1970s, where—singing in excellent Japanese—she quickly became wildly popular. From there she skyrocketed to fame in her homeland of Taiwan and in Hong Kong and Chinese communities in Southeast Asia. She even performed in the United States, and was the first Chinese singer to give a concert in Las Vegas. In China, demand for tapes of her albums was so strong that they sold for ridiculously high prices. People began to say, "We'd rather have Little Deng [meaning Teresa] than Big Deng [meaning Deng Xiaoping]," and "By day, Deng Xiaoping rules China. But by night, Deng Lijun rules!"[5] The effect of her music even on sophisticated listeners could be intensely personal and moving. Jia Ding, one of China's leading songwriters, declared: "The first time I heard Deng Lijun's songs was in 1978. I just stood there and listened for a whole afternoon. I never knew before that the world had such good music. I felt such pain. I cried. I was really very excited and touched, and suddenly realized that my work in the past had no emotional force."[6] For some time the authorities attempted to ban her songs, but relented in 1986 and went so far as to declare one of her romantic hits, "When Will You Come Back Again?"—a reworking of a popular tune dating back to the 1930s—a "revolutionary patriotic song." Then came the Tiananmen Incident of June 1989. Teresa made her sympathy for democracy and the demonstrators amply clear on several occasions in Taiwan, Hong Kong, and elsewhere. This led the Chinese authorities to ban her songs again and to denounce them as "nothing but pornography."

Around the same time Teresa and other singers from Taiwan became popular in China a genre of pop music known as Canto pop exploded across the country, and after several years it does not appear to have lost any of its immense popularity. Canto pop—pop music from Hong Kong (where the dialect is Cantonese, hence "Canto pop")—has taken hold of the Chinese listening audience like no other music. It was reported that in 1989 all of Shanghai's top-10 pop hits were from Hong Kong.[7] One can easily believe it: walking down the streets of Shanghai and other cities one cannot avoid Canto pop pouring from CD players in private apartments, restaurants, and shops. Nowadays not all Canto pop is from Hong Kong: mainland Chinese performers have gotten savvy and have begun to record their own version of Canto pop, sung in Mandarin or local dialects, but often with a put-on Cantonese accent. The public is free to participate in this phenomenon not simply as passive listeners but as ersatz performers thanks to the thousands upon thousands of karaoke bars that emerged in China's cities in the 1980s. By the year 2000, karaoke had become old hat, but nonetheless still remained popular. Young people in particular seemed to find karaoke bars an appealing place to get together with friends and let down their hair, and also to express their individuality.

Appealing to a somewhat different audience is Chinese rock, which also emerged in the early 1980s. The grandfather of Chinese rock is Cui Jian (b. 1961), a classically trained instrumentalist (he played the trumpet in the Beijing Symphony Orchestra for six years) who seems to have discovered some of the Western mega-star bands (the Beatles, the Rolling Stones, and others) around 1986. In that year, he began performing his own compositions in Beijing and quickly became the biggest "big name" rock musician. By the 1990s, Cui and other rock musicians had released China's first music videos. As these were disseminated around the country, rock began to gather an enthusiastic, young audience. To Western ears, Cui's music may not sound "cutting edge," but it does boast a Chinese flavor, with some Chinese in-struments (such as the suona) thrown in with the usual guitar, saxophone, keyboard, and drums. Over the years, Cui has been in and out of the official doghouse several times. In 1988, he was praised in an article in *People's Daily* and later that year gave a concert that was broadcast worldwide in conjunc-tion with the 1988 Seoul Olympic Games. In the following year, his first album was released simultaneously in China, Taiwan, and Hong Kong. In

1989, Cui performed in Tiananmen Square, in solidarity with the demonstrators who were camped there. This earned him an official ban, but as is so often true in China today, a ban may not be total or may be impossible to enforce everywhere at all times. In 1990, Cui performed a series of benefit concerts for the Asian Games, and throughout 1991 and 1992 performed in the provinces and even occasionally in Beijing.[8] If there were any doubt about the popularity of rock, it should have been dispelled by a private concert in Beijing in 1990 that featured Cui's band (ADO) as well as several other big-name bands (Tang Dynasty, Black Panther, and many more) and drew an audience of at least 30,000.[9] Things got so rowdy that no other concert was approved by the authorities for a year.[10]

The authorities must be perplexed and uncertain about rock and pop music. In 1991 an album of songs from the Cultural Revolution—all paeans to Chairman Mao updated into disco-like arrangements—was released in Shanghai by the China Record Company. This album, *The Red Sun*, became an instant best-seller. Does its popularity reflect the public's continuing faith in the Communist Party, or a nostalgia for the heyday of the revolution (and hence an implicit questioning of the Party's current reform program)? Are listeners really imbued with love for Mao Zedong, or are they secretly sniggering at the Chairman? Or does politics have nothing to do with it—are people simply expressing the human desire to make connections with the past, the same way elementary school children in the United States today enjoy "fifties days" at school? Undoubtedly, different listeners have different motivations.

The popularity of pop and rock, and the concomitant decline in traditional music, is a complicated phenomenon. Hong Kong and Taiwan are part of the Chinese cultural sphere, but have been much more closely tied to the West than has mainland China. Thus listening to Hong Kong and Taiwan pop music is a way of being modern and "with it." While the government promotes modernization at every turn, it is leery of Westernization (which it periodically condemns as "bourgeois liberalism"). For the listening public, Canto pop is a relatively safe and comfortable way of partaking of a heavily Westernized culture associated with romantic notions of wealth and sophistication, but the music is not too Western nor so overtly political as to get a person in trouble. Finally, pop music is commercial music. "To get rich is glorious"—these words sum up the sentiment that rules China today. Taiwan and Hong Kong symbolize dynamic, freewheeling, internationalized moneymaking. Listening to their music can be an escape into another, and exciting, world: the songs seems to shout out "you too can dream of having glamorous and sophisticated friends, of driving a Mercedes Benz, of vacationing in Paris."

Rock music is more a matter of the fringe. Although most devotees of rock probably live quite conventional lives, the rock subculture, with its wild hairdos and fashions and unconventional lifestyles, holds an appeal for youth, although only a minority of youth. To be a "rocker" or a "punk," even if one only dresses the part and otherwise lives a fairly conventional life, is a way of rebelling against polite society and declaring one's independence. But paradoxically it can also be a way of conforming to the drive for modernization and commercialization. The biggest rock groups smack of money and international ties. Many have toured abroad, a sure measure of having really "arrived," and some have even been inducted into the temple of international commerce by having recorded abroad.

In the face of an onslaught of pop and rock music disseminated by television, videos, CDs, and so forth, traditional Chinese music has tended to follow a "join them if you can't fight them" philosophy. Some traditional music concerts have also included performances with electric guitars, rock drum sets, and synthesizers. Following the same philosophy, scholars and musicians of traditional music are increasingly embracing commercialization and "fishing for profits." Florid performances of "revived" ancient music (of doubtful authenticity), with "modern stage lighting techniques and colorfully stylized stage decor . . . reminiscent of a spectacular Broadway show," have been staged for money-paying tourists and for appreciative audiences in Japan and elsewhere.[11] Thus it appears that music in China today, whether it be traditional, pop, rock, or symphonic, is caught up in a culture increasingly fixated on the glory of getting rich.

EXUBERANCE AND RESTRAINT: DANCE IN CHINESE CULTURE

The Origins of Chinese Dance

The earliest representation of Chinese dance is on a Neolithic painted pottery bowl (ca. fourth millennium B.C.) from far western China that presents several groups of dancers, each with a braid or feather hanging from the hair, holding hands and dancing in a circle. Looking at this bowl, it is easy to imagine those dancers of long ago swaying and stomping their feet to the sound of music and song. The joy that seems to animate these figures also suffuses the ancient *Book of Songs*, which contains many references to dance. These poems reveal that while ancient dance was often, but not always, performed as part of ritual, it could be exciting and joyful:

> Drumming and dancing in the gully,
> How light-hearted was that tall man!

Subtler than any of them at capping stories.
And he swore he would never forget me.[12]

In later times, Confucianists railed against "irregular, debauched, feminine, quick, mobile, violent and excessive" dances,[13] but the common people and the aristocracy alike continued to find unbridled joy in dance. A ruler of the semi-legendary Xia dynasty (ca. 1900 B.C.) is said to have kept 30,000 dancing girls (probably an exaggeration). He was convinced that "the bigger the better, the more the merrier."[14] In later centuries, we find many large, sometimes huge, and magnificent secular dances. The Tang dynasty Ten Movement Music dance, for instance, encompassed dance and music from Korea, India, Persia, and Central Asia, as well as from many places in China. Performances of this magnificently lavish dance featured the best dancers in the country.

As far as technique is concerned, the wielding of long plumes, which dates back at least to the Shang dynasty (sixteenth to eleventh century B.C.),[15] has survived in ceremonial dances performed at Confucian temples. In addition, dancing with long feathers may have provided the inspiration for sleeve dancing, which features performers with extremely long sleeves that are waved and swung in a sinuous, flowing manner. Folk dances and classical dances such as these, as well as dances featuring long streamers (such as those seen in women's gymnastic exercises all across the globe), remain popular to this day.

In traditional times, dances of all sorts were an important part of festivals and folk entertainment. At least by the Han dynasty, variety shows—which included conjuring, acrobatics, martial arts, comic performances, music recitals, and music and dancing—were performed all across the country. From these roots sprouted the many regional forms of Chinese opera.

Traditional Opera

Around the thirteenth century A.D., Chinese opera began to enter its golden age. It continued to develop and grow in popularity right down to the end of the imperial period, early in the twentieth century. As we have noted in Chapter 3, Chinese opera is a composite art, incorporating music, singing, dialogue, acrobatics, martial arts, and dance; it is an art that invites all in the audience to exercise their imagination to the utmost. Scenery and stage sets are absent or nearly so. Instead, the stage is set, so to speak, through the skillful movements and gestures of the performers. To show that he is entering a room, the actor raises his foot as if stepping over a threshold and strides forward. In the imagination, a small stage immediately expands to great distances when the actor trudges around the perimeter to represent a long journey. And from atop stacked chairs, a performer executes a spectacular somersault to indicate that he is running down a mountain. Through exaggerated movement of the body and the eyes, through the way the torso is held, and through a myriad of other techniques, the actor communicates the traits and personality of the character. The hero swaggers onto the stage, swinging his arms with sharp powerful gestures that make his sleeves snap to-and-fro, showing that he is resolute and decisive. The villain, on the other hand, enters the stage with short, rapid footsteps, and with his eyes darting from side to side, in imitation of a rat.

Also crucial to the pageantry and action are lavish period costumes and props as well as face painting. Although the conventions of face painting vary a bit from one style of opera to another (and a few styles use no face painting at all), in general makeup—which is still another element that reveals the personality and nature of the character—is extremely colorful. Red usually represents loyalty and courage; green and blue, perfidy and scheming; white, deceitfulness; and black, boldness and incorruptibility. The greater the extent of white makeup, the more villainous the character is; conversely, the blacker the character's face, the greater is his steadfastness. The popular character Bao Gong, an upright official of the Song dynasty who during the day is a judge in this world and during the night judges souls in the next world, has his face painted entirely black to show his absolute impartiality and incorruptibility, save for only a yellow moon on his forehead, which indicates his determination to go into hell itself to see that justice is done.

Half the fun and excitement of traditional opera took place off the stage, among the audience. Performances were usually all-day affairs, with one play after another, and with people constantly coming and going. An illustration of a theater in Shanghai from the late nineteenth century (Figure 4.4) provides us a glimpse of a typical performance. Some in the audience (the smaller part, it would seem) are intently watching the action on stage, where the actors are engaged in a mock battle, while others are chatting with their neighbors ("chatting" may be too weak a word, since they would have had to shout to be heard over the din), and still others are craning their neck to see some interesting action that appears to be taking place outside the frame of the illustration, to the left. Is a patron choking on a tidbit (food and drink were served in the theater), or maybe shouting "hao, hao!" (bravo!)?

Folk Dance

From ancient times, on traditional holidays the people of China have delighted in watching or participating in dancing in the streets or at temples

Figure 4.4. A theater in Shanghai, in 1884, complete with all the most modern conveniences (note the gas lights, including the footlights) combined with traditional hospitality (note the waiter serving tea to the patrons in the balcony box). *From* Dianshizhai huabao *(Dianshi Studio pictorial), 1884.*

or open marketplaces. A Ming dynasty observer recalled how the colorful Lantern Festival was celebrated in the city of Shaoxing, in Zhejiang province. Lanterns of all sorts were hung along the streets, giving the night a magical air. "Besides that, there were lion dances, drums, wind and string instruments and singing. Fireworks were set off. The main streets and twisting alleys were packed with people. The 'Monk with a Big Head' was danced where there was space. . . . Everywhere people crowded round to look."[16] The lion dances mentioned here have a very long history and to this day are performed in parades and public celebrations among Chinese communities everywhere. The "lion" consists of two men within a single "animal" made of cloth and papier-mâché or wood. To a vigorous beat provided by accompanists with a drum, cymbals, and a gong, the lion leaps and rolls and sometimes jumps onto an enormous ball on which it balances itself as it rolls along. The dragon dance—also a very old and still popular form—requires seven to 25 men, all of whom support the billowy body of the "dragon." As the dragon runs along, twisting this way and that, its back arches, rises, and falls in a sinuous and convincingly serpentine manner (see Figure 8.4).

Dance and song, as in many places in the world, are also used in work, almost like a magical ingredient to lighten heavy loads and inject fun into what might otherwise be pure drudgery. The 1825 gazetteer of the city of Hangzhou records that "in the spring, the peasants walk in the fields side by side. They use their feet as hoes to move the earth as they advance. A drum is beaten in rhythm at the side of the field. They go backwards or forwards quickly or slowly. It is partly as entertainment."[17] Around the same time, an essayist noted that "in the springtime, women and children by the dozens would go to the fields to plant rice-seedlings. At the sound of a drum beaten by an old man, they competed together with group songs which lasted all day. It was called yangge."[18]

The word *yangge* came to be used to label folk dance in general, particularly that of northern China. Some of the same intellectuals who early in the twentieth century collected folk songs also collected folk dances, and subjected them to the same sort of "improvement." Often this meant "Hollywoodization"—adding fancy and spectacular choreography suitable only for professional dancers—and in other instances it meant the opposite: making the dances as simple as possible. The greatest simplifiers were the Communists, who launched a "new yangge" movement in the early 1940s. Under their leadership the yangge became an elementary matter of three-quick-steps-forward, one-step-backward, pause, and repeat. Soon it seemed that everyone, including—or perhaps, especially—soldiers in the People's Liberation Army, in the Communist-controlled area in Northwest China was singing and dancing. The army continues to be actively involved in dance, and still has several dance troupes, the largest of which has 100 dancers.[19] These are professional troupes, of course. Today, when most ordinary people want to dance for fun they hardly give a thought to folk dance but instead move to the beat found in discos and clubs all over the country.

Ballet and Bullets

By what quirk of history did ballet, that most aristocratic of Western dance forms, become the inspiration for dance in the Revolutionary Model dramas during the Cultural Revolution, that most pristine and fervent of revolutionary eras? The influence of the Soviet Union during the 1950s, when the People's Republic of China and the Soviet Union were still friends, played a role. The first Chinese ballet school—staffed with some outstanding Russian teachers—was established in Beijing in 1954, and in following years performed such conventional, *haute culture* ballets as *Swan Lake* and *Romeo and Juliet.* Sino-Soviet relations collapsed by 1959, and in that year the Russian teachers departed, but left as a legacy a particularly Russian style of ballet that China has been slow to give up.[20]

Indigenous Chinese opera also played a role. The popularity of the action-packed acrobatics of Chinese opera assured the ready acceptance of the athletics of Western-style ballet. Ballet features assertive and "highly extended postures, which enable the human body to be shown in its most imposing and least subservient aspect."[21] Thus postures like the arabesque, where the body is bent forward from the hip on one leg with the other leg and one arm extended backward and the other arm extended forward, were perfect for conveying strength and determination, especially when the hand at the end of the outstretched arm held a pistol or hand grenade, or was at least clenched in a fist (Figure 4.5). Similarly, flying leaps were used in the Revolutionary Model dramas to good effect by heroes and heroines, who seemed to soar above the villains, a marvelous metaphor of the downtrodden rising up to smite their oppressors. At the same time, some of the softer, more prissy postures and movements of ballet were abandoned, and the pas de deux—where so often the role of the male dancer seems to be primarily to support, lift, and toss the female dancer—was severely curtailed, presumably because male-female romance, which often is the theme of pas de deux, has no place in revolutionary drama.

In the Revolutionary Model dramas female characters figuratively and literally leapt ahead. The protagonists were often females, with the male dancers relegated to a supporting role. The heroines typically were assigned the most spectacular and assertive choreography; the heroes often were limited to simpler ballet movements or to steps similar to those of the old Beijing opera;

Figure 4.5. From a 1970 performance of the Revolutionary Model drama *The Red Detachment of Women*, set in the 1930s. The inscription on the flag reads "Women's Detachment of the Chinese Worker and Peasant Red Army." The leaping dancer is clutching hand grenades. *From* China Pictorial, *Special Issue no. 10, 1970.*

the roles of the villains (male and female alike) rarely included anything that could be called part of the "ballet vocabulary."[22] The Revolutionary Model dramas also represented a great step forward—or backward, depending on one's point of view—in the sense that they were mass entertainment, a status to which ballet in the West could never aspire. During the Cultural Revolution, no one asked audiences their opinion of the Revolutionary Model dramas. But, whether they were liked or not, the Revolutionary Model dramas were the only features on the program and hence became mass entertainment by default.

In the reform era, ballet lives on in China, and in some respects thrives in an environment of financial backing from the government and the business community. Chinese ballet companies have resurrected the classical Western ballets—*Swan Lake, Nutcracker, Romeo and Juliet,* and all the rest—but many have also retained in their repertoire the Revolutionary Model ballets. Whatever the reasons for this curious combination, it seems that Chinese ballet companies are at their best when performing the "old faithfuls" of the Cultural Revolution, but rarely rise above the mediocre when presenting the

Western classics. A Western critic has summed up *The Red Detachment of Women* as an "amusingly earnest . . . portrayal of an abused young woman's flight away from an evil landowner. . . . Its movement vocabulary is hidebound with tradition, its depiction of a contemporary woman's anger is wearyingly superficial."[23] That same critic nonetheless praised a performance of *The Red Detachment*: "The victim Qionghua dances with a curious mix of surface delicacy and heroic stamina. . . . She slugs it out . . . with one of her boss's henchmen one moment, then flees a squad of captors in a beautifully arching series of Plisetskaya jetes the next. It's the passion of the subject enacted in *The Red Detachment* that seems to push the full cast to heights of expression."[24]

Modern Social Dance

When, around the end of the second decade of the twentieth century, a few Chinese men and women began to practice Western social dance, with men and women in each others' arms, they probably had no idea of the profound significance of what they were doing. Just a few years earlier it would have been unthinkable—in fact, it would have been almost impossible—for men and women of decent families to dance together. In part this would have been because of moral strictures against a young lady being touched by any man but her husband. But it would also have been because of Chinese women's unique physical disability. For reasons that are not entirely clear, from around the eleventh or twelfth century A.D., foot binding became common in China. Foot binding involved tightly wrapping a three- to five-year-old girl's feet with bindings so as to stunt the foot's growth and bend the front and back of the foot together. After being wrapped in a crushing grip for a few years, the foot was thoroughly deformed. The object was to produce a tiny foot, which was considered lovely and sexually alluring. The crippled, deformed stump of a foot transformed walking into clumsy waddling. The thought of such a hobbled woman dancing the fox trot, the Charleston, or other popular dances of the 1920s was ludicrous. However, late in the Qing dynasty, foot binding began to decline, and then with the fall of the empire in 1911 and the rise of the New Culture Movement— with its proselytization of "science" and "democracy"—it almost disappeared. For instance, in Ding county, about 130 miles south of Beijing, among women born before 1890 foot binding was nearly universal at 99%. But in just a few years the situation was completely reversed: among those born between 1910 and 1914, 80% had *unbound* feet, and among those born after 1919, *all* had natural feet. In a few places among a few families foot binding lingered on until the 1950s, when it was finally and totally ended.[25]

The physical liberation of women's feet was inextricably attached to notions of women's health and women's social liberation, which in turn were tied to ideas of the health and liberation of the nation. During the first three decades of the twentieth century, many Chinese feared that the nation might not survive, that the Chinese people—small, weak, and scrawny—were not fit for the struggle with large, strong, and brawny Westerners. To redress the imbalance required physical cultivation—the building up of strong bodies, including those of women. Only healthy, strong women could bear healthy, strong babies, on which the future of the race depended. Both public schools and missionary schools began to teach physical education, including, in a few schools, dance. In 1915, the Shanghai YWCA opened the first girls' normal school for physical training, and in the early 1920s, Liangjiang College was founded near Shanghai as a school for female physical-training instructors. Group dancing was included in the curriculum.

Most of this dancing, to be sure, was single-sex group dancing. Yet over the years, ballroom dancing grew in popularity, especially among young, well-educated people, and especially in the big cities, but for most people, and particularly for the most conservative, it continued to have a somewhat unsavory reputation. During the early 1950s ballroom dancing was quite acceptable in the cities, but gradually it became frowned upon as a manifestation of "decadent" Western culture, and during the Cultural Revolution, with its overpowering streak of Puritanism, it essentially disappeared from everyday life. However, in recent years there has been gossip that even during the most fervid revolutionary years of the 1960s, the elite—including Chairman Mao—enjoyed private dance parties.

In the reform era, private discos, clubs, and dance halls have proliferated and attracted flocks of young people, as well as some middle-aged couples. The patrons are, presumably, out to have a good time: to escape from the confines of tiny apartments where one's actions are scrutinized by one's parents or by nosy neighbors, to meet with friends and make new friends, and to let one's hair down and perhaps find romance.

The authorities have tried to respond by promoting "healthy collective dance parties" where the lights are bright, the music is subdued, and couples are kept from dancing cheek-to-cheek by vigilant floorwalkers. Dancers who prefer a more spontaneous and unrestrained atmosphere can find plenty of alternatives, including dances—with hefty cover charges—given at hotels that have found it profitable to transform restaurants and meeting rooms into ballrooms.

When it comes to dance, as in so many other areas, popular culture is extraordinarily powerful and resistant to governmental manipulation. The present Communist government faces an insoluble dilemma: on the one hand

Figure 4.6. Early morning ballroom dancing in Ritan Park, Beijing, 1998. Public dances of this sort attract people of all ages, from their twenties to their seventies. © *Stuart Franklin/Magnum Photos.*

it promotes modernization, a consistent theme in Chinese life throughout the twentieth century, and commercialization, a concomitant of economic development in today's world, while on the other hand it struggles to control and suppress inevitable and unavoidable outgrowths of modernization and commercialization. These outgrowths—rebelliousness, hedonism, indiscipline, willfulness, and all the rest—it considers to be subversive excrescences, which it labels "bourgeois" or "Western" or "decadent." The real problem for the authorities is that the Chinese people do not seem to share this fear of "Western decadence," nor do they seem to weigh each element of culture for its "Western" content. In the words of a young man of Beijing, "I go dancing to have fun. I don't need anyone telling me what to dance or how to dance."[26]

NOTES

1. John Hazedale Levis, *Foundations of Chinese Musical Art* (Peiping: Henri Vetch, 1936), p. 10.

2. Liang Mingyue, *Music of the Billion: An Introduction to Chinese Musical Culture* (New York: Heinrichshofen Edition, 1985), pp. 197, 203.

3. Ted Shawn, *Gods Who Dance* (New York: E.P. Dutton, 1929), p. 51.

4. Richard Curt Kraus, *Pianos and Politics in China: Middle-Class Ambitions and the Struggle over Western Music* (New York: Oxford University Press, 1989), p. 5.

5. Gu Canxiu, "Teresa Teng Forever," *Sinorama* 20, no. 7 (July 1995): p. 15.

6. From interview with Jia Ding, quoted in Andrew F. Jones, *Like a Knife: Ideology and Genre in Contemporary Chinese Popular Music* (Ithaca, NY: East Asia Program, Cornell University, 1992), p. 16.

7. Geremie Barmé, "Official Bad Boys or True Rebels?" *Human Rights Tribune* 3, no. 4 (winter 1992), http://www.nmis.org/gate/film/badboys.htm (Feb. 12, 1999).

8. "Cui Jian: A Short Biography," http://www.cs.berkeley.edu/~zyang/cuijian (Mar. 3, 1999).

9. Tong Wei, "Rock 'n' Roll China," *Nexus: China in Focus* (summer 1990): pp. 18–21.

10. "Development of Rock Music in China," http://zero.com.hk/rock/history.html (Mar. 1, 1999).

11. Liang Mingyue, *Music of the Billion*, p. 160.

12. *The Book of Songs*, no. 56.

13. The words are those of the Marquis of Wen (ca. 485 B.C.), recorded in the *Book of Rites* (*Liji*), Chapter 2.

14. Wang Kefen, *The History of Chinese Dance* (Beijing: Foreign Languages Press, 1985), p. 9.

15. Li Chi, *Anyang* (Seattle: University of Washington Press, 1977), p. 252.

16. *Recollections of Tao An*, in Wang Kefen, *The History of Chinese Dance*, p. 81; quoted here with revisions.

17. Cited in Wang Kefen, *The History of Chinese Dance*, p. 85; quoted here with revisions.

18. Ibid., p. 85; quoted here with revisions.

19. Ou Jiang-ping, "Star Power," *Dance Magazine* 67, no. 11 (Nov. 1993): pp. 110–11.

20. Beryl Gray, *Through the Bamboo Curtain* (New York: Reynal, 1965), pp. 29–31.

21. Gloria B. Strauss, "Dance and Ideology in China, Past and Present," in Adrienne L. Kaeppler, Judy VanZile, and Carl Wolz, eds., *Asian and Pacific Dance: Selected Papers from the 1974 CORD-SEM Conference* (New York: Committee on Research in Dance, 1977), p. 35.

22. Ibid., p. 43.

23. Janice Ross, "Central Ballet of China," *Dance Magazine* 70, no. 1 (Jan. 1996): p. 102.

24. Ibid.

25. David Wakefield, "Translator's Postscript," in Feng Jicai, *The Three-Inch Golden Lotus*, trans. David Wakefield (Honolulu: University of Hawaii Press, 1994), p. 37.

26. Interview, June 2, 1999.

5

Food and Clothing

A COMMON CHINESE expression encapsulates the four basic necessities of daily life in a simple, straightforward list: "clothing, food, shelter, and transportation" (*yi, shi, zhu, xing*). To put clothing before food may seem odd since food is obviously essential for life, but this order fits perfectly with the prominent place in Chinese culture of the Confucian notion of *li* (propriety) and moreover clothing is the sole item on the list that distinguishes humans from beasts.[1]

While clothing may be in the foreground, so to speak, it is clear that looming behind it is the huge and formidable matter of food. In Chinese culture, food is much, much more than a necessity. It is an art, a passion, a joy; it is something to be ranked with the most weighty matters of life. In few other cultures have serious authors and scholars written entire books on cooking, and written them with such care and devotion. For instance, Yuan Mei (1716–98), a renowned poet, late in life finished writing a splendid little book—*Suiyuan shidan* (Menus from the garden of contentment)—which ranks as one of the world's great works of gastronomy. Indeed, the Chinese passion for food and for the connoisseurship of good eating reaches such depths that at times food seems a national obsession. No wonder Lin Yutang could declare that "if there is anything we [Chinese] are serious about, it is neither religion nor learning, but food."[2]

FOOD

It is sometimes said that while every nation has its own, characteristic ways of cooking, only a few possess a cuisine. What elevates "cooking" to "cuisine" has less to do with the nature of the food on the plate than with how people approach the question of eating. When they have an intellectual and aesthetic appreciation of cooking; when they treat it as a serious subject to be cultivated, discussed, and written about; when they prepare meals with creativity, engagement, and dedication; when they have a sophisticated repertory of ingredients and techniques—in short, when cooking becomes an art—then we can say such people are the lucky possessors of a cuisine. On each of these counts, and others, Chinese cooking qualifies as one of the world's very greatest cuisines.

Fan and *Cai*: The Culinary Foundation

A Chinese meal stands on two legs, so to speak: *fan* and *cai*. These two words have no precise English equivalent, nor an equivalent in any other European tongue, because the concept is uniquely Chinese. Fan consists of grains and other starches, and cai of meat, vegetables, fruit, and everything else. A complete meal contains both fan and cai. Fan, however, is the more fundamental—it is often referred to as *zhushi*, "primary food," while cai is relegated to the status of *fushi*, "secondary food." The words *chifan* (literally, "to eat fan") have come to mean simply "to have a meal."

The preeminent form of fan is steamed rice. In fact, in much of China fan is also a synonym for cooked rice. Moreover, rice is generally the preferred and most widely available form of fan. However, rice is far from ubiquitous. While since prehistoric times rice has been the staple grain crop of Central and South China, the people of northern China relied on other grains, principally, since the dawn of Chinese civilization, on millet. From around the Tang dynasty millet was gradually superseded in most areas by wheat, and in some areas by *gaoliang* (a variety of sorghum), which in turn in still more recent centuries has been generally superseded by corn from the New World. China today is the world's second largest producer of corn—the United States is the first—although, as in the United States, most corn is for animal feed.

It is often said that rice has not been raised much in North China because the climate is too cold. This is wrong: the growing season in most of North China is sufficiently long and hot to support rice cultivation. The limiting factor has been the availability of water. When irrigation networks, developed in the 1950s, brought sufficient water to the fields of Northeast China (Manchuria), rice flourished.

Grains are cooked whole or ground into flour, and consumed in a number of forms. All of them (rice, wheat, corn, millet) can be eaten simply as cooked grain, or made into gruel or noodles, while wheat, corn, and millet can also be made into skins or wrappers for dumplings, such as *huntun* (wonton) and *jiaozi* (a shallow-fried or boiled dumpling), and a variety of cakes, such as *mantou* (steamed breadlike loaves) and *baozi* (steamed, filled buns).

The range and variety of cai Chinese cooks have prepared for the table is staggering. In any particular area, many farmers can identify almost every edible wild plant, although only in times of famine would people resort to eating uncultivated vegetation. The crops cultivated and livestock raised vary from area to area, naturally, which has supported a great number of local cuisines. However, on the whole the Chinese throughout history have eagerly adopted new foods and ingredients. Farmers have tended to plant whatever thrives and has a market, and consumers have tended to buy whatever is tasty and nutritious. About the only food group that has not made a deep impression on the Chinese diet is milk and milk products. Traditionally, milk was considered rather exotic and did not find a place in the diet of most people, although during the Tang dynasty various milk products graced the table of the wealthy. Today ice cream is popular, powdered and canned milk are widely available, and fresh milk and yogurt can be found, but still China has no equivalent to the important role played by milk, cream, butter, and cheese in Western cooking nor to the role of milk and butter in Indian and Central Asian cooking. The latter is particularly remarkable inasmuch as China absorbed Buddhism from India, via Central Asia. While the Chinese accepted the religion, they rejected the foodways.

Countless explanations and speculations have been offered for the negligible role of milk in Chinese cuisine, among them the fact that the cow is an inefficient producer of food, consuming a great deal of food itself in return for a relatively meager yield of milk. In a densely populated land, the pressing need is to secure the highest possible nutritional output per unit of land, which—the environment permitting—almost always means that food crops will be favored over pasturage. In addition, Chinese cuisine possesses some alternatives to milk products, notably *doufu* (bean curd, or *tofu* in Japanese) and soybean milk (soy meal in sugared water), a favorite breakfast beverage, and one, when made fresh at a local shop specializing in breakfast foods, is a delectable drink to which the bland, packaged soy milk sold in supermarkets bears little resemblance. Still another explanation is that from time immemorial the Chinese have been at pains to differentiate themselves as settled agriculturalists from the pastoral nomads who lived nearby. One way to punctuate the distinction, so the argument goes, was to eschew the milk products of the pastoralists. There are countless other explanations, too numerous, and some too silly, to explore.

In any case, aside from milk and milk products, the ingredients in Chinese cuisine are not fundamentally different from Western cooking. If one were to buy at a Western market some pork, onions, carrots, oil, and so on, one might prepare fried pork chops and boiled carrots, or, with the same ingredients, one might prepare an identifiably Chinese meal. With more characteristically Chinese ingredients, the Chineseness of the meal would increase of course, but even with typically Western ingredients cooked in a Western kitchen, the result can still be a Chinese meal.[3] If it is not so much the ingredients, then what makes Chinese cuisine characteristically Chinese? The answer lies primarily in the method of preparing foodstuffs before they are cooked and in the concoction of dishes with attention to a combination of flavors, textures, aromas, and colors. In the words of Lin Yutang, "the whole culinary art of China depends on the art of mixture."[4]

Food: Preparation and Perception

Depending on who is counting, China boasts about 20 cooking methods, including steaming, boiling, roasting, deep frying, red cooking, smoking, drying, clear simmering, salting, cold mixing, and sizzling. The most common methods, especially at home, are, first, stir frying, which involves tossing ingredients into a wok (*guo* in Mandarin) with some hot oil, stirring them around a bit, and fishing them out while they still retain their nutritional value, color, and texture; second, deep frying, which is also done in the wok; and third, steaming, where again the wok is used, this time filled with steamer racks with a cover over the whole.

The basic utensil found in every Chinese kitchen is the cleaver, a 4×7 inch rectangle of honed steel with a handle used to cut, chop, slice, dice, shred, crush, mash, and crack foodstuffs of every description. Wielding this well-sharpened instrument, the Chinese cook attacks the item on the chopping block, reducing it to bite-sized morsels or slices that cook quickly and uniformly. A common explanation for cutting foodstuffs into small pieces is that China is a fuel-poor country: small pieces cook quickly, hence fuel is saved. On the other hand, the Chinese insist on cooking almost everything they put in their mouths; save for fresh fruit, almost nothing is eaten raw. This would seem to fly in the face of the fuel-economizing explanation. Perhaps a more plausible explanation for turning food into bite-sized bits has to do with the utensil used to move food between plate and lip: chopsticks (*kuaizi*). Chopsticks were on the scene at least from the Shang dynasty if not before. To this day, together with the spoon for drinking soup, they remain the sole personal utensil used at the table.

Which came first, chopsticks or bite-sized bits of food? We may never know. What is clear is that if the Chinese had prepared food along the lines favored by medieval Europeans, who heaped mountains of roasted meat on platters, chopsticks would have been useless. The correct utensils for a medieval European meal were the hands augmented by a knife, which were precisely what people used. Instead, with chopsticks in hand, the Chinese diner requires food precut into pieces that can be picked up and placed directly into the mouth.

The other requirement of the Chinese diner is that food be fresh. It is commonly thought that certain foods are unfit to eat if they are even a day old, and the preference is always for the freshest possible foodstuffs. Hence, markets feature live fish and other seafood in tanks or pools and live poultry. If the shopper sees fish swimming in a tank, obviously they are fresh; if they are laid out on ice, how can a person know if they last swam earlier the same day, or yesterday, or—heaven forbid—even the day before yesterday. Packaged and dressed fish and meat are available, and are cheaper than the live variety, but they are also less desirable. The search for fresh foodstuffs means that for most families in towns and cities marketing is a daily affair, and it is not unusual for some shoppers to visit the markets even more than once a day.

The issue of freshness may be related to ideas about the role of food in health. The current Western interest in "healthy" foods and the organic food craze may seem terribly modern, and scientific—and "Western"—but similar ideas have a very long and elaborate history in China. Traditionally, some foods were considered *yin* and others *yang*, or, following the same sort of thinking, were either *liang* (cool)—examples are persimmons, most water plants, and crabs—or *re* (hot)—examples are peanuts, oily and fried food, and fatty meat. The actual temperature of the food is irrelevant; it is its effect on the body that determines whether a food is "cool" or "hot." Health depended on eating a proper amount of foods in each category, thereby keeping yin and yang in balance. Similarly, food could be a medicine: if one suffered from, for example, a fever, rash, or sores, "cool" foods could help. Westerners long dismissed such thinking as superstitious, and many Chinese today would probably agree; however, there is some scientific validity to these principles as, for instance, high-calorie foods really are heating since they help keep the body temperature up on a cold winter's day.

Old Standbys

The Chinese way of eating is remarkably inventive, creative, and flexible. Since the typical cai dish is a mixture of ingredients, if a particular ingredient is not available, a tasty dish can still be prepared omitting that element or using a substitute. In recent decades, cleverness in the kitchen stood Chinese cooks in good stead since most foodstuffs were rationed and in short supply from the 1950s to the early 1990s, meaning that many favorites were only occasionally available, and then almost always in very small quantities, or were not available at all. Cooks had to be creative and inventive if they wished to turn out palatable meals. The one foodstuff that seemed to be available almost without limit was cabbage. In winter in Beijing, huge pyramids of cabbage erected in the streets left no doubt about what was on everyone's table for dinner. But we can be sure that the best cooks found or created enough ways to prepare this leafy vegetable to minimize the monotony.

What people missed most was the ready availability of the old standbys, which means (to quote from *Merriam Webster's Collegiate Dictionary*) "a favorite or reliable choice or resource" in food. Soy sauce, that ubiquitous condiment known to the Chinese at least as early as the Zhou dynasty, must surely head the list of old standbys. A thirteenth-century scholar included soy sauce among the seven things that "people cannot do without every day." After soy sauce, the list of old standbys would go on, and on, and on to include a huge variety of seasoning agents; preserved foods—grains, meat, vegetables, fruit, and eggs—preserved by smoking, pickling, salting, sugaring, steeping, and drying; and spices, all used (if available) frequently, if not daily, by the Chinese cook. Also included on the list would be prepared foods, primarily snacks or "little eats" (*xiaochi*) as they are called, which now once again are found in profusion in hole-in-the wall shops and cafés and street stalls in cities and towns (Figure 5.1). The types of popular snacks vary somewhat from region to region, but high on most lists would be various kinds of bean preparations, such as dried doufu simmered in a soy sauce and tea stock together with eggs, many kinds of noodles in soup, wonton soup, fried peanuts, and other tidbits to accompany alcoholic beverages, baked sweet potatoes, and "oily sticks" (*youtiao*), a deep-fried dough stick rather like a cruller or doughnut but without the sugar, a favorite breakfast food. Also included in breakfast favorites would be dim sum (in Mandarin *dianxin*, literally "dot hearts"), a Cantonese specialty that comes in hundreds of steamed and fried forms, including *shaomai* (*siumai* in Cantonese), *chashaobao* (a bun stuffed with barbecued pork), and fried rice wrapped in lotus leaves, all washed down with tea, which is also available in scores of varieties.

Finally, any list of old standbys must include special foods for holidays and festivals, such as moon cakes, which are enjoyed all over China at the Moon Festival in autumn. These small circular cakes containing a sugary paste, ham, dates, walnuts, candied apricots, watermelon seeds, or other ingredients, like other special foods for China's many traditional holidays are enjoyed not merely for their good flavor or to fill the stomach. Rather, gazing upon, then holding, and finally nibbling these treats stimulates the memory, one could say, causing the eater to experience the bittersweet pleasure of

Figure 5.1. Curb-side food vendors in Xi'an, 1998. The "restaurant" consists of a table (a few boards placed on the back of a tricycle), a tablecloth, and some benches. *Courtesy of Thomas DuBois.*

recalling holidays in past years and remembering times gone by. Since holiday treats are enjoyed with family and friends, sharing them implies also sharing memories of the past and creating new memories for the future. Thus, eating with others contributes to a sense of social togetherness. Food, then, is more than a source of nutrition and gustatory satisfaction; it is also a vehicle of social interaction.

The Sociology of Eating

In China, food is a source both of social cohesion and of social division. Important events of all sorts—weddings, births, deaths, graduations, business deals, forging of political alliances, visits by dignitaries, and so on—are marked by dinners or banquets. In cities and towns, such dinners and banquets are usually held at restaurants (as a rule private homes are much too small to accommodate many guests and in any case lack the cachet of a fancy restaurant), while in the countryside they are often held in convenient open spaces (temple grounds, private courtyards, etc.). The kind and amount—and cost—of the food served must suit the occasion. Spending "too much" for a banquet can get the host criticized as a vulgar showoff. But failing to "spend enough" when the occasion or guest of honor warrants it, can get the host dismissed as a miserly tightwad. Getting it just right—spending just the right amount for just the right kind of food—is a fine skill that takes years to develop.[5]

Moreover, the food itself is not the only marker of the importance of the occasion. The host must be mindful of the relative status of each guest, and while all may be warmly welcomed, only one can sit in the seat of honor next to the host. Those deemed lowest in status—and of least importance—will be seated far away, perhaps at a distant table, and will be served last, when the food may already be cold. Thus, at the same time that a banquet joins people together in a social event, it also separates them.

Food also acts to reinforce social distinctions because it is an index of wealth. The bus driver cannot dream of competing with the manager of the bus company when it comes to entertaining. He likely will never even enter the kind of expensive restaurant where his boss entertains. The boss, safe from that sort of competition, will nonetheless entertain before the watchful eyes of other patrons, and each will be comparing the food on his or her table with what is being eaten by other parties. Failure to keep up with what other patrons are eating can lead to a humiliating loss of face. To lessen the anxiety, most expensive restaurants, and some that are not so expensive, have private dining rooms.

Face is a key element in Chinese social psychology. "Face," meaning reputation, dignity, or prestige, has entered the English vocabulary, and English speakers talk of "losing face" or "saving face" precisely in the same way that Chinese do.

At a Chinese banquet, if the occasion and the guest of honor are important enough, the host may be trapped into spending a ruinously large sum. Many adults can tell tales such as the one about the unhappy man in the provinces who had to entertain a visiting delegation of dignitaries. The guest of honor, in a lax moment and without adequate thought for the consequences, mentioned to the host that he had heard that the restaurant was noted for some fantastically expensive dish. The host took this to mean that the guest of honor wanted this dish, and thus felt compelled to order enough for everyone.

Why play the game? Why not opt out of this extravagant custom? The answer lies in the fact that in China the individual lives within a social network, or many social networks, some of which are very tight. To some extent it is possible to escape these networks, to turn one's back on custom, to turn one's back on one's family, colleagues, and associates, but the costs of doing so are very great—prohibitively great in the eyes of most people. This is clearest in the countryside, in the thousands upon thousands of villages that dot China. Socially speaking, villagers live in close proximity to one another. Over the years, one will surely need the help of one's family and neighbors: to borrow tools, to get help in repairing machinery, to borrow money if need be. How can one expect to get assistance if one fails to live up to what family and neighbors expect; if, in other words, one fails to live up to one's social obligations? For city people, too, networks of relationships—*guanxi* or "connections"—are crucial to life.

The custom of entertaining has also endured because some people can participate without bearing any financial cost. A school principal can afford to throw a lavish banquet for each important person passing through since it is the school, not the principal, who pays the bill. Similarly, government and Party cadres, who are very numerous in China and who, like officials everywhere in the world, are sensitive to status and relationships, can afford to entertain on a grand scale since the state picks up the tab. The Communist government no doubt recognizes that excessive official banqueting jeopardizes its claim to being as close to "the people" as "fish and water," and the official press periodically rails against grand banqueting and other profligate customs, but with limited effect. Not surprisingly, "the people" look upon officials lavishly entertaining one another as a form of corruption, and, according to surveys, the public today considers corruption China's biggest problem.[6]

The largest changes in Chinese foodways are likely to come not from government exhortations but from deeper, systemic changes in Chinese society. How else can we explain the phenomenal popularity in China of McDonald's fast food restaurants, that exemplar of Americana? In 1992 the world's biggest McDonald's restaurant—with 700 seats and 29 cash registers—opened in Beijing. One observer quipped that the McDonald's onslaught represented, insofar as cuisine is concerned, a "Great Leap Backward."[7] Be that as it may, on opening day, 40,000 customers were served, setting a new one-day, worldwide sales record for the McDonald's chain.[8] A fascinating study conducted in the mid-1990s found that the city's McDonald's restaurants are often jammed with patrons—yuppies, young couples, and children (accompanied by their parents or grandparents). What attracts them? It is not that the food is "fast"; patrons often occupy a table for hours on end. Nor is it that the food appeals to the patrons; on the contrary, most customers (save for children) say they do not care much for the food. And, finally, it is not that the food is cheap; while McDonald's is cheaper than an expensive Chinese restaurant, it is more expensive than eating at a middling restaurant or a food stall. Instead, the answer is status. Eating at McDonald's, and just *being* at McDonald's, is a way of partaking of modern, Western culture. As one patron declared, "The Big Mac doesn't taste great; but the experience of eating in this place makes me feel good. Sometimes I even imagine that I am sitting in a restaurant in New York City or Paris."[9] McDonald's is clean, it is quieter than most Chinese restaurants, it is reliable, and in the eyes of many people, its food is "scientifically designed." In short, McDonald's represents modernity and Westerness. Another patron commented, "I want my daughter to learn about American culture. She is taking an English typing class now, and I will buy her a computer next year."[10] Eating at McDonald's presumably is part of a strategy of learning about and absorbing American culture and getting ahead.

At the same time, through a clever strategy of "localization"—hiring local staff, including managers; giving small gifts to first graders at local schools at the start of each term; sweeping the streets in front of the restaurants; and so on—McDonald's appeals to patrons as friendly, concerned, civic minded, even patriotic (the Chinese national flag is hoisted every morning in front of the McDonald's near Tiananmen Square, the center of Beijing). Patrons can follow custom, but in a modified, comfortable, modern fashion. Many patrons, especially younger, college-age people, entertain at McDonald's.[11] In this way they avoid the "food competition" that takes place at banquets at Chinese restaurants, because everyone has mostly the same food, and nothing is terribly special or expensive. Thus, for many people without a lot of money but who need to host a meal, McDonald's has become the restaurant of choice.[12]

Changes in Chinese foodways, and indeed changes in so many other aspects of Chinese culture, perhaps can best be understood not as the result of tension between modernity and tradition, or between Chinese and Western, but between *yang* and *tu*. Yang (this is a different character from the yang of yin and yang) refers to things that are of identifiably foreign (especially Western) origin, and are also modern, fashionable, and sophisticated. Tu—a word redolent with meaning—connotes just the opposite: rustic, backward, old-fashioned, simple. Bare feet encrusted with dirt is a perfect image of tu. So is an itinerant butcher, wheeling a cart from which hangs a hunk of pork, fresh no doubt but also covered with flies. Increasingly it appears that people want, and are able to afford, to turn away from tu toward yang. As they do so, many of the old standbys are slipping from popularity. A case in point is spring pancakes (*chunbing*), a low-budget but tasty delight once eaten in Beijing to celebrate the coming of spring. The tortilla-like chunbing is seasoned with some savory brown sauce and spring onions and then loaded with any of a sufficiently wide variety of stir-fried and marinated dishes to please most palates—bean sprouts with shredded green pepper, red-braised doufu and pickled bamboo with celery and peppers, stir-fried onions and squid, and others—before being tightly rolled up into a leak-free little sandwich.

However, today spring pancakes are hard to find in Beijing. According to an octogenarian customer at one of the few restaurants still featuring this treat, back in the 1920s spring pancakes were very popular. "We used to make it at home, but the ingredients were so expensive for us back then that we only made it on special holidays. . . . Nowadays, spring pancakes are hard to find because it is traditional Beijing food; it isn't fashionable."[13]

The same sort of process has eroded a once seemingly impregnable Chinese institution, the teahouse. No one is sure when tea drinking began in China; probably in the Han dynasty, although tea did not become a beverage enjoyed daily by all classes of people until the Song dynasty. Even today there are people who in order to economize or out of personal preference occasionally drink what is euphemistically called *baicha*—literally "clear tea" or "plain tea"—which is actually nothing but hot water. At the opposite pole are connoisseurs of tea, who created and sustained an art that involved an exceedingly refined appreciation of tea itself, naturally, and also of teapots, methods of preparing tea, ways of pouring tea, and even the very water used to make tea. In enthusiasm, tea connoisseurs in China were like the connoisseurs of wine in the West today, except the tea fanciers were probably more fanatical. In recent years, tea connoisseurs have managed to make the "tea tastings" that are conducted at conferences to promote the beverage look like Chinese versions of French wine degustation, with the tea served in—of all things—wine glasses, the better for nosing the "bouquet" of the tea and for appreciating its color.

Subtracting the connoisseurs of tea and those people who are satisfied with hot water, leaves those who simply enjoy tea as a beverage and drink it daily, without ceremony or rigamarole—just about everyone in China. For a while—from the late 1970s to the mid-1990s—it looked like tea was in trouble, that like many other traditions it was going by the wayside. Faced with the onslaught of such yang beverages as Coca-Cola and other soft drinks, consumption fell roughly in half during those years. But by 1998, annual tea production was up by 66% compared with output between 1993 and 1995, to about 1.3 pounds per capita.[14] Most tea is consumed at home or work, although many people also patronize teahouses. Without question the most important institution associated with tea has been the teahouse. By the nineteenth century, when teahouse culture reached its zenith, most towns and cities had a variety of teahouses—the larger the town, the greater the variety—that catered to virtually all pocketbooks, from little, simple shops that sold hot water for bathing and cooking and also served tea and snacks as a sideline, to teahouses that catered to porters and other manual laborers, to fancier teahouses that served a wealthier clientele. Many teahouses featured singers, musicians, storytellers, and other entertainers. For the small price of a pot of tea plus some snacks, a patron could simultaneously enjoy a simple, relaxing repast and, for no additional charge, be entertained. In some establishments in the city of Chengdu, one did not even have to pay. There, late in the nineteenth century, any thirsty person was free to drink the tea left over from paying patrons.[15]

Teahouses were also often nodes of social networks. Particular teahouses became associated with a certain profession or occupation or avocation. In the town of Nantong, near Shanghai, for instance, the teahouses on Eastern Street, which had many fabric shops, served as gathering points for retailers and shop customers.[16] All across China, in a relaxing and convivial atmosphere, merchants discussed business trends, exchanged news, and concluded deals; matchmakers arranged marriages; seers told fortunes; doctors diagnosed patients; and scholars discussed poetry. The range of activities—business and pleasure—conducted in teahouses was almost without limit.

Teahouse culture has undergone an inevitable transformation. With private enterprise severely curtailed in the years after 1949, much of the relevance of teahouses evaporated. In truth, the teahouse was under assault long before the Communists came to power. Early in the republican period, the new cultural elites came to consider teahouses old-fashioned, backward, and a drag on China's effort to modernize. In this view, teahouses were places where people idled away their time and where unsavory characters gathered. In other words, teahouses were considered definitely tu, a reputation that continues to dog them today. The solution for enterprising entrepreneurs has been to reinvent the teahouse. It is said that all of the chain teahouses in Shanghai are run by Taiwanese franchise groups. The customers are mostly young and are attracted by gimmicks, such as personal computers with internet connections free for the use of any patron, and swings instead of booths.[17]

CLOTHING

The 2,000-year-old Chinese idiom "to wear a silken robe but walk by night" (yi jin ye xing), meaning "hidden talent," hints at the fact that clothing serves more than the utilitarian purpose of protecting the body but is also a matter of show, proclaiming the wearer's social and economic status. Thus changes in fashion are often reflections of deeper, underlying social changes. When looking at any slice of Chinese history—any period of, say, two or three decades, or often just a slice of a year or two or even of a few months—it becomes clear that fashions in clothing sometimes changed dramatically. Even changes that appear to us subtle, or which we might miss entirely, almost always were significant and meaningful for the people of the time.

This is simply further evidence that Chinese society was never static, never frozen in time. Because of this considerable variation, it is impossible to generalize about "traditional" clothing as if it were constant and unvarying. In the discussion that follows, unless a time is specified, it should be understood that we are talking about China during the Qing dynasty, especially late in the dynasty, on the eve of the modern era.

Verities in Clothing

If there is any enduring verity in Chinese clothing it is—at least until recent years—that layers of clothing were added or subtracted according to the dictates of the weather and season. As it got colder, in an eminently sensible way, people put on additional layers of clothing, and as it grew warmer they doffed clothing—so much so that today in sophisticated cities like Beijing and Shanghai on hot summer evenings working-class men lounge outside their homes stripped down to their boxer shorts.

This sort of utilitarian approach particularly influenced what babies and children wore—or did not wear. Until well into the twentieth century, babies were wrapped in swaddling clothes, generally made from the cast-off clothing of older members of the family. Diapers were not used. After a few weeks, babies were usually given clothing tailored along the same lines as adult clothing—namely, trousers and a shirt or jacket—except that for babies and children up to the age of three or so, the crotch in the pants was not sewn up, allowing children to squat and relieve themselves whenever and wherever they found it convenient. Crotchless pants are still *de rigueur* for toddlers in much of the country. In the cities, however, disposable diapers are becoming popular.

Frequently, young children wore a *doudou*, a small triangular affair that was fastened with cloth tapes around the neck and waist (see Figure 8.2). This garment can be thought of as a type of underwear, and into the early years of the twentieth century Chinese women also wore the doudou, often as their sole undergarment. But when the weather was hot, for toddlers the doudou often became outerwear. Clad only in a doudou, little children were undeniably cute. But as someone once remarked, wearing this single garment, which covered only a bit of the body, was like putting on symbolic apparel rather than a real piece of clothing.

This charming picture needs to be balanced by a recognition that customs in clothing varied a bit—in some instances, quite a bit—from place to place. To this day, in some rural areas of North China people always keep themselves well covered, and the men almost never go shirtless, even on the most sweltering of days, indeed they rarely even wear short sleeve shirts. This may be less a matter of modesty than of ideas about health: people in these places say that if one is not well clothed, one might catch cold—even if the temperature is over 90°F. This may also reflect a matter of cost. Until recently, men had few shirts and needed the flexibility afforded by long sleeves: long sleeves were of course better for cool weather, but also protected against the beating rays of the sun when one worked in the fields all day. Yet even here, when the hot season arrives, people remove layers of clothing, so that by mid-summer they are down to one or two.

Aside from adding and subtracting layers of apparel, the other verity of Chinese clothing has to do with fabric. From the very beginning, China has been mostly a two-fabric society. The first fabric of China, in more ways than one, was silk. Silk was already known to the people of Neolithic North China, and by the Shang dynasty sericulture—the raising of silkworms and the production of silk—had become highly developed. We think of silk as a luxury, but through much of Chinese history it was worn, on various occasions, by a wide variety of people, not just the wealthy. The second, and more utilitarian and economic, fabric for most of Chinese history was hemp (supplemented, or replaced, in much of Southwest China by ramie). By around the eleventh century, cotton began to be grown in northern China, and it gradually spread all around the country, to become for most people *the* fabric, used for every conceivable article of clothing. By sometime in the fifteenth or sixteenth century, cotton was worn by 90% of the population.

Until the twentieth century, leather and wool were rarely used. Shoes, for instance, were made of cotton or silk and trousers were held up not by leather belts but by fabric tapes or soft, fabric girdles. The dearth of leather and wool may in large measure be a reflection of the fact that China's agricultural land has been overwhelmingly devoted to crops and not to the pasturage that would be required to raise large animals.

Traditional Clothing: The Long and the Short of It

The trendy idea of unisex clothing, which became a rage in Europe and America toward the end of the twentieth century, would have been quite passé to the people of late imperial China. There, on the eve of the modern era, the everyday utilitarian apparel of the common people—both men and women—was an essentially unisex outfit consisting of unshaped, baggy trousers and a tunic. This outfit could be supplemented or replaced by a range of other garments that varied according to the wearer's sex, social status, needs, and personal taste. Men could wear over their trousers (which both men and women often bound around their ankles with strips of fabric tape) a long gown (known as the *pao* or *changpao*), which fastened on the right and had slits along either side extending some distance upward from the bottom hem, and long straight sleeves that, in the nineteenth century, usually reached beyond the hands. Westerners have sometime called this a "scholar's gown." Actually, the long gown was not limited to upper- and middle-class gentlemen, although it was rarely worn by working-class men. So it was that the length of one's coat signaled one's social class. In his short story "Kong Yiji" (1919), Lu Xun mentions a tavern where most of the customers who stand drinking at the bar "belong to the short-coated class," and only those in long gowns "go into the inner room to order wine and dishes and sit drinking at their leisure."[18]

Over the long gown was usually worn a waist-length "riding jacket" (*magua*), either with sleeves or without. The magua, probably patterned after Manchu apparel (the Manchus were fine horsemen), originated sometime in the Qing dynasty as military dress, but toward the end of the dynasty had become standard men's apparel. Hats were sometimes worn, particularly a brimless skullcap with a knotted cord button on the top, looking rather like a beanie. These caps can sometimes still be found in shops in Hong Kong, although today they are strictly for tourists. Footwear consisted predominantly of cotton socks and black cloth shoes (usually of cotton and sometimes of silk). Such was the uniform of the gentleman: trousers, over which went a long gown, over which went a magua, the whole outfit occasionally crowned with a skullcap.

Working-class men wore trousers and a utilitarian tunic or a thigh-length jacket (*shan*) with sensible sleeves that stopped at the wrists. A wide variety of headwear was available, depending on the weather, the region, and so on. Large straw sun hats, worn by both men and women, were found just about everywhere, as were skullcaps for men. Especially in North China, many men wore simple turbans; and some farmers still do. Again, footwear consisted of cloth shoes or straw sandals—or was completely absent. Most rural men usually worked barefoot if the weather permitted.

The standard attire for women in the late imperial era consisted of the aforementioned trousers—the same sort of formless baggy trousers worn by men—plus a tunic. For many women—except those at the lowest rungs of the social ladder—a long skirt was worn over the trousers, especially on dressier occasions, and over all this was worn an ample surcoat (*ao*), usually of waist length or three-quarters length, with wide, wrist-length sleeves. Fashions in hairstyles were very changeable, and varied greatly according to the time and place. Entire books have been written about women's hairstyles of the late nineteenth century alone. Footwear for women with bound feet—which included most Chinese women in late imperial times—consisted of, first, bindings (long strips of cloth wound about the foot), over which went

Figure 5.2. School boys, ca. 1910, dressed much like their fathers, except their clothing is a bit more colorful, as befits youngsters. All the boys are wearing *changpao*, and some also are wearing sleeveless *magua*, and a few magua with sleeves. Each boy has a ribbon pinned to his chest: for outstanding cousework, or perfect attendance perhaps? We can only speculate. *Courtesy of Zhang Weiming and Shanghai on the Internet.*

cotton or silk socks (tied up with ribbons), then cotton or silk shoes. Women with bound feet never went barefoot—that would have been unimaginably indecent. Pornographic art of the period depicts women nude, but not totally nude: always they are shoed.

Underwear for men consisted of a simple loincloth, and for women, as we have noted, the doudou and, sometimes, slender undertrousers. Some people simply dispensed with specialized undergarments and wore old trousers and tunics as underwear, or wore no underwear at all. And, as we have suggested, when the weather grew cold, people tended to put on additional layers of clothing and/or clothing filled with padding of cotton or old scraps of cloth. In cold climates fur coats were common, with the fur turned inward, as a lining. Padded or fur-lined clothing was bulky and gave the wearer a roly-poly look, but it was certainly an effective and economical solution to the problem of keeping out the cold. Similarly, in hot weather loose-fitting pajama-like trousers and tunics of thin fabric were an effective means of keeping an insulating layer of air around the body. When it got really muggy, one could don an undervest of delicate, airy woven bamboo, a marvelous invention that kept one's sweat-soaked shirt away from the skin.

Clothing could be as fancy and colorful as one wished, albeit within limits set by one's pocketbook, local fashion, and sumptuary laws that restricted the use of certain colors and designs. Everyday cotton clothes of the common people were dyed a solid color—usually navy blue—and bore little if any decoration. But that was just the starting point, what we might call the baseline of basic blue. From there one could add embroidered or appliquéd decoration of the most florid sort, or turn to silk garments of delicate colors— lilac, turquoise, creamy white, and so forth—or of intense, vibrant colors— vermilion, bright yellow, and so on—all of which were typically covered with magnificent designs and decorations. The quality of the needlework in many households was not remarkable, but the work turned out by professional seamstresses and tailors, and by some amateurs, was usually of superb quality, revealing a level of skill, patience, and dedication far above what can be found today. About the only clothing that was purposefully colorless was funeral attire, which was white—the color of mourning—and usually made of hemp.

Being richly attired when the occasion called for it was not beyond the reach of most people. In 1930 Mao Zedong commented on the women of Xunwu county in the province of Jiangxi, a completely unremarkable place:

> It does not matter whether they are workers, peasants, merchants, or poor peasants or rich peasants, they all wear jewelry in their hair or on their hands. All of it is silver except for the gold jewelry worn by women in large-landlord families. Every woman puts silver hair clasps in her hair and wears silver earrings. No matter how destitute the woman, she has these two kinds of jewelry.[19]

And if one could not afford to buy fancy attire, one could, at least in some places, rent it. For women, especially in the countryside, brightly colored clothing was usually reserved for unmarried young women. Elaborate, colorful, highly decorated clothing was not worn by women alone; men too could make themselves up into prancing peacocks. Writing in the 1920s, a journalist complained that "costume in our country often shows no differentiation between male and female forms, whether in style or color. The fabrics used by men are frequently of the flowing sort, such as silk, which do not lend themselves to the display of the strong beauty of the male."[20] By the 1920s of course, China was in the midst of its painful struggle for cultural identity—what did it mean to be both Chinese and modern?—a struggle in which clothing figured prominently.

Twentieth-Century Clothing, Part 1: Fusion and Confusion

In the revolution of 1911 that ended two thousand years of imperial rule, one of the first and most defiant acts of radical young men was to change their hairstyle. To be more specific, they cut off their queue, that long single plait of hair that for almost two and a half centuries had been universal among Chinese men. The queue had actually been the hairstyle of the Manchus, who had, by government fiat, forced it on Chinese men after the Manchus conquered China in 1644. At first, the Chinese resented this as a humiliating imposition, but gradually they warmed to the queue until, after time, they seemed positively to cherish it. To be called "tail-less" came to be considered an insult.[21] Bald men did not hesitate to solve their problem by wearing a cap with a false queue attached.

Reminiscent of the biblical story of Samson, a certain Second Simpleton, a character in a novella by Feng Jicai (b. 1942) set in the closing years of the empire, possesses a "miraculous pigtail" that, cracking it as if it were a whip, he wields to defeat his enemies. But, in the end Second Simpleton discards the queue in favor of a quintessentially modern, Western alternative: a pair of six-shooters. When Motley Glass, the novella's protagonist, expresses shock at the transformation, Second Simpleton explains: "However good the things of our ancestors, when the time comes to discard them, then discarded they must be."[22]

With these words, Second Simpleton nicely sums up the sentiment of a great many Chinese in the early years of the twentieth century: it was time to discard "the things of our ancestors," including their hairstyles and their clothing. But what was to take their place? In the eyes of some cynics, such as a journalist writing in the Shanghai daily *Shenbao* in 1912, in fleeing from tradition people were liable to run directly into confusion: "Chinese are wearing foreign clothes, while foreigners wear Chinese clothes, men are adorned like women and women like men, prostitutes imitate girl students, and girl students look like prostitutes."[23] This overwrought statement is at least accurate in capturing the fluidity of clothing styles early in the twentieth century.

The spectrum of choices in clothing became remarkably wide. Men could stick with what they had worn late in the empire or they could go to the opposite extreme and gussy themselves up in Western woolen suits (or linen suits in the summer) together with leather shoes and the obligatory necktie— so attired, they would have been perfectly at home on the streets of New York or London. Or, they could, as most urban men of the middle class and above did, dress somewhere in between, depending on the occasion and personal preference, dressing more Chinese on some occasions and more

Western on others. Commonly, urban men added identifiably Western bits and pieces to their clothing, starting literally at the top. The trilby (a soft felt hat with an indented crown) and the boater (a stiff straw hat with a flat crown) became very popular among gentlemen, and continued to be worn—with the changpao—right down to 1949.

In some minds, dressing in purely traditional style or in purely Western style or mixing the two did not make the proper political statement. What was needed for "new China" was a new style that was distinctively Chinese *and* modern. Such a style was bestowed on the men of China by none other than "the father of his country," Sun Yat-sen. Working with a tailor, Sun designed a suit replete with symbolism. The trousers were like those of a Western-type suit while the jacket borrowed heavily from Japanese school uniforms, which in turn had been influenced by contemporary Western military attire. The jacket featured a row of five buttons down the front, symbolizing the "five powers"—legislative, executive, judicial, examinational, and supervisory—in Sun's political theory, an extension of the three branches of government scheme in the West. It also had two breast pockets, usually with flaps, and two hip pockets, also usually with flaps, all the flaps being in the shape of an inverted writing-brush stand, symbolizing the enduring role of learning in Chinese culture and making it clear that this was not a military uniform. The jacket featured a Mandarin collar (as it is known in the West), a reflection of contemporary fashion. High collars were the rage in both men's and women's clothing in the decade or so before 1920, not only in China but also in Japan and in the West. In Japan, the English words "high-collar" came to mean "sophisticated" and "high class." The globalization of fashion that we see at the dawn of the twenty-first century has deep roots.

Appropriately enough, the suit designed by Sun was dubbed the Zhong-shan suit (*Zhongshanzhuang*), after the Mandarin pronunciation of Sun's name (Sun Zhongshan).[24] In the West, this suit has become known as the Mao suit. Mao had nothing to do with its design, but in "Mao's China" after 1949 it became the proper dress attire for men, to the exclusion of nearly everything else (Figure 5.3).

The vicissitudes of women's attire mirrored the development of men's clothing. To begin with, the analog of men cutting off their queue was women rejecting bound feet. The latter did not signify defiance of the Manchu Qing dynasty, but nonetheless it was, like lopping off the queue, a strongly symbolic rejection of tradition. Just like the men, women, now with natural feet, had to decide on what to wear. And, just as for the men, the available choices were plentiful. Women could continue to dress more or less as they had in the nineteenth century—trousers and a tunic—although the cut was becoming increasingly form fitting. Women often added Western

Figure 5.3. Mao Zedong, attired in a *Zhongshanzhuang*, from a poster dated 1965. Already by the 1930s the Mandarin collar of the early *Zhongshanzhuang* was losing out in popularity to the pointed collar, such as that on the suit worn by Mao. Behind Mao, in the background, is a sea of waving red flags, a symbol of communism. The pine tree in the right foreground is a traditional symbol of long life and integrity. The inscription at the bottom of the poster, in both characters and pinyin romanization, reads "Long Live Chairman Mao." *Photograph provided by the author.*

accoutrements—for instance, high-heel leather shoes. Furthermore, wearing both trousers and skirt simultaneously became increasing rare. A skirt—without trousers—topped with a blouse became the uniform in many girls schools. Things went even further in some of the more progressive schools. Girls there exercised in shorts and thin, revealing blouses—a situation unimaginable during the imperial period.

But most characteristic and influential of all was the *qipao* (literally meaning "Manchu banner gown"), better known in the West as the *cheongsam* (a Cantonese word meaning "long gown"). The qipao emerged in the 1920s as an authentic indigenous modern form of female dress (although as the name implies it was patterned after Manchu dress), and to that extent it was the female equivalent of the Zhongshan suit. The qipao was indeed novel. Its distinguishing feature was that it was a single, one-piece garment, something which had been alien to the Chinese women's wardrobe in the late imperial period. But the qipao was not *too* new. At first it looked very much like a man's changpao: a long, rather formless gown. But it quickly became an attractive form-fitting dress. The details were highly variable, and fashion seemed to change with each season: the qipao could have long sleeves, elbow-length sleeves, short sleeves, or no sleeves; it could be ankle length or knee length or any length in between; the slits along the sides (again, reminiscent of the men's changpao) could be short or long; the collar was usually high and closely fitted around the neck (Figure 5.4).

The qipao survives to this day, although it went into a long period of sartorial dormancy from the Cultural Revolution to around 1980. It has been resurrected not as a flourishing everyday garment but as more or less a novelty, worn as a uniform by hostesses in some enterprises and the like. Even during its heyday (from around 1925 to 1950), it was hardly universal. Urban women, especially middle-class women, wore it, and so did shop girls, students, and others. On the other hand, rarely did women in the countryside, especially poor women, wear it.[25]

Twentieth-Century Clothing, Part 2: Sartorial Severity

In 1956 the French journalist Robert Guillain published a book on contemporary China under the offensive title of *The Blue Ants: 600 Million Chinese under the Red Flag*. With these words, Guillain intended, presumably, to encapsulate several "facts" about the People's Republic, including that the people all dressed in identical cheap, drab, androgynous clothing—the Maoist uniform, as it has been called. As a description of clothing during the 1950s, this was completely inaccurate since, for instance, women could continue to wear colorful dresses (including the qipao) or skirts. But the trend was undeniably toward utilitarian clothing befitting a nation now supposedly led by "workers and peasants." Even then, distinctions that might be missed by an outsider were important. The wearer's status was clearly marked by such things as fabric (choice wool for those high on the ladder of power; cotton for everyone else), or whether the wearer sported a fountain pen in the breast pocket (a hint that this was a person of importance), and so on. In any case, clothing in the old, politically incorrect styles was not thrown

Figure 5.4. An ad for cotton fabric, from the late 1930s or 1940s. The model is wearing a *qipao*. Written vertically on the right side of the ad is an endorsement: "Using Yindan Shilin colored fabric for a variety of clothing will help you be more beautiful." *Photograph provided by the author.*

away—that would have been unthinkably wasteful. Cloth was rationed, after all, and one could not buy more than the rationed amount even if one wanted to. Instead, people used patterns that showed how to cut up and refashion a man's long gown into a "uniform" (*zhifu*, an informal work suit based on the Zhongshanzhuang; see Figure 8.6), and tailor shops advertised "Reconditioning of Western Suits" (by which they meant transforming them into Zhongshan-style suits). In the words of an old tailor, "uniforms (*zhifu*) were recognised as the mark of state employees; to wear one was progressive. If you wore a [Western] suit people thought you were a capitalist. . . . You had to follow the fashion and, in clothing, the model was Chairman Mao. . . .

Foreigners like talking about 'Mao suits,' but for us that uniform . . . was the national dress."[26]

During the height of the Cultural Revolution from 1966 to 1969 it became just about impossible to wear anything but the zhifu (going out in public in a qipao, for example, would have been an invitation to mayhem), yet even then children's clothing remained colorful and "personal statements" in clothing, although subtle, were still possible. One could always wear a bright red bandanna around the neck—who could object to this accessory in revolutionary red? And the olive drab military uniform became popular; demobilized soldiers and others who could get their hands on these uniforms proudly wore them on the streets. Yet, anyone contemplating going beyond the exceedingly narrow confines of acceptable fashion had to think twice, for Red Guards roaming the streets eagerly waylaid pedestrians attired in a "bourgeois" style and cut their clothing to shreds on the spot.

Twenty-First Century Clothing: Fashion Once Again Fashionable

A China International Young Fashion Designers Contest held in March 1999 had as its theme "We have just one planet." Through "the language of fashion," some of the contestants "eulogized the beauty of the earth" while others "reviewed the development of modern industries, expressing their terror of its pollution."[27] These concerns are, of course, those of people all across the globe. When it comes to the globalization of fashion, China today is definitely no outsider.

Today most people walking down the streets of Shanghai or any other Chinese city or town are dressed pretty much as people dress in St. Louis, or Sydney, or Seville. A short story by Chen Jiangong (b. 1949) published in 1988 mentions a certain "chick" who was "real pretty, pretty enough to be a film star, and she had a fantastic body. She was wearing a fine pair of jeans; her cream-coloured sport jacket was unbuttoned, and inside she had on a blue sweatshirt with foreign lettering on it."[28] The description could, of course, fit millions of young women all over the globe.

Chinese suffer from no shortage of knowledge of global fashion. China's first fashion magazine in contemporary times, *Shizhuang zazhi* (Fashion), was launched in 1979. Since then it has been joined by more than a score of others, including a Chinese-language edition of *Elle*. International fashion shows have become commonplace since Pierre Cardin held the first post-reform extravaganzas in Beijing and Shanghai in 1979. In 1998, designer Shi Yanqin made a big splash in Paris with a showing at the Louvre of ancient clothing (actually, clothing Shi had made according to what she thinks is the ancient style), including some supposedly from the Xia dynasty (21st to 16th century B.C.),[29] a good trick since there is neither archaeological nor documentary evidence of Xia clothing. People who do not read fashion magazines or attend *haute couture* shows learn of global fashions through photographs in advertisements in glossy magazines, and of course through television and the movies and through tourism. Finally, many Chinese have a ringside seat on international fashion by virtue of the fact that China is by far the world's largest producer and exporter of clothing: it is rare to find a closet anywhere in the world that does not have at least a few pieces of clothing with a "Made in China" label.

Global fashion has even invaded the countryside, and it is not unusual to see a farmer dressed in "going to town clothes"—the same sort worn by young men out for the evening in Los Angeles—riding a tractor or walking behind a water buffalo. At the same time, the zhifu, often worn with a cloth cap, remains very much in evidence, both in the cities and in the countryside. For a great many working-class men, it is the preferred on-the-job attire, and also for many, especially the middle aged and older, it is the leisure attire of choice. This is also true of many working-class women. Some older women dress in trousers and tunic very much reminiscent of those worn in the nineteenth century.

Rarely are choices in clothing nowadays conscious attempts to make a political statement. However, today when political leaders wear the Zhongshan suit, it is invariably to send a political message. In 1989 when the television newscaster came on the air to announce the imposition of martial law in Beijing, he was wearing not the usual Western-style suit but a Zhongshanzhuang. Before he even opened his mouth, viewers knew that he was going to announce something politically momentous. And on October 1, 1999, when China's top leaders stepped out onto the reviewing stand to watch the parade celebrating the 50th anniversary of the founding of the People's Republic, President Jiang Zemin was wearing a Zhongshan suit. The fact that the president, and no one else, was so attired was certainly not a matter of happenstance, but rather a calculated demonstration that this man was China's supreme leader. Standing there, before a television audience of several hundred million, Jiang was announcing, by the suit he was wearing, that clothing can still carry a political message.

NOTES

1. On the four basic necessities of life, see Hanchao Lu, *Beyond the Neon Lights: Everyday Shanghai in the Early Twentieth Century* (Berkeley: University of California Press, 1999), pp. 252–53.

2. Lin Yutang, *My Country and My People* (New York: John Day, 1935), p. 337.

3. This point is made by K.C. Chang, "Introduction," in K.C. Chang, ed., *Food in Chinese Culture: Anthropological and Historical Perspectives* (New Haven, CT: Yale University Press, 1977), p. 8.

4. Lin Yutang, *My Country and My People*, p. 340.

5. K.C. Chang, "Introduction," p. 17.

6. "Corruption Tops List of Major Concerns," *China Daily* (Sept. 24, 1999), http://www.chinadaily.com.cn (Sept. 27, 1999).

7. Jan Wong, *Red China Blues: My Long March from Mao to Now* (Toronto: Doubleday Canada, 1996), p. 362.

8. Yunxiang Yan, "McDonald's in Beijing," p. 39, and James L. Watson, "Introduction," p. 203 n.1, both in James L. Watson, ed., *Golden Arches East: McDonald's in East Asia* (Stanford, CA: Stanford University Press, 1997). The discussion here of McDonald's is based upon Yunxiang Yan, "McDonald's in Beijing."

9. Yunxiang Yan, "McDonald's in Beijing," p. 49.

10. Ibid., p. 65.

11. Ibid., p. 57.

12. Ibid., p. 42.

13. *Beijing Scene* 5, no. 8 (May 7–13, 1999), http://www.beijingscene.com (Aug. 30, 1999).

14. *China News Digest*, Global News no. GL99–141 (Oct. 18, 1999).

15. Di Wang, "Street Culture: Public Space and Urban Commoners in Late-Qing Chengdu," *Modern China* 24, no. 1 (Jan. 1998): p. 40.

16. Qin Shao, "Tempest over Teapots: The Vilification of Teahouse Culture in Early Republican China," *Journal of Asian Studies* 57, no. 4 (Nov. 1998): p. 1012.

17. K. Sima, "Shanghai versus Taibei," *Shanghai Daily* (Sept. 9, 1999), http://www.shanghai-daily.com (Sept. 16, 1999).

18. Lu Xun, "Kong Yiji," *Lu Xun: Selected Works*, vol. 1, trans. Yang Xianyi and Gladys Yang (Beijing: Foreign Languages Press, 1980), p. 52.

19. Mao Zedong, *Report from Xunwu*, trans. Roger R. Thompson (Stanford, CA: Stanford University Press, 1990), p. 108.

20. Quoted in Antonia Finnane, "What Should Chinese Women Wear? A National Problem," *Modern China* 22, no. 2 (April 1996): p. 115.

21. Valery M. Garrett, *Chinese Clothing: An Illustrated Guide* (Hong Kong: Oxford University Press, 1994), p. 81.

22. Feng Jicai, "The Miraculous Pigtail," *Chinese Literature* (Spring 1986): p. 148.

23. Cited in Antonia Finnane, "Military Culture and Chinese Dress in the Early Twentieth Century," in Valerie Steele and John S. Major, eds., *China Chic: East Meets West* (New Haven, CT: Yale University Press, 1999), p. 130.

24. On the origin and symbolism of the Zhongshanzhuang, see Hanchao Lu, *Beyond the Neon Lights*, pp. 253–54.

25. Finnane, "What Should Chinese Women Wear?" pp. 119–20.

26. Cited in Sang Ye, "From Rags to Revolution," in Claire Roberts, ed., *Evo-*

lution and Revolution: Chinese Dress, 1700s–1900s (Sydney: Powerhouse Publishing, 1997), pp. 46–47.

27. Tang Min, "Peng Wins with Design for Life," *China Daily* (Apr. 3, 1999), http://www.chinadaily.net (Sept. 9, 1999).

28. Chen Jiangong, "Curlylocks," *Chinese Literature* (summer 1988): p. 47.

29. Ji Tao, "Ancient Chinese Culture Inspires Designer's Work," *China Daily* (Dec. 31, 1998).

6

Architecture and Housing

THE BUILDINGS and other structures that humans make are, like food and clothing, a combination of art and practicality. To appreciate China's highest achievements in this regard, one might turn to the country's so-called monumental architecture (mainly large buildings such as temples, government offices, palaces, etc.), which today throng with tourists. But to find the greatest ingenuity and creativity in combining art and practicality in architecture, one must turn to the simple everyday buildings—especially the homes—of the common people. It is there that can be found the art of taking whatever inexpensive materials are available locally, even if nothing more than common dirt, and transforming them into a useful structure, however simple and crude. Yet most housing being built today is thoroughly modern, which is to say anonymous and universal, using materials such as concrete and techniques and plans that make little allowance for regional diversity.

ARCHITECTURE

Toward the end of the nineteenth century a French diplomat declared that "the first impression one gets when looking at a Chinese town . . . is of a certain monotony which results from the predominance of a single architectural type. After a long stay, this impression persists, with only a few buildings appearing not to fit the general formula."[1] With equal justification—or perhaps equal lack of justification—one could complain about the "monotony" of the contemporary Parisian skyline. Nonetheless, this gentleman's sweeping generalization contains a good deal of truth. The architectural tradition in

China was more continuous than in Europe and lacked radical disjunctures such as that between classical Greek and Roman architecture and Gothic architecture. Furthermore, in China monumental architecture tended to follow a fairly uniform pattern in materials, structure, layout, and proportions. Architecturally speaking, there was no fundamental difference between a Buddhist temple, a palace, a large school, or almost any other sizable traditional building or complex of buildings. Depending on one's feelings, this can be condemned as monotony or praised as coherence.

But this is only part of the picture. The other part is that in a country as large and diverse as China, with its variety of climatic and topographic settings, its many styles of living, and its varied economic conditions, architecture was bound to be rich and variegated. This is particularly true of everyday buildings, especially houses. The building style in one locale may be more or less uniform, but a person has only to travel to another locale to see a quite different style, and to still another locale for still a different style. In some places in North China people live literally underground, in dwellings 30 feet below the surface; in some places in South China, people live in houses on stilts. These two extremes suggest the wide variety of creative adaptations to different local environments.

Framework and Philosophy

Above all else, architecture in traditional China meant creating small worlds within larger worlds, within still larger worlds. "A man's home is his castle" may capture how an Englishman feels about his home, but it is much too puny a formulation for how a Chinese regards his domicile—his home is his world. At least since the Han dynasty, and probably before, the home was a secure, self-contained compound—not just a free-standing house—that turned its back on the world outside. Typically, the exterior walls of the house formed the perimeter of the compound, with a courtyard in the center. With the exception of the rooms that opened onto the courtyard, few if any of the walls had windows. Entrance to this little world was usually through a single gate. This remains the most popular layout for Chinese homes.

The private compound was a re-creation of the layout of the town itself. By around the first millennium B.C., the broad outlines of city planning had been set. The ideal city was square shaped, with roads laid out in a grid pattern, and enclosed within walls with gateways opening in all four directions. Also ideally, the city was arranged symmetrically along a north-south and an east-west axis. The most important buildings—government offices or palaces—were usually located at the intersection of the two main axes at the center of the city (symbolizing that the ruler is at the center of the earth, just as the sun was thought to be at the center of the universe). Such buildings faced south; ideally houses also faced south, toward the life-giving sun. Important buildings themselves were laid out on an axial plan and were usually symmetrical. Finally, important buildings tended to be placed within compounds containing a hierarchy of courtyards. Entering the first, and least important, courtyard, one faced its main building, with subsidiary buildings on the left and right. Walking through or around the main building of the first courtyard, one entered a second and more secluded and more important courtyard, again with the main building straight ahead and subsidiary buildings on the left and right. Depending on the size and grandeur of the compound, there could be still more courtyards, each more secluded than the previous one, each a progressively more intimate world.

All these features were attempts to re-create on earth, in increasingly smaller units, the supposed layout of the universe. They were, however, only ideals, not rigid rules. Never has a Chinese city followed the ideal plan in all its particulars, just as Chinese houses by no stretch of the imagination adhere to an invariable layout. Instead, the pattern has been various degrees of divergence from the ideal. Towns and cities that were administrative centers and housed important government offices tended to be walled. Yet cities that arose from trading centers, and developed and grew with little or no planning, often displayed no symmetry and had no walls whatsoever.

Still, the Chinese surely stand at the forefront of wall-building cultures. Their premier achievement in this realm is the Great Wall, which once stretched 4,000 miles from the Yellow Sea to the edge of Central Asia, and which is sometimes said—erroneously—to be the only man-made structure visible from space. Most of what tourists see today of the Great Wall are restored remnants, albeit most impressive remnants, some 30 miles north of Beijing, that were built during the Ming dynasty (1368–1644), although many earlier walls were built along roughly the same route. The heyday of wall building was the Warring States period, before the third century B.C., when most of the contending kingdoms erected long stretches of walls along their frontiers. Even if these were not as large and massive as the latter-day Great Wall, they nonetheless represented a staggeringly huge investment of labor and other resources. These walls testify to the wealth of China, and to the overriding concern for a safe, well-organized, and secure world.

Fengshui

According to legend, General Meng Tian, the reputed builder of the first Great Wall (ca. 210 B.C.), lamented just before his death by suicide that "I have committed a crime and I must pay for it. . . . I have constructed walls and moats stretching for more than 10,000 *li*. Surely in that expanse of land I must have severed a vein of the earth. That is my crime." This is one of the first references to geomancy (a belief that human fortunes are affected by geographic features and human intrusion on the natural environment), which still has currency in China and beyond.

Fengshui (literally, wind and water), as geomancy came to be known in China, is premised on the notion that flowing throughout the earth are *yin-yang* currents of *qi*, vital force or cosmic energy. Fengshui serves the purpose of locating these veins of energy and of ensuring that everything added to the landscape is properly designed and placed so as to harmonize with the forces of nature. A house, a grave, a temple, or any other structure that is improperly placed or improperly designed will lead to bad luck.

The rules of fengshui are a combination of common sense (such as, do not build a house at the end of a busy T intersection) and nonsense (such as, if the front and back doors of a house are aligned in a straight line wealth and happiness will escape). Thrown in for good measure is a degree of aesthetic sensibility, which may or may not be related to practical considerations. For instance, a building with excellent fengshui would face south and have a hill behind it and gently flowing water (a stream, river, lake) before it. The analysis of fengshui can get complicated and even with the help of a manual, penetrating the esotericism may be difficult. A nineteenth-century fengshui handbook directs that "on a rock hill you must take an earthy site; on an earth hill you must take a rocky site. Where it is confined, take an open space; where it is open, take a confined space. On a prominence, take the flat; where it is flat, take the prominence. Where strong comes, take weak; where weak comes, take strong."[2] With instructions such as these it is no wonder that people wanting guidance often turned to professional geomancers who conducted fengshui analyses and dispensed advice. Since potential clients presumably sought relief from some adversity—a financial setback, troubled relations with in-laws, bad teeth—it must have been a rare geomancer who announced, "The fengshui here is perfect. Don't change a thing." Instead, giving the client his money's worth, the geomancer judged that the client's windows were in the wrong place, that his door was slightly out of line with a vein of energy, that the graves must be moved, and so forth—hence the saying that "if you invite those who inspect houses and graveyards, you might as well move your dwelling altogether." The smart geomancer, recognizing that the client wanted relief but not at the expense of an extraordinary "solution" such as tearing down his house, offered artful alternatives such as using a mirror to redirect a vein of energy or putting up a screen to deflect malevolent forces.

It is difficult to judge the depth of belief in fengshui in China today. The

Communist government has consistently condemned it as superstition, but even Communists have betrayed evidence of "backward thinking." The first officially published book on fengshui since 1949 appeared in 1990, and quickly sold out. According to a study of rural Sichuan and Jiangsu in the early 1990s, almost everyone who had recently built a house, buried a family member, or restored an ancestor's grave had consulted a fengshui practitioner.[3] In rural Longchuan, consisting of 18 villages with 28,000 inhabitants, there were 10 full-time fengshui specialists, all so busy they were rarely at home.[4] City dwellers are less likely to indulge in fengshui, either out of a lack of belief or because people living in apartments cannot enjoy the luxury of minutely arranging the siting of their dwelling. On the other hand, even some people who consider themselves well educated and sophisticated are taken with fengshui, including people outside China. In its weekly real estate section, the *Los Angeles Times* has a column (written by a non-Chinese) devoted to dispensing advice about fengshui. Finally, even in cities, paying attention when possible to fengshui and other so-called superstitions may be a way of both respecting tradition and playing it safe. The Jinmao Tower in Shanghai, China's tallest building when it was officially opened in 1999, is a case in point. The building is replete with references to the number eight, which is considered lucky because, in the Cantonese dialect, it is a homophone of a word that generally suggests wealth and because its shape 八 suggests a pouring out of riches: it is 88 stories tall, the vertical parts of the tower are octagonal shaped, and it has eight exterior composite megacolumns and eight outer steel megacolumns.[5]

Classical Architecture

The Chinese have not been good at preserving their architectural heritage. The task has been difficult because the main material of traditional buildings, wood, is highly perishable. But wanton destruction due to warfare, neglect, and unconcern has also taken its toll. One example was the pulling down of the walls of Beijing by the Communist government after 1949. Liang Sicheng, China's most noted architect and architectural historian of the time, decried the destruction of Beijing's magnificent walls as painful as having one's own flesh or skin torn off. At the same time the authorities removed a number of magnificent stone memorial arches (*pailou*), treasures sacrificed for the sake of improving traffic flow.

The ancient buildings that are left (the oldest surviving wooden building dates to around the ninth century) and the archaeological record reveal that the broad outlines of a consistent style began to emerge very early, probably before 1000 B.C., and continued to develop, expand, and sometimes degenerate during the following millennia. Furthermore, there has long been a close relationship between monumental architecture and so-called vernacular architecture, that is, simple, everyday buildings. The latter, in fact, has been the more varied, interesting, and creative of the two.

The three features that mark most traditional Chinese buildings, both great structures and simple houses, are, first, a structure of wooden post-and-beam construction. In this system, walls are merely screens and do not hold up the building. Second is a lack of diagonal bracing. Diagonal bracing provides critical resistance to the strain of high winds and earthquakes, and was common in European post-and-beam buildings even in countries free of earthquakes, but strangely absent in China, where earthquakes are frequent. Chinese carpenters were acquainted with diagonal braces, and used them to reinforce buildings under construction. But as soon as the building was far enough along to stand on its own, off came the braces. Third is tile roofs, especially with curved, up-turned eaves. Roofs of tile—the most characteristic and most immediately recognizable Chinese element—appeared first in the Zhou dynasty, and soon became standard for important buildings and for houses also, although thatched dwellings were also common. Two more features, almost universal among monumental structures but rarely found in simple houses, were an elaborate system of eaves brackets and the construction of buildings on a platform or podium of tamped earth. Eaves brackets (*dougong*), sitting on the tops of the posts, served to support the long, cantilevered eaves. Visitors to any traditional Chinese temple, or palace, or other great building, should first look up under the eaves—the dougong there are a marvelous bit of construction. The wide podium on which important traditional buildings sit was evidently introduced as a means of preventing moisture from reaching the posts that hold up the building. Setting buildings up on a platform gives them an imposing and monumental air and makes them particularly "Chinese." When shown fanciful drawings of a traditional Chinese building erected at grade level rather than on a podium, Chinese respondents are apt to say that the building "just doesn't look right," or "it doesn't look Chinese," even if they cannot put their finger on the reason.

It is these shared features that give monumental buildings the sameness or coherence that we have noted. They are such an integral part of tradition that they were applied even to circular or polygonal buildings and were imitated in brick buildings. The sameness also arises from the multifunctionality of design, that is, from the fact that the same sort of building could be secular, such as a library, or religious, such as a Buddhist temple. One of the very few structures that was exclusively religious was the pagoda, that Buddhist tower that served to enshrine relics and guide pilgrims (Figure 6.1). The pagoda developed from two roots: the Indian stupa, which looked rather

Figure 6.1. Great Goose Pagoda, near Xi'an, built in the mid-seventh century. *Courtesy of Daniel C. Waugh.*

like a huge overturned bowl, and the native Chinese tower, which dated back to before the Han period. Unfortunately, none of the towers that predate the pagoda have survived. About the only part of the stupa design that the Chinese retained was the tall finial or spire on top. Otherwise, they stretched the structure into a multistory tower, with a generally square, or circular, or polygonal floor plan, and often built it of masonry.

Gardens

The perfect counterpoint to the axiality and symmetry in Chinese architecture is the Chinese garden. Historically, for all their concern about strict, even rigid, city planning and the precise layout of monumental buildings, the Chinese have also been addicted to rurality and to the irregularity and freedom of nature. Town dwellers thus sought to re-create on a small scale the rural scenery they adored. The wealthy were, of course, able to give free rein to their fancy, and have left us some small but magnificent gardens.

The object was to use every square inch of the garden with great care and planning to create a series of dramatic scenic effects. In this scheme, flowers were not of much importance. What was important was *shan-shui*—mountains and water. To re-create a mountain or group of mountains in an area no bigger than a typical American backyard required ingenuity. Large rocks were carefully selected and artfully placed to suggest mountains; the more interesting and unusual the shape and character of the rocks, the better. As for water, if the garden were large enough it might have actual ponds; if not, pebbles could be arranged to suggest a lake or river.

Until the twentieth century, all gardens were private except for those attached to temples. Today, the best surviving gardens are publicly owned, and the gardening tradition among individuals has just about died out. The vast majority of city dwellers today live in small apartments; if they want to enjoy a re-creation of a magnificent landscape, they must settle for a few potted plants or hang a picture on the wall.

Homes and Vernacular Architecture

In 1986 the Chinese post office issued a series of 14 stamps depicting Chinese traditional folk houses, followed by an additional issue of seven more stamps in 1989. Taken together, the houses on these 21 stamps fit no pattern; each represents a different, unique solution to the problem of putting a roof over one's head. Furthermore, these 21 comprise only a fraction of the extremely wide variety of housing in China. As everywhere else in the world, the dwellings and other everyday structures built by the common people grew out of the local, natural, and cultural environment. This means that the materials used were generally the most economical available, and until modern times, were, as a rule, the most plentiful and readily available in the locale and, based on common sense, experience, and tradition, were judged the most suitable for local conditions. In a country as large as China, with such widely varying climatic and topographic conditions, with huge cities and tiny hamlets and everything in between, it is hardly surprising that there has been an extremely rich, creative, and diverse answer to the problem of housing. Single story, two story, and multistory; wood, earth, masonry, bamboo, and grass; above ground and below ground; permanent and seasonal: just about every building material and type have been put to good use.

To search for "the typical Chinese house" is therefore fruitless since such a thing simply does not exist. If instead, we begin to journey about China with a notebook in hand, jotting down the various types of housing we see, we will quickly fill up the notebook but also discover that there are a few types that reappear time and again. A good place to begin the journey is the seaport town of Lianyungang, in the province of Jiangsu, about a third of the way down the coast, and the eastern terminus of a railway that stretches across China and then onward, all the way to Rotterdam, in the Netherlands. Downtown Lianyungang looks like many other small- and medium-sized cities in China. The most prevalent dwellings are medium-rise reinforced concrete apartment houses, more or less the same sort of rectangular slabs that fill the cities of much of the world. In fact, an apartment house plucked off the streets of Lianyungang and plopped down in Tokyo, or Cairo, or Buenos Aires would fit in seamlessly. Most of these nondescript gifts of modern architecture were built in recent years, after the opening of the reform era in 1978, but still they look like they could use a fresh coat of paint or at least a good scrubbing. On the other hand, almost every apartment has its own balcony, a perfect spot for the householder to hang out the wash, keep some potted plants, or sleep on a scorching and humid summer's night. Here and there in town are what real estate agents would call "upscale" apartment houses, attractive edifices with elevators, hot running water, and central heating. But again, these apartments, most of which were built in the past few years and some of which were built for sale not for rental, are anonymous and would pass unnoticed in any of the world's cities.

Driving out of town along the coast brings us to the real architectural treasures of Lianyungang. There, in the suburbs, we find attractive communities of small, rectangular single-story houses built of magnificent cut and dressed granite stone. Almost all the homes have the same sort of simple gabled roofs, clad with orange flat tiles. Such tiles are rather unusual elsewhere in China. A bit unusual too are houses of stone, but a quick glance at the hills that surround Lianyungang reveals why this material is so popular here. The hills—barren except for some scrub growth that clings to life here and there—appear to be pure granite, with boulders as big as two-story houses scattered about everywhere. Stone is so plentiful that it is used for the walls that surround many homes, for paving, and for seawalls. Almost all the stone houses have been built within the past 10 or 20 years by newly risen shopkeepers and other entrepreneurs who have taken advantage of the opportunities created by the reform program. Only a "newly industrializing country," as scholars like to call places like China, could afford this luxury: there are enough people with enough wealth to buy homes of stone, while labor is still plentiful enough and cheap enough that such homes are affordable.

Proceeding south and west about 200 miles toward the interior, we reach our next destination, the town of Shengze, long famous as a silk-producing center, located at the southern tip of Jiangsu province. In the town itself, most of the older houses are roofed with charcoal-gray clay tiles. Tiles like these can be found all across China. The older homes in the town center, some of which are two-stories, are mostly of wood frame construction, with walls of lightly fired brick covered with plaster. Many of them are laid out in a courtyard fashion, often with the courtyard surrounded on all sides by rooms. Some houses have several courtyards, some of which are so small that they are scarcely more than an open skylight (indeed, they are called "sky wells" in Chinese). All these design features are very common and can be found in a great many places in China.

In the countryside surrounding Shengze, the older homes are essentially of the same construction as the houses in town, except that some are of plastered sun-dried mud brick and many are single-story and do not have enclosed courtyards. Perhaps the privacy assured by the courtyard style is not required by rural families because the farmsteads are dispersed, separated in many instances by hundreds of yards of rice fields, wood lots, mulberry bushes, and canals that crisscross the landscape. Dispersed farmsteads, as in Shengze, are found in many regions of China. But just as common are concentrated villages, where farmers' homes are gathered together into compact villages.

A striking feature of the countryside outside Shengze is the many new homes built in the past decade or two. These are almost all two-stories, built of concrete and brick, plastered and painted white, and with charcoal-gray tile roofs. Most of these homes have similar floor plans and elevations: they are rectangular, one room deep, with a balcony across the entire façade. The doors (usually French doors, which open wide and provide light and ventilation) and windows are numerous and of a generous size. By any reasonable standard, these homes are attractive and comfortable.

Both Shengze and Lianyungang have been part of a building boom that has swept rural China since the late 1970s. Comfortable—and sometimes imposing—homes, some boasting three stories and several thousand square feet of floor space, are found in a great many places. In relatively poor regions, such large and expensive homes are rare, but even there modest but still comfortable new homes abound. Such a region is our next destination.

Traveling about 500 miles northwest we arrive in Pinglu county in the province of Shanxi, a world apart from Shengze. While Shengze is flat, well watered, and verdant, Pinglu is a veritable badlands, with little water, hills almost bare of vegetation, and steep gullies that rend the landscape. The soil in this part of North China is loess, the fine loam that is carried from the west on strong winds and threatens to be but a quick visitor, ready to blow still further away unless anchored by vegetation. Loess is the single treasure of Pinglu for it is fertile and can support good crops if only enough rain falls.

In this region building materials are scarce. Here and there a few scrawny trees dot the hillsides, but they would not yield sufficient lumber to house all who need shelter. The loess can be made into sun-dried bricks, but only with much labor. Unlike clay, loess cannot be simply slapped into brick-shaped molds, but must be pounded into the molds with heavy stone hammers so that it becomes sufficiently compacted to hold together.

In this environment, which covers much of North China, people long ago devised a clever solution to the problem of housing: caves. Dug into the face of cliffs, the caves have several advantages, not the least of which is that they cost almost nothing. Sheltered by tons of earth, they are relatively cool in summer and warm in winter. Winters on the loess plateau are cold, and the cave dwellers, like the residents of conventional above-ground houses in rural North China, have a marvelous device to keep themselves warm, the *kang*. The kang is a raised platform or dais of brick, often located on the south side of the house up against the windows, containing a warren of flues through which flows the hot smoke from the cook stove. During the summer, the kang is bypassed, but during the winter, with the smoke directed through it, it becomes a warm and welcoming platform. And, best of all, heating the kang costs little since it uses heat that would otherwise just be vented out of the house. The kang is where the family puts down bedding and sleeps, but it also the place where much of the family life takes places. It is a good spot for sewing, for the children to do their homework, and for just sitting and chatting.

However clever, cave dwellings are still caves and to many people they smack of primitiveness and poverty. Just about no one builds traditional cave houses any longer. People who can afford it are building conventional above-ground houses of brick. But about 300 miles to the northeast in Ansai county, in the neighboring province of Shaanxi, people still appreciate cave dwellings, although here too traditional cave houses are no longer excavated. Instead, people are turning to what they call stone caves, which have frameworks of attractive, buff-colored cut stone, over which is placed a thick layer of sheltering earth. Often these so-called stone caves are built on long terraces, with each terrace filled with a row of houses side by side. Looking at the interior of these homes, one hesitates to call them caves. The rooms are still rather long and the ceilings are arched, as in traditional caves, but the walls are plastered and painted, the floors are covered with ceramic tiles or stone, and the opening of the cave is almost entirely filled with glass, so that there is plenty of light. The impression is of comfort and newfound prosperity.

The final leg of our journey involves doubling back to Pinglu, since we missed some interesting homes there. It is understandable that we overlooked these houses since they are, in a sense, invisible. Not all of Pinglu is rent by gullies. There are flat areas too, without hills into which caves can be cut. What is the solution to housing here? Sunken caves (see Figure 6.2). A large

Figure 6.2. A pit house in Shanxi province, 1998. *From Hong Kong China Tourism Photo Library.*

square pit 20 or 30 feet deep is excavated, and then along the faces of the pit are dug caves for houses, a privy, storage rooms, work rooms, and domestic animals. Long stairwells lead from the surface down to the sunken courtyard, and sometimes long ramps too, so that farmers can ride their motorbikes down to their homes. Homes of this sort, which can be found in several places on the loess plateau, are definitely no longer fashionable, and many people have built conventional above-ground houses in which they live most of the year, retreating to the old sunken homestead during the winter. Others have abandoned the underground life entirely, and now live contentedly in modern homes on the surface.

Thus, in just a quick trip from coastal Lianyungang to Shengze in South China to the loess plateau we have encountered a variety of markedly different types of dwellings. Anyone wanting to inventory *all* the types of vernacular architecture in China would have to look forward to a lifetime of travel. However, perhaps before long the trip can be shorter and quicker because unique traditional varieties of homes are passing from the scene and being replaced by more standardized and anonymous structures. A cave dwelling, for instance, is very much *local,* using local materials and responding to and taking advantage of local circumstances. It is unlike a house of concrete, built

Figure 6.3. A luxurious contemporary rural home (left) and a nineteenth-century watchtower-and-house combination (right), on the Pearl River delta, Guangdong, 1998. *Courtesy of William Hocker.*

according to a professionally drafted plan that can be followed in humid South China or dry Northwest China or anywhere else. This transition from regional and traditional to universal and modern is taking place in China's cities also, where entire communities housed in century-old dwellings are disappearing at a dizzying pace (Figure 6.3).

The Cityscape Yesterday and Today

In the past quarter century, China's cities have undergone such sweeping changes that even long-time residents who return after being away but a year or two become disoriented and scratch their heads in puzzlement as they try to find neighborhoods they once knew so well, but which have now entirely disappeared. An architectural revolution has engulfed the cities as countless old buildings have been torn down and replaced by new structures, some impressive, some imposing, and some nondescript. In the process, acres of traditional housing, mostly built between the middle of the nineteenth century and the 1930s, have been demolished to make way for new high-rise apartments.

A quarter of a century ago, each of China's great cities, with few exceptions, had a characteristic type of dwelling that was, in some instances, unique to that particular city. In Shanghai it was the two-story brick alleyway house, which made up about three-quarters of that city's dwellings. In Beijing it was the single-story courtyard house. It some parts of Guangzhou it was the rectangular two-story "big house" with intricately carved window frames and doors and spectacular eaves. Most of these buildings had been designed as single-family residences, but over the years, as cities became increasingly crowded, they were haphazardly subdivided and what was intended to house one family became a home to four or five or even more households. Furthermore, maintenance was usually slack, especially after the Communist "liberation" in 1949. Finally, many homes were converted into retail stores, workshops, schools, and the like. Thus neighborhoods of once-stately homes became poor, crowded, and noisy. The circumstances of Liang Xi, his wife, and teenage son, residents of an 80-year-old "big house" in Guangzhou, are typical. The Liang family lives in a single 100-square-foot room. They share a kitchen and toilet with four other families. Rainy days, plentiful in Guangzhou, are a misery because the roof leaks. "It's not only inconvenient but also dangerous to live in this house," Liang complains.[6] With tens of millions of people in similar circumstances, the need and demand for new housing, even if it is simple and architecturally undistinguished, has been urgent.

Despite sporadic efforts to save some old homes, the drive for redevelopment is well-nigh irresistible. In the rush to tear down old housing and put up new, it seems only a matter of time before a distinctive architectural legacy is lost. Occasionally architects have tried to incorporate traditional notions of housing in the design of modern multistory apartments, such as arranging apartment houses around enclosed open spaces reminiscent of traditional courtyards.[7] But looking down from a little sixth-floor apartment on a "courtyard" that is available to hundreds of people is hardly the same as enjoying a private courtyard that one steps into directly from one's home. Besides, most large urban residential developments show little evidence of concern for traditional Chinese architectural aesthetics.

Commercial districts are also undergoing a transformation. It has been said that on any given day during the 1990s there were more cranes at work erecting skyscrapers in the city of Shanghai alone than there were in the entire United States. Most of the new buildings are rigorously "international" in style and have no particularly Chinese look. Nonetheless, many architects and others are concerned about perpetuating "national characteristics" in monumental buildings, although there is an ongoing debate about how to make a modern large building characteristically Chinese. On one side are those who favor incorporating the supposed Chinese "spirit" in large buildings. Theirs is a difficult position since concrete and steel have no nationality whatsoever. On the other side are those who emphasize Chinese "appear-

Figure 6.4. Artist's rendition of the Cultural Palace of the Nationalities, in Beijing, completed in 1959 as one of the so-called Ten Great Buildings constructed in celebration of the tenth anniversary of the People's Republic of China. *Photograph provided by the author.*

ance." Theirs is a much easier task since it usually involves little more than grafting some Chinese-looking designs onto an otherwise anonymous building. The results are often Disneylandesque. The most egregious examples are often hotels and public buildings that sport tacked-on upswept tile roofs that have no functional rationale at all but are added merely to announce that the building is "Chinese."

The public seems to like this. A survey of readers of the *Beijing Daily* revealed that, in their eyes, the "most handsome structure in the capital" is the Cultural Palace of the Nationalities (Figure 6.4), which other observers have dismissed as "a Stalinist monstrosity built in the 1950s."[8] However, the Palace does have a sweeping, curved Chinese roof. One architect declared that "there's no rule that new buildings have to have these roofs, but the leaders make suggestions about the designs, and they like the roofs."[9] Not only Chinese architects but also foreign architects designing buildings for China apparently find this sort of political correctness congenial. The Jinmao Tower, for example, designed by the noted American architectural firm of Skidmore, Owings, and Merrill, looks rather like a huge pagoda.

While the postmodernism that is currently the rage in architectural schools in the West gives intellectual justification to such kitsch, adding Chinese features to non-Chinese buildings is not something new. From the middle of the nineteenth century to the middle of the twentieth century, when the European imperial powers threw up buildings in their concessions in the Chinese treaty ports, they assiduously shunned the slightest hint of "Chineseness" and instead insisted on buildings that looked exactly like those back home. For instance, walking through the German concession in the city of Qingdao in the 1910s, if the visitor avoided looking at the people in the street but kept his eyes riveted on the buildings, he could easily have believed he was in Berlin. Chinese designers of important buildings, on the other hand, tended to favor eclecticism, with bits of Western style thrown together with bits of Chinese style. Even during the period of "learning from the Soviet Union" in the 1950s, when the accepted practice was to imitate the dehumanizing and ponderous style of Stalinist Russia, Chinese architects—following the dictum "socialist in content and nationalist in form"— tended to tack on Chinese-style roofs. This elicited jibes from people with modern tastes: "the Communists are atheists, but why do they build temples?"[10]

The final item on our inventory of urban architecture requires that we direct our gaze downward from skyscrapers and look upon what are figuratively (and often also literally) the lowest structures in China's cities: shacks, shanties, and hovels of every sort, built by squatters who have flowed into the cities since the start of the reform program in search of a better life. The word architecture hardly seems applicable to such humble structures, but their very existence highlights China's ongoing struggle to find decent housing for all its people.

HOUSING

A basic fact of life for much of the Communist period was the rigid division of the entire population of China into two enormous groups: urban dwellers and rural residents. By 1958 this separation was enshrined in law: each person was assigned a permanent registration as either an "urban resident" or a "rural resident." Under this law, people registered as rural residents were prohibited from moving to cities. Sneaking into the city was pointless because one could not get a job (since that required an urban registration), nor rent an apartment (since most apartments were assigned), nor get clothing (since buying fabric required ration coupons), nor get much to eat (since essential foods were also rationed). The authorities did not have the least concern with urban residents moving to the countryside since an urban registration entailed tremendous privilege, as we shall see; the last thing in a city dweller's mind was to move to the countryside. While this system was intact, China avoided the problem suffered by most developing economies where poor farmers flood into the cities, gather in squalid shantytowns, and compete for miserable jobs paying subsistence wages.

To understand the reasoning behind the rigid separation of the Chinese population requires understanding the economic program that gave rise to it. The model of economic development followed from 1949 to the start of the reform in 1978 was summed up in the expression "agriculture as the base and industry as the leading sector." This meant that agriculture, then by far the biggest sector of the Chinese economy, was to be squeezed to extract from it the capital necessary to develop industry. Thus almost all agricultural products, except what rural people needed to survive, were purchased by the state, and at low prices. The state invested almost nothing in the rural sector. The countryside was left to its own devices, to develop as best it could from the meager capital that it was allowed to retain.

In the urban sector, the state very tightly controlled the economy and invested primarily in heavy industry and little in light industry (which turned out consumer products) or in essentially nonproductive infrastructure, such as housing. The rationing system ensured that consumption was held down and that products that in other systems might have been consumed by the public were instead directed toward industrial development. Therefore, in the cities (as well as in the countryside), all sorts of consumer products were in short supply. Urban wages were also kept low. The other side of the coin was that prices were also kept low and stable.

It may seem strange, but many city people today, when the economy is booming, look back to the Maoist era with nostalgia. In those days, there was much apparent equality in the cities; everyone was in the same boat. Wage differentials were much smaller than in any capitalist system, and private enterprise, especially on a large scale, was prohibited. No one got rich, it is true, but also no one got left behind in abject poverty. There was— despite the political toll taken by the Maoist system—economic security. This the Chinese called "the iron rice bowl." In the cities almost all work-places—factories, shops, schools, and all sorts of enterprises—were owned and run by the state. Since the state did not require its enterprises to be profitable, workers did not have to worry that their employer (their "work unit" as it was called) would go bankrupt and that they would lose their jobs. Wages were mostly based on seniority, not on performance. On the other hand, bonuses, which came under attack during the Cultural Revolution era, were typically performance based, and there were many instances of favoritism in pay, which points up the importance of *guanxi* in the workplace. And, finally, the state or the work unit provided employees with a wide range of free or low-cost benefits, including health care, pensions, and housing.

Urban Housing

Housing in China's cities from 1949 to the dawn of the reform period in 1978 can be summed up in one word—stagnation. During the 1950s, most urban housing was nationalized, and thereafter, until the 1980s when the reform period got rolling, virtually all new housing in China's cities was built by the state. But since housing was a low priority, not much was constructed. At the same time, the urban population grew—by 55 to 60 million between 1949 and 1977. The result was to make already crowded cities even more crowded. In 1949, per capita living space was around 63 square feet. By 1962 it had fallen to around 30 square feet, although by 1976 it had recovered a bit to 50 square feet.[11] The recovery was principally the result of the program of sending millions of mostly young urban residents down to the countryside after 1968, partly as a way of ending the violence of the Cultural Revolution. Following the introduction of the reform program in 1978, almost all of these "sent down" youth filtered back to the city, making living space especially tight in some places. In the core of Shanghai, for instance, population density toward the end of the 1970s was around five times greater than that of London or Paris and almost three times greater than that of Tokyo.[12] Living space there was perhaps 25 square feet per person or less: enough space for a person to lie down, but not much more than that. In most households no one even dreamed of having a private room. As with the Liang family in Guangzhou, often the entire family lived in but one room, where everyone ate, entertained themselves, and slept. In conditions such as these, it is almost impossible to speak of privacy. Some of the most intimate details of one's life were known not only to one's family but also to one's neighbors.

The upside was that rent was incredibly cheap, at about 1% or less of household income, making it no more costly in some instances than the electric bill. The downside was that the money the state or work units earned from rent was insufficient to fund proper maintenance; hence the condition of housing deteriorated. Even if a family wanted to fix up its own apartment, there was the nearly insurmountable obstacle of a lack of building materials, which were almost unobtainable at stores and shops. Furthermore, with little new housing being built and with practically no investment in the modernization of existing housing, amenities were primitive. Almost everyone had electricity, but as late as 1985 only 73% of city dwellers had running water (but not hot water), only 70% had access to a kitchen, and only 34% had a flush toilet (and almost 30% of those had to share a toilet with other families).[13] As late as 1985, in other words, the majority of city residents still used chamber pots. People either put out their chamber pot each morning to be emptied by a night-soil collector or they took the pot to a public dumping station. Human waste was hauled out of the city and used by farmers to fertilize their fields. While that took care of the waste, it still left urban families with a dirty chamber pot to be cleaned each morning.

Another daily chore was lighting the cook stove each morning. Cook stoves were fired mostly by coal briquettes. In the past two or three decades, sooty coal has been giving way to bottled gas, and even more recently to natural, piped-in gas. Until very recently, whether an apartment had heating or not depended mostly on where it was located: apartments in the north, where winters are severe, usually had heating, but those in Central and South China—even in places that experienced winter freezes—did not. Thus people in Shanghai complain that the winter in the Northeast (Manchuria), with heavy snowfall and really frigid temperatures, is more comfortable than in Shanghai—where the temperature rarely drops below 20°F—since apartments in the Northeast are at least heated. Furthermore, for most apartments the only source of hot water is what can be heated on the cook stove or lugged home from a shop that sells hot water. Thus bathing is a problem. The usual solution has been to go to a public bath.

Until recently, there was no rental housing market quite like that in capitalist countries. Housing was controlled by city or district housing offices or in some cases assigned by the work unit. The best a dissatisfied renter could hope for would be to find another dissatisfied renter and for the two to swap apartments. Many cities had semi-official offices, usually operated at the community level, where people could post want ads and then negotiate with potential "customers" who were interested in exchanging apartments.

Since the reform program hit its stride in the 1980s, the housing situation has been turned upside down. The state greatly increased investment in the construction of new housing and also allowed private real estate development. The result was that in the 20 years between 1979 and 1999, tens of billions of square feet of new apartments were built, many times what had been constructed during the 30 years from 1949 to 1979. By 1997, per capita living space had mushroomed to about 95 square feet. And since 1979, about 60% of urban families—around 75 million persons—had moved into new housing, a phenomenal accomplishment.[14] The spillover has benefited many people. With all those new apartments needing to be furnished, the furniture industry has grown from a midget (with a few thousand employees and $156 million in sales in 1978) to a giant (2 million employees and $10.5 billion in sales in 1998).[15] And interior decorators, an unknown occupation before the 1980s, can now be found in almost every big city.

The boom in housing construction has been so great that by the end of 1999 an over-supply of apartments had developed. Shanghai alone had a staggering 100 million square feet of empty new apartments.[16] At the same time, many people have ended up in shanty towns, where they huddle together in crude shacks thrown together from cast-off materials. People living in substandard housing while comfortable new apartments sit empty is an inevitable outgrowth of a reform program that has sought to crush the "iron rice bowl" and introduce a large dose of capitalism.

As a key part of the reform, the state has closed or sold off many enterprises, throwing millions out of work and turning tens of millions of others into employees of collectively owned or private enterprises, where wages are set by the market and job security is only a memory. In the new system, most people have done well, and some have done very well (China now has its small but growing share of BMW-driving millionaires), but others have not prospered and now live a precarious existence. Insofar as housing is concerned, the hallmark of the reform program has been not only the construction of a vast amount of new residences, but also the end of housing as a benefit. This has entailed an attack on the old housing system along two fronts: the raising of rent, and the sale of apartments. While rents have indeed been raised, so much so that some renters are paying 20 or more times what they paid in the late 1970s, given the general inflation since the 1970s and the fact that wages have also risen, the real cost of public housing is still cheap (at around 8% of household income).[17]

Compared to raising rent, the sale of housing is a much more fundamental change for it undermines one of the principal props of socialism in the city. In 1998 the central government announced that it would stop providing public housing and that urban families would have to buy their own homes. Sales of apartments had started in some cities in the 1980s, but by 1998 publicly owned housing still predominated. In any case, most city dwellers with the means are eager to purchase a home, especially since the price can be attractive. In one "affordable housing" development in Beijing, for instance, apartments sell for about $30,000. With a downpayment of $13,000, a buyer can move in and pay off the balance in monthly installments of $125 to $250. Typical wages in state-owned enterprises are around $1,200 to $3,000 a year, but the pay in private enterprises and joint-venture companies often reaches $7,000 or more a year. With husband and wife both working (which is usual), $30,000 does not seem an inordinately large sum of money. "Around 1,000 yuan [$130] per month is not a problem for me and my husband," said a woman who works for a newspaper. "My newspaper office is not likely to give me a house," she continued. "Even if it did give me one, it would be a small one. So why not buy a large house myself?"[18] Apparently many people feel exactly the same way. A sales manager with a Beijing real estate company declared that with prices as low as they are today, purchasing an apartment "is not buying, it's snatching." His company had completely sold out 24 affordable apartment buildings and has a waiting list of 1,600 people for four newly completed buildings.[19] And some work units have sold apartments to their employees at giveaway prices, equivalent to about one year's household income. A 56-year-old academic working for the Chinese Academy of Sciences made the buy of his life in 1996. The Academy, which had also been his landlord, offered to sell him his 450-square-foot apartment for a paltry $3,400, about 10% of the market value. He could have gone on renting the apartment at $5 a month, but with the asking price so enticing, and with the right to resell the apartment—which is sure to result in a hefty profit—in five years, how could he resist the offer?[20] Another couple, residents of the city of Changzhou, about 100 miles northwest of Shanghai, did even better. When the husband retired in the mid-1990s, the power station he worked for sold the couple their three-bedroom two-bath apartment (built in 1986) for the princely sum of $1,500.[21]

The shift from housing allocation and ownership by the state to allocation by the market and private ownership has been bumpy. China has had to work out the rules as it goes along: What does the buyer really get when purchasing a state-owned apartment? Actually, a 70-year lease (after which the apartment theoretically reverts to the state). Can apartments be inherited? Yes, and there is no inheritance tax—for now. Can apartments be resold? Yes, with certain limitations, according to a law adopted in 1999.

Finally, while people moving into modern apartments get most of what they are looking for—three or four good-sized rooms; a modern kitchen; clean heating; an up-to-date bathroom with a Western-style flush toilet and a bathtub; but usually still no hot water (in 1997, just 2% of Chinese households had hot running water)—they often also find they are losing something. In the old neighborhoods people were always getting in each other's way, but there was some value to this. Residents could usually count on their neighbors to lend a hand when it was needed, and company and camaraderie were easily available when one wanted them (and often when one did not). On summer nights one could always pick up a chair and join one's neighbors on the street, to play music, or watch TV through an open window, or just sit and talk. At best, there was a genuine sense of community. And at the very least there were usually enough attentive (or nosy) neighbors around to deter burglars. But, much like everywhere else in the world, high-rise residents in China find that they often do not know their neighbors, that their lives have become increasingly focused on their own household isolated within four walls, and that they suffer disproportionally from assault and other crimes.[22]

Rural Housing

In olden days, Chinese scholars delighted in passing the time in rustic huts and crude pavilions in the countryside where they could escape the pressures of the everyday world, drink wine, and write beautiful poetry. The delight of farmers, however, was not in escaping *to* these kinds of crude buildings but in escaping *from* them. Thus, when farmers had money one of their first acts was to build a new home or enlarge and improve their existing home. This remains true to this day.

Yet from 1949 to the beginning of the reform in 1978, most farmers could only dream of a better home. Once farmland was collectivized in the 1950s, doing better than one's neighbors and getting ahead was nearly impossible. The income of the collective—in cash and in kind—after deductions for taxes, schools, fertilizer, and so on was lumped together and then doled out to each member according to the number of "work points" each had earned during the year. Driving a tractor, for instance, earned more work points than feeding the hogs. The value of a work point depended entirely on what the collective earned. If the collective prospered, everyone more or less prospered together. If the collective did poorly, everyone starved together, and indeed starvation was widespread in the horrific famine of 1959–63.

Homes generally remained private property. However, ownership was rarely an issue because there was little market for homes, and certainly no market for farmland, which was now owned by collectives. People were stuck in the village into which they had been born or into which they had married. Of course, the population grew, and new families were started, and in response there was some expansion of existing homes and some building of new homes, but not much.

The reforms that began in 1978 were like a dam suddenly bursting. Collectivization was effectively swept away as farmland and the "means of production" (tractors, trucks, mills, etc.) were privatized. (Technically, "ownership" of land still resides with the collective, but practically speaking use, control, and profit and loss are entirely in private hands.) The state raised the price it paid for produce, and gradually allowed a free market to emerge. Each household was now responsible for its own success or failure. In most regions the majority of households have done very well under the new system; and some families have positively prospered. One of the greatest proofs of this is the building boom that began with the reform and still continues. By 1982, just four years after the start of the reform, one in three households was involved in expanding its living space, either by building an entirely new home or enlarging and renovating its existing home.[23] The boom in new construction is absolutely colossal. Fully 66% (nearly 60 billion square feet) of all the rural housing that was constructed between 1949 and 1987 was built *after* 1979, that is, after the reform.[24] Living space per person increased from about 110 square feet in 1978 to about 165 square feet in 1984, and it has continued to grow since then.[25]

Amenities have also improved and life in general is more comfortable. Electricity is nearly universal, and is put to good use: almost every household has a television and a great many have a variety of electric appliances (CD players, fans, refrigerators, etc.). Air conditioning has even appeared here and there. But many households still draw their water from a well by hand or share outside water taps with several families. On the other hand, in most regions new homes have piped-in water. As a rule, kitchens still feature a brick stove fired by wood or straw. Also found in the kitchens of a great many families is a niche for the Kitchen God, a symbol of domestic harmony.

Flush toilets remain rare, and most households rely on a privy in an outhouse. Squat toilets are usual in most places. The privy itself is not just a hole in the ground, but a tank or large pot from which the contents are removed and, after fermenting, applied to the fields. In many places, farmers continue a long tradition of maintaining "public" privies along the road, and welcome contributions from passersby.

The tremendous amount of new construction in the countryside also has its negative side. Each year more than 600,000 acres of land are consumed by new housing along with its accompanying open spaces and roads. Since China has precious little arable land as it is, this is a loss it can ill afford. Moreover, uncounted acres are lost through the excavation of clay to make the hundreds of billions of bricks required each year for new construction. The search for suitable soil for brick making has even led to cemeteries being dug up. Furthermore, as sun-dried mud bricks have fallen out of favor, kilns have popped up all over the country, and these consume nearly 20 million tons of coal a year, about half of all the coal used by the building materials industry.[26] Of course, finding suitable building material is an age-old problem. The tradition of reusing salvageable materials, especially wooden posts and beams, when an old house is demolished continues. And throughout history, unscrupulous individuals have felt free to pilfer from monuments and public structures. One woman reported that when she visited a village outside Beijing in 1977 she was stunned: "All the bricks in their houses, pigsties and public toilets had come from the Great Wall! . . . I understood then why, all along the way, the Great Wall had been reduced to mounds of earth!"[27]

Fortunately, more and more construction today is of concrete. In addition, for several years there has been a movement to create "new villages" with two-, three-, or four-story row houses, which not only saves land, but makes it easier and cheaper to provide paved roads and utilities. Many of the residents of these new villages are now part-time farmers or no longer farm at all. Rural industry, which sprang up in the pre-reform era, is a big employer. Furthermore so-called specialized households—which earn their living by running little transportation companies and the like—have emerged. And millions of rural people have deserted the countryside and flowed into the cities to work as construction workers, waiters, and factory hands. Nonetheless, it is unavoidable that providing better housing for the 800 million or so people who still reside in the countryside exacts a huge cost in natural resources. In housing, as in so many other areas of life in China, solving one problem seems inevitably to lead to another.

NOTES

1. M. Paléologue, *L'Art Chinois* (Paris: Alcide Picard, 1910), p. 82.

2. Quoted in Ronald Knapp, *China's Traditional Rural Architecture* (Honolulu: University of Hawaii Press, 1986), pp. 110–11.

3. Ole Bruun, "The Fengshui Resurgency in China: Conflicting Cosmologies between State and Peasantry," *China Journal*, no. 36 (July 1996): p. 52.

4. Ibid.

5. "Eight Is a Magic Number," *Civil Engineering* 66, no. 12 (Dec. 1996): p. 61.

6. Ou Shuyi and Ou Chijun, "Historical Homes Endangered," *China Daily* (Oct. 31, 1998), http://www.chinadaily.com.cn (Jan. 4, 1999).

7. See Li You, "Culture and Form: A Study of Contemporary Housing Development in China" (M.A. thesis, University of California, Los Angeles, 1990), pp. 77ff.

8. "Provided They Have Curly Tops," *Economist* 332, no. 787 (July 16, 1994): p. 80.

9. Ibid.

10. Gao Yilan, *Architecture in New China* (Berkeley: Center for Environmental Design Research, University of California, 1987), p. 3.

11. R.J.R. Kirkby, *Urbanization in China: Town and Country in a Developing Economy, 1949–2000 A.D.* (New York: Columbia University Press, 1985), p. 165.

12. Ibid., p. 164.

13. Ministry of Urban and Rural Construction and Environment Protection, and the State Statistical Bureau, *The Reference Collection of the First National Survey of Urban Housing Situation 1986* (Beijing: Ministry of Urban and Rural Construction and Environment Protection, 1987).

14. Chen Zhili, "Reform of the Housing Sector Has Become a National Priority," *China 2000*, http://www.china2thou.com/9809p2.htm (Jan. 4, 2000).

15. "Furniture Industry Faces Bright," China International Economic Consultants Co., http://www.chinavista.com/business/ciec/en/ciel19991102.html (Nov. 2, 1999).

16. *China News Digest*, Global News no. GL99–081 (June 9, 1999).

17. Xinhua News Agency (Apr. 20, 1999).

18. Xinhua News Agency (Dec. 9, 1999).

19. Ibid.

20. "The Great Haul of the People," *Business Week* (international edition), http://www.businessweek.com/1997/18/b3525154.htm (Jan. 5, 2000).

21. *Affordable Housing in China: A Study of Pilot Housing Estates in Three Cities* (Hong Kong: Department of Architecture, Chinese University of Hong Kong, 1997), p. 157.

22. Solvig Ekblad et al., *Stressors, Chinese City Dwellings and Quality of Life* (Stockholm: Swedish Council for Building Research, 1991), p. 94.

23. Knapp, *China's Traditional Rural Architecture*, p. 124.

24. Kate Hannan, ed., *China, Modernisation and the Goal of Prosperity* (Cambridge, UK: Cambridge University Press, 1995), p. 176.

25. Ibid., pp. 124–25.

26. Knapp, *China's Traditional Rural Architecture*, pp. 147–48.

27. *Chinese Literature* (winter 1985): p. 10.

7

Family and Gender

THE FAMILY has been central to life in China, so much so that each family is like an atom in the universe that is Chinese society. Of course, the particles within each atom—the husband/father, wife/mother, and children—have by no means been equal. The Western perspective, with its emphasis on individualism, deplores this inequality. But another perspective, the traditional Chinese view, emphasized the unity of the household and the necessity of each individual performing his or her socially assigned role in assuring the family's survival.

Throughout the twentieth century Chinese families have undergone great changes, and in recent years truly revolutionary changes. If present trends continue, Chinese families soon will look very different from those of the past. In particular, the long and arduous struggle of women for liberation from traditional norms, for equal status with their husbands, and for a productive and valued role as individuals *outside* the bounds of the household, is contributing to a fundamental reshaping of the family and, indeed, of all of Chinese society.[1]

FAMILY

Families in Traditional Times

To say that the family has been central to Chinese society is another way of saying that marriage and having sons were central. Traditionally, it was simply accepted that under normal circumstances everyone would get married and would have a son or sons. In practice, marriage was not quite universal, especially among men, but, except for some Buddhist monks and nuns, this was almost never a matter of choice. In the past two or three centuries in many places in China there has been a surplus of men, resulting in a competition for potential brides. There always seemed to be some men— "bare sticks" they were called—who were so utterly poverty stricken that they could not attract a bride. Almost all other men, and virtually all women, got married.

The unwritten traditional cultural law that everyone get married and have sons sprang from several sources. One was the great importance placed on honoring one's ancestors. The people of China have been particularly sensitive to the fact that each individual is a link in a long chain of descent from the ancestors, or more accurately, that each male is a link, since in the Chinese scheme descent is entirely through the male line: genealogies (records of descent, rather like family trees) record only the males. It was considered a great misfortune if not a tragedy for a couple to break the chain by failing to produce male offspring. In the third century B.C., the philosopher Mencius, in a statement that has doubtlessly been repeated billions of times throughout Chinese history, declared that "there are three things that are unfilial, and to have no posterity is the greatest of them." Thus, the law in late imperial times allowed a man to divorce his wife if she failed to bear a son and it also allowed him, if he preferred, to take a concubine (a collateral or secondary wife), actually as many secondary wives as he liked. The cost of supporting more than one wife, and other factors too, limited concubinage. It may have been more common for a couple without sons to adopt a boy, usually from relatives with surplus males, or to adopt a son-in-law.

A second source of the norm of marriage and having sons was economic. China was overwhelmingly an agricultural country, and running a farm, however small it may be, is difficult for a single person, all alone. Additional labor, such as can be provided by a wife and children, can be essential. In some places by tradition women did not work in the fields, but even there women played an indispensable role, obviously by bearing and caring for the children, but also by tending the garden, making the family's clothing, raising the chickens and pigs, and in many cases producing handicrafts for market. "Men till and women weave"—a popular saying in imperial times—described the division of labor for countless households. In a great many families, the income earned from handicrafts produced for the market by the wife and her daughters formed an indispensable part of the household budget. In some families, the wife accounted for a bigger share of the household income than did the husband.

This most assuredly did not lead to male-female social equality. China was patriarchal and in many ways women existed as appendages, first to their fathers and then, after marriage, to their husbands. This is clearest perhaps in the question of inheritance. In imperial times, by law real property could belong to men alone, although a widow might in fact control and manage her deceased husband's property if her sons were not yet adults. A watershed event in each family was the so-called division of the household (*fenjia*), which usually occurred either when the head of the household (the husband/father) died or when he retired. At this time, each son received an equal share of the family property. The head of the household and his wife (or widow) might, depending on local customs and their wishes, keep some property, but more typically they now relied on one of their sons (in some places it was usually the eldest son, in others it was the youngest) to take care of them.

Daughters received nothing. This was not as unreasonable and unfair as it may seem at first glance because a daughter was only a temporary member of her father's family. When a woman married, she left her father's family and became a member of her husband's. Thus, although she received none of her father's property, she was not without means of support. Furthermore, inheritance rights carried with them "inheritance responsibilities." Since by tradition sons, not daughters, were responsible for supporting the aged parents, it was sons who inherited the family property. In any case, as a daughter or as a wife, the woman was legally without property (except in some cases for the dowry she brought with her when she married). Thus it was difficult—almost impossible usually—for a woman, if even she were so inclined, to refuse to get married.

The point also is that sons were a form of social security. Pity the man or woman who reached old age and had no son. Who would support such an unlucky old person? A daughter could not since she had married out, and was now responsible for helping to support her husband's parents. The fact was that sons were essential for the survival of the elderly.

Families: Construction and Composition

Familial relationships in traditional China spread outward, into larger and larger circles. At the center was the nuclear family, consisting of the husband/father, wife/mother, and their unmarried children. In addition, as we have mentioned, many households contained a parent or both parents of the father. Anthropologists call these "stem families." Finally, some households, known as "joint families," also contained at least two married brothers, with or without children.

Although no comprehensive survey of family types was ever undertaken in traditional times, it appears that nuclear families were the predominant variety, and increased in number as one went down the socioeconomic ladder. In other words, the poorer the household the more it was likely to be a nuclear family.

No matter whether a household was a nuclear family or some sort of extended family, relationships with kin, both inside the household and without, were of great importance. Moreover, kinship and the rights and obligations associated with it were hierarchical. These facts were evident in the rich language used to describe relationships. Unlike in English, where siblings are merely "brothers" and "sisters," in Chinese there are specific words for "older brother" (*gege*), "younger brother" (*didi*), "older sister" (*jiejie*), and "younger sister" (*meimei*). And unlike English, which has merely the word "cousin," a term that makes no distinction of sex or of whether the "cousin" is the offspring of the father's siblings or the mother's siblings, Chinese used separate words that clearly indicated the relationships. And for "uncle," a simple, single word in English, the Chinese drew a number of clear distinctions based on paternal or maternal line and age hierarchy: there were separate words for father's elder brother, father's younger brother, and mother's brother (sometimes differentiated into mother's older brother and mother's younger brother). Chinese also had many other kinship terms, in common use, that specified relationships for which there is no English word. These terms are still used today.

Furthermore, all households existed within a larger world of lineages. A lineage is simply a group of people with the same surname in the same community who claim descent from a common ancestor. In many places, especially in South China, lineages were well organized and powerful. They often owned property that supported such institutions as schools and ancestral halls. In the latter, where tablets with the names of important ancestors were kept, members of the lineage gathered to worship their forebears. Essential to the maintenance of a lineage was a genealogy, which specified how each male in the lineage was related to the ancestors. In the 1930s, the Kong family clan (a clan being a group of lineages), which claimed descent from Confucius (whose surname was Kong), compiled a grand genealogy comprising no less than 108 volumes and 9,000-odd pages.[2] Actually, most genealogies, including that of the Kongs, contain a good deal of fiction; it is hard to imagine that any person living today could accurately trace his descent back 2,500 years. Yet, as a cultural instrument the genealogy is less important for its accuracy than for its role as evidence of the importance attached to establishing and maintaining ties to one's ancestors and to the living whom one considers kin.

Sometimes members of voluntary organizations who were not related by blood or marriage and who did not share the same surname treated each other as if they were related. Sworn brotherhoods, formed by men who gathered together to fight injustice and protect the weak, have a long and noble history in China. Similarly, members of bandit gangs frequently formed a large fictive family wherein the elders were "uncles" and the rank and file addressed each other as "brothers."

In short, the rugged individualist was not much esteemed in China. Instead, society emphasized the nurturing and mutual respect and responsibility that being members of a family implies. On the other hand, it will not do to romanticize the traditional Chinese family. The Chinese were well aware of the faults of their family system, of the conflicts it engendered, and even of its humorous aspects. Traditional literature did not shy away from the oppressive features of extended families nor from the petty intrigues and jealousies that inevitably arose in large households. It is hard enough for one man and one woman to live together under the same roof; imagine what life was like in households where men maintained several wives. Of course, these particular problems may have been confined to wealthy families that could afford to keep all sorts of people—related by blood or marriage—together in one big household. Yet even small and poor families were susceptible to the tensions and fighting that seem to be an unavoidable part of living together. Sometimes family members ended up in court suing each other, although this sort of public squabbling was very much frowned upon, and sometimes they ended up murdering each other.

One can add up the pluses and minuses of the traditional family system, and, depending on one's values, praise or condemn it. But, in the end, no one can deny that the traditional family was the bedrock of Chinese society and that, as an institution, it was spectacularly successful.

Wedding Customs and Marriage, Past and Present

So far we have discussed marriage as a social and economic institution, but have not mentioned love between the husband and wife. This is because in the traditional scheme of things romantic love was rarely a motive for marriage. Most marriages were arranged between the parents of the parties concerned, usually with someone acting as a go-between. This might be a professional marriage broker but more often was a well-connected older woman who performed several useful functions, including the gathering of valuable and delicate information. The parents of the prospective groom could hardly ask the parents of the prospective bride, "Does insanity run in your family?" But a third party could make inquiries of this sort without anyone losing face.

It was not unusual for the bride and groom to meet for the first time on their wedding day. The daughters of many elite families were kept in seclusion so that rarely did anyone outside their household see them. But even young people in average households found it difficult to meet prospective marriage partners. In large part this was because customarily families looked for marriage partners outside their own village. Of course, young men and women often found ways of meeting, and people did fall in love, although not always with the person they ended up marrying. The results were often tragic, with people married their entire adult life to someone they did not care for. The grounds on which a woman could obtain a divorce were exceedingly limited; a lack of love between husband and wife was not one of them. And even if a woman could get a divorce, her value as marriageable material was greatly reduced since men wanted a fresh young bride, not an "old shoe," her children, if any, would remain with their father (and the mother would have no visitation rights), and her prospects for survival itself were dim unless she immediately remarried or her father accepted her back. The last option was by no means certain. Accepting a daughter back usually entailed a messy and unpleasant fight with the family of the spurned husband and also imposed an economic burden on the father. Frequently, the solution for a woman who could not endure a loveless marriage or mistreatment by her husband and his family, and who could not secure the agreement of her father or did not even want to ask, knowing the burden this would place on his shoulders, was suicide.

To some extent, traditional attitudes and practices survive to this day, albeit with crucially important differences. In the first place, arranged marriages still exist, especially in the countryside, although it has been illegal to force people to marry against their will since the Marriage Law of 1950. In the vast majority of marriages today, however, compulsion plays no role at all. Reflecting the continuing importance of networks of social relationships (*guanxi*), frequently friends, work associates, and family members introduce marriageable young men and women and help smooth the way toward matrimony if the couple is so inclined. In a survey undertaken in Beijing in the 1990s, 35% of the couples reported that they had met through go-betweens; 1% said they had met through computer dating or dating agencies; the rest (64%) said they found each other and married because of love.[3] In places less cosmopolitan than Beijing, the rate of marriage through introduction is higher.

Survey after survey undertaken in the 1980s and 1990s has confirmed that most people are very practical and not the least bit starry eyed when it comes to selecting a marriage partner. Material comfort and financial security head the checklist. At first glance, this appears to be a major shift from the heyday of radical socialism in the 1960s and early 1970s when political reliability— did the prospective spouse belong to one of the favored classes such as "worker" or "poor peasant"? had he or she been a member of the Communist Youth League? and so forth—was supposedly the norm. But even in those days young women might not give a second thought to a suitor who could not provide "the goods," such as the "three things that go around" (a bicycle, a sewing machine, and an electric fan).

The material or economic basis of marriage is a carry-over from traditional times when brides were expected to have a dowry, mostly consisting of a trousseau (clothing, bedding, housewares, etc.). In return, the groom's family was usually expected to provide gifts to the bride's family. Furthermore, the wedding itself tended to be a lavish affair, often a community-wide or village-wide celebration, with much eating and exchanging of gifts. The cost often represented a huge expenditure for the parents of the bride and groom.

After 1949, the Communist authorities denounced traditional, costly weddings as "feudal." The government advocated modest ceremonies and, legally speaking, made getting married simple. According to the Marriage Law of 1980, the man must be at least 22 years old and the woman 20, the couple must not be blood relatives up to "the third degree of relationship," and neither must suffer from a disease "rendering a person unfit for marriage."[4] Qualifying couples go to the local government office and register for a marriage certificate, and when the certificate is issued the couple is considered married. While every couple must follow this simple businesslike procedure, it is clear that the people of China have decided that they still want splashy and expensive weddings.

The content and character of wedding ceremonies varies from place to place and, of course, also varies according to the financial circumstances of the couple and their families. In some areas in the countryside, the bride, wearing a traditional wedding costume, in red, the color of happiness and joy, is picked up at the house of her father and paraded to the home of the groom's father, where most of the ceremony takes place. It was traditional for the bride to be carried in a sedan chair and to be accompanied by an entourage of family, friends, musicians, and sometimes porters carrying the furniture and other items in the bride's trousseau, all on public display. Today, brides in the countryside ride in horse carts, trucks, bicycles, taxis, or rented cars. Sometimes the bride wears a Western-style wedding dress, often in red. Grooms wear their best clothing, usually a Western-style business suit, and they often sport a red shirt or red socks. It is typical at wedding ceremonies for there to be lots of bantering and joking at the expense of the bride and groom (Figure 7.1).

In cities, many couples turn to wedding service agencies, which make all of the arrangements: getting the bride and groom photographed (which, with pose after pose and many changes of costume, can take half a day), organizing

Figure 7.1. Bride and groom getting their picture taken on a street in Beijing, 1998. © *Jeff Booth.*

a sumptuous banquet, providing the decorations, videotaping the ceremony, and providing the costumes for the groom and bride (the bride will sometimes change costumes once or twice in the course of the ceremony, appearing in a somewhat traditional costume for part of the ceremony and then in a white Western-style wedding dress). Other couples prefer slightly less elaborate ceremonies held in a restaurant or at home. In any case, wedding ceremonies usually involve some clever adaptations of traditional practices to contemporary possibilities. The bridal procession still survives even in the most cosmopolitan of cities, but now the bride rides in a rented car or a limousine complete with a television and mini-bar. When the car arrives to pick up the bride and she emerges from her door, the tape-recorded "bang" of firecrackers (real firecrackers were outlawed in Beijing and some other cities in the 1990s) starts and people within earshot gather round to enjoy the spectacle. During the ceremony itself, the bride and groom will drink wine from the same cup (an old tradition) and walk from table to table toasting all the guests and getting toasted in return. They also give the guests gifts (cartons of cigarettes are common) and in return the guests give them gifts (packets of money are traditional—and still appreciated). After the main ceremony, the new couple—accompanied by close friends and family—retire to their new home (literally a new house in many instances) where they

Figure 7.2. A woman, recently arrived from the southern province of Yunnan, selling tea on the sidewalk in front of a bridal shop in Beijing, 1998. © *Jeff Booth*.

proceed to "raise the roof" with more drinking, games, and teasing and joking.

Honeymoons were not traditional, although in many places it was customary for newlyweds to pay a visit to the parents of the bride on the third day following the wedding. Today, an increasing number of couples are indulging in a honeymoon, traveling to some local scenic spot or, depending on their wishes and pocketbook, to some glamorous overseas destination (Figure 7.2).

While the wedding ceremony itself can be expensive by any standard—into the thousands of dollars—the overall cost of getting married can add up to a staggering figure, by Chinese standards, in the tens of thousands of dollars in some instances. This is because parents are under great social pressure to provide the newlyweds with as much material wealth as they can. Wide-screen televisions, microwave ovens, housefuls of expensive furniture, his and her cellular telephones, computers, even new houses—these sorts of transfers of wealth from the parents to the children do not even raise an eyebrow today. This is not merely a question of continuing a tradition at a much higher level. Rather it is part and parcel of a complicated revolutionary transformation of family attitudes and structures, of a movement of the central axis of the family from the parent-son relationship to the husband-wife relationship.

Parents & Children and Husbands & Wives: The Rise of Conjugality

In traditional times when marriages were decided by the parents, when married couples did not—until the division of the household (fenjia)—have the economic wherewithal to survive apart from the husband's parents, and when social norms emphasized obedience to the parents, the relationship between the husband and the wife was almost incidental to matrimony. Conjugality—where the primary tie in the family is between a man and a woman living together as companions in a mutually supportive relationship—was not only *not* the ideal, it was often beyond reach. Indeed, society seemed to conspire against young couples having a mutually supportive life together independent of the parents.

In the first place, many people were married at an age when they were barely more than children themselves. In Zouping county in the northern province of Shandong, for instance, in the early 1930s the modal age at marriage for males was 15, and for females 17.[5] Although age at marriage varied considerably from place to place, the figures for Zouping are not the least bit unusual. Under the best of circumstances what kind of conjugal relationship could there be between a teenage couple who hardly knew each other when married, and who had little or no experience with such essential familial matters as handling money?

In the second place, society emphasized and reemphasized obedience to parents, or what the Chinese called filial piety. Children were expected to cherish, honor, and obey their parents as long as the parents were alive and to honor them in death through protracted mourning. This was sometimes carried to extremes. One parable approvingly told of a young woman who cut flesh from her own arm and cooked it in a broth to feed and cure her sick mother-in-law. Presumably no one ever took this story literally, but it certainly brought home the lesson that daughters-in-law were to sacrifice everything for their parents-in-law. The suffering of women at the hands of their domineering mothers-in-law, with the husband standing silently by or even taking the side of his mother, was a perennial theme in Chinese popular literature.

In the third place, age itself carried great prestige. To be called old (*lao*) was a compliment. It was also a sign of respect and usually of affection. To this day, the word "old" has a generally positive connotation in China and is used with a sense of comfort and familiarity in a great many informal terms, such as *laoshi* (teacher) and *laoban* (boss). Unlike in the United States where people nowadays resort to euphemisms such as "senior citizen" in order to avoid the unpleasant word "old," the Chinese are more direct and describe the elderly as "old people" (*laonianren*).

In traditional times, within the family the senior members expected respect and power. Women, who started out married life in the lowliest of lowly positions as a bride, tended to look forward to old age as a time when their views would not only be respected but might become the single most powerful force within the household. In such an environment, it was difficult for a married son to be more than his parents' child, still obedient, still tied to his mother with a bond that could be stronger than the bond with his wife.

By the beginning of the twenty-first century, familial relationships had undergone a radical transformation. The family ideal has been redefined as people have become increasingly convinced that married couples should live on their own, apart from and independent of the older generation. Not only has the ideal changed, but it is now achievable: a great many people today are sufficiently wealthy to afford independence. At the same time, power has shifted from older to younger generations and the prestige of age has waned. This sea change, contrary to what one might think, has not been the result of the younger generations rebelling against their elders, but rather has evolved gradually. It is, in other words, the result of a transformation that was not planned but emerged from the complicated interplay of a variety of social forces.

Today, it is not simply that younger couples want to live apart from their parents—one suspects that couples in years gone by wanted this too, although it was then beyond their reach—but that an increasing number of older people now also want to live independently. A middle-age farmer reflected this yearning for independence when he complained to a researcher that on hot summer days he "likes to wear only his shorts when at home, but after his son married (and brought in a daughter-in-law) he had to dress more formally, no matter how hot it became. Thus, when his son moved out last year he felt happy that he had recovered his freedom."[6] A woman in the same village was even more outspoken: "You cannot imagine how smart they [the young people] have become nowadays. They want me to be in charge, but I have to do everything: cook for the family, raise chickens and pigs, keep the family savings, and baby sit for their children. What do they do! They do nothing except watch TV and complain. I am an old servant in the family."[7] Older people are doing more than complaining; an increasing number are living on their own and liking it. In a survey taken in China's cities in the late 1980s, fully 53% of older people with married children were living on their own, in their own household. Furthermore, a large percentage of those living with a son were unhappy with the arrangement, but felt they had no alternative since they needed "to get economic support from the children."[8]

It is difficult to explain why attitudes have changed, or if they have not changed (since it may be that people throughout the ages would have preferred independence), why at least now it is accepted that the old ways are not necessarily the best ways. Part of the answer lies in the fact that people are getting married at an increasingly older age, a trend that seems to have been building up all during the twentieth century. In 1996 the average age of people marrying for the first time was 24 years (25.77 for men and 22.75 for women). In the larger cities, the age was higher still (26.16 years in Beijing and 25.73 in Shanghai).[9] People of this age have worked for several years, have learned something of life, and are, emotionally and psychologically speaking, able to stand on their own two feet. Furthermore, life expectancy for both men and women in China in the past four decades has jumped from about 41 years to more than 69 years. In the 1940s, men and women aged 50 years were considered old and not expected to do much work. Today, men, and women to a lesser extent, can and do work well into their sixties, and sometimes beyond. Older people now are able to earn an income and need not become dependent on their children, at least until an advanced age.

On the other hand, China's social security system is not well developed, especially in the countryside, and many couples still feel the need to produce a son. In a survey of 25 villages conducted in 1990, more than 50% of the women questioned said the most important reason for childbearing was "security in old age." (Those who gave the "joys of family life" as the most important reason were only about 1%.[10]) Furthermore, surveys have confirmed that there continues to be a strong preference everywhere—and in the countryside, an overwhelming preference—for boys. Very traditional attitudes, one might say.

Yet, in many respects attitudes today on these matters are remarkably different from those of the past. Most importantly perhaps, there has been a shift away from the traditional preference for large families. In the survey conducted in 1990 mentioned above, a majority of the women indicated that the ideal number of children is two. Furthermore, all the women surveyed who preferred two children said they would ideally like to have one boy and one girl, not two boys.[11] These preferences in themselves represent a great change from the past, and also hint at some revolutionary transformations lying below the surface.

Part of the change in attitudes is related to the one-child-per-family policy pursued by the government since around 1980. To control population growth, the state has decreed that couples should have but one child—however, there are many exceptions (the policy is not enforced in politically sensitive regions inhabited by ethnic minorities, for instance) and in any case enforcement is in the hands of local bureaus, and this inevitably means in China that the interpretation and application of the regulations varies from place to place. A great many rural communities have followed a two-child policy, and in some places even that policy is laxly enforced. In the cities, however, enforcement can be rigorous. The authorities there wield various rewards and punishments—sometimes quite draconian—to see that couples limit themselves to one child. This sort of state intrusion into family planning angers some Westerners, particularly Americans, but without it the result could be a horrendous population growth that would completely overwhelm China's ability to cope.

The one-child policy has probably helped convince some people that big families are bad. It is even more likely that it has induced many people to be careful about expressing their true feelings regarding family size since big families are very politically incorrect. Thus, when interviewees say that the ideal number of children is one or two, we cannot be certain that they are not merely repeating the politically correct answer. There is absolutely no question that many people want more than one child and struggle to find ways around the regulations. The Chinese press from time to time reports on violations of the policy, such as happened in the town of Tanba where, from 1997 to 1999, over 5,000 women gave birth to children in excess of the regulations. This was possible because of the connivance of local officials, who accepted bribes to look the other way and then reported false figures on births to higher authorities. Nonetheless, nationwide the number of children born to women of reproductive age reportedly fell from 2.4 children in 1989 to 1.8 children in 1996—less than in the United States (where the rate is 2.0).[12] In Shanghai the rate may be an astonishingly low 0.96.

While the one-child policy has undoubtedly played an important, even crucial, role in shrinking the family, other, unplanned forces have also been at work. In China, as is generally true all over the world, as people have become wealthier and better educated, they have had fewer children. Also, children have become less and less an investment or a form of old-age insurance and more and more of an expense. In a nationwide Gallup poll conducted in 1994, people were asked about their savings goals. The goal shared by the most people (64% of the respondents) was saving to finance "a child or children's education." Number five on the list was "paying off your children's marriage" (a goal shared by 39% of the respondents), followed by "saving for old age" (32%).[13] In the past decade or so, China's spoiled "little emperors," as the children of new, one-child families have been dubbed, have become notorious. Children are not only indulged, they are increasingly demanding, and getting, a crucial say-so in family expenditures, especially when it comes to the things that children really care about, such as toys. One enterprising fellow has taken advantage of this by founding a boarding school that aims to reform "little emperors" and curb their dictatorial ways.[14]

The biggest costs of all typically come at the time of marriage, for young couples now demand and get such a great share of their parents' wealth that household division often must begin when the first son marries and takes his share of the family property. When other sons, if any, subsequently marry, they too take their share, leaving the parents in the end, as is often said, "naked," with little or no wealth. To cope, many parents start saving for their child's marriage when the child is born. For self-preservation, many also squirrel away money for themselves, which they do not consider part of family property and hence do not include in the household division. It is not surprising that many couples do not want more than one son: in their eyes, the cost would simply be too great.

At the same time, adult children are acting in ways that would have been considered deplorably unfilial in traditional times. Young men are not at all reticent about siding with their wives in disputes with the man's parents. In a study conducted in the 1990s, a majority of parents claimed that their sons "never" take their side. Almost all the sons denied this, but as one old woman commented, "They just try to make excuses for themselves. At each and every time, they can find a reason for their wives to be right and for their parents to be wrong. This is true, and I can speak for all parents."[15]

At its worst, the precipitous decline in the prestige of age manifests itself in elder abuse. Mistreatment of oldsters certainly existed in traditional times, although it was little talked about, perhaps because it was very rare and also probably because people plotted to keep it hidden since it was such a gross violation of cultural norms. Today it is harder to keep hidden and, moreover, evidence suggests that, while still rare, it is a growing problem, despite laws that adult children must provide "economic and spiritual" support for their parents and in-laws.

The socialist system introduced in the 1950s played an important role in reducing the prestige of age and the power of parents. In the cities, as businesses were nationalized and in the countryside as land was collectivized, parents lost most of the valuable property that, in earlier times, they would have passed on to their children. Adult children, who now worked as employees of the state in the cities or who earned their own "work points" in the collectivized farms, no longer were completely beholden to their parents for support until the division of the household. In short, parents lost their power base. Since the beginning of the reform program in 1978, private ownership (or at least, private control) of businesses and land has reappeared with a vengeance. However, the system today is far from being a mere copy of the old days. Opportunities for earning a living have expanded dramatically, especially in the countryside. Many young people find work in local rural industries and enterprises or gravitate toward the cities. Dependence on one's parents for a livelihood is the rare exception.

Education has also played a role in eroding the power of parents. In the 1950s illiteracy nationwide stood at about 80%; by the 1990s, it was down to around 15%. People in their forties and fifties today typically find that they are more poorly educated than their children and in many respects less sophisticated and knowledgeable about the world.

Finally, a consumer fever has swept China since the introduction of the reform and has helped to reshape young people's concepts of what constitutes the good life. Old-fashioned thrift and self-denial have little appeal for young people who are eager to keep up with fads and fashions as touted on television, in the movies, and in slick magazines. Young people not only spend more on food, clothing, and entertainment than do their parents, but they often dismiss their parents' choices as "ridiculous" and decide themselves how they are going to spend their money. Polo brand T-shirts, Nike shoes, Levi jeans, Playboy belts and socks—such are the emblems of youthful good taste, a subject that most middle-aged people cannot fathom. Young people today are, as a slogan promoted by the reformers in the 1980s put it, "capable of making money and knowing how to spend it."

GENDER

The history of China for the past 150 years or so—particularly the story of China's difficult march into modernity—has been inseparable from the history of Chinese women. The two are so intertwined that at times they appear as one. During the May Fourth period in the early 1920s intellectuals frequently took Chinese women as a symbol of the nation: for instance, the unequal status of women symbolized in some eyes China's unequal status vis-à-vis Japan and the Western powers, and the oppression of women likewise symbolized the oppression of the peasants by the landlords. For many intellectuals the subjugation of women was a metaphor for all that was wrong with China. In this view, the liberation of China was impossible without, and inseparable from, the liberation of women.

When the Communists came to power they acted quickly to "liberate" women. The Marriage Law of 1950 proclaimed women's equality and guaranteed them the right to choose their own mates and to seek divorce. Thereafter, insofar as governmental policy was concerned, the struggle for women's rights became submerged in the larger struggle for "socialist construction." With the success of the latter, the "women's problem" in the eyes of China's leaders was "basically solved."

In fact, both the view that traditional society crushed and oppressed women and the view that Communist society emancipated them are political rhetoric. The actual position of women in the family and in society at large, both in traditional times and today, is a complicated question. Although the norm for women traditionally was the obedient wife and dedicated mother, alternative role models were also available. For instance, Ban Zhao (A.D. 41–ca. 115), early China's most famous female scholar and writer, was renowned for her work on one of China's most esteemed histories. Standing opposite the woman of letters was the woman of action, such as Hua Mulan (a semi-mythical heroine said to have lived in the fifth or sixth century A.D. and made famous in the West by the recent Disney feature-length cartoon *Mulan*), who, masquerading as a man, went to war in her father's place. Ban Zhao and Hua Mulan, and women like them, were celebrated in Chinese history not because they struggled for women's liberation—they certainly did not do that—but because they exemplified filial virtue expressed in an unusual and interesting way. Ban Zhao completed a great historical work that her brother left unfinished at his death, and Hua Mulan risked her life to protect her father. These alternative models of womanhood thus were not the least bit subversive of the patriarchal tradition.

Today women have made great strides and are now barred from no professions—they are engineers, doctors, political leaders, university professors, entrepreneurs, and soldiers (since 1949, about 15 women have attained the rank of general). Nowadays, most people profess to believe that men and women are equal. In a large survey conducted in 1990 by the All China Women's Federation, 81.3% of the women thought they enjoyed equal rights with men, and 82.4% of the men said they regarded women as equals. Yet this too is rhetoric. One does not have to look far to see that women, despite the great strides they have made in the twentieth century, still have not attained equality with men.

Employment and Education

One of the most notable changes in China in the past several decades is the nearly universal employment of women. Today, better than 9 out of 10 women between the ages of 18 and 65 are working—perhaps the highest rate of anywhere in the world. In 1949, around 600,000 women were in the workforce; today there are more than 50 million. Actually, these figures need to be multiplied severalfold because a great many women in the countryside may not show up on official employment statistics although they work on the family farm. We should consider them "working women" because the work they do earns money and contributes to the family budget. And some women make a crucial contribution: various surveys undertaken in the 1980s and 1990s found that from 20% to 25% of women are the chief breadwinners in their family. Women make a crucial contribution in another sense also: they feed China. In the 1990s, it has been estimated that women accounted for 60% to 70% of agricultural output because more and more rural men are now farming only part time or have given up farming entirely to work in more lucrative rural industries and enterprises.

Surveys have also found that most women work because they want to. In the mid-1990s, 88% of married women interviewed said that they would work even if their husband's income were sufficient to support the family. About 35% of them considered work as an opportunity to express themselves. Only 8.5% said they worked in order to gain financial independence.[16]

Employment figures for women would probably be still higher were it not for the fact that women tend to retire, sometimes against their wishes, earlier than men. For physically demanding work, such as stevedoring, the official retirement age is 55 for men and 50 for women. For other types of work, women generally are retired at age 55, while men can continue to work until age 60 or beyond. Thus, in the age group 50 to 55 years, about 30% of women are retired compared to only about 8% of men. This discrepancy may have less to do with discrimination against women per se than with several other factors related to the employment of women.

The first of these factors is that women tend to have less skilled jobs. For instance, nationwide women account for over 60% of sales clerks, but only 22% of scientists and technicians. Presumably, enterprises want to hang on to workers with valuable skills, most of whom are men, while they are more inclined to part with workers with less valuable skills.

The second factor is that women are less well educated than men, and therefore fewer are qualified for higher-paying, skilled jobs. In a nationwide survey conducted in 1990, in the age group 16 to 65 years, women on average had completed only 4.75 years of schooling, while men had completed 6.63 years. About 27% of women had never been to school, compared to less than 10% of men. About 51% of men had graduated from middle school, but only 34.6% of women. And about 3% of men had received a college education compared to 1.7% of women. The education discrepancy between men and women is largest among those born before 1949. After 1949 educational attainment for both males and females skyrocketed, at least until the late 1970s, so that younger people tend to be much better educated than their elders. Yet, the male-female education gap still exists, and in recent years may even be getting wider, especially in the countryside. Equally disturbing is the gap between rural women and their urban sisters. In 1990, one in 10 rural 16-year-old girls had not completed primary school; in the cities, less than two in 100 girls of the same age had failed to finish primary school.

A third factor militating against women's equality in the labor force is the notion that employing women can be expensive or troublesome. Some employers are quick to point out that it costs the enterprise plenty when a woman worker gives birth. By law, female workers in state-owned enterprises are entitled to 90 days of maternity leave and, for one year after they return to work, to two 30-minute rest periods each day, so they can breast-feed their babies. Furthermore, state enterprises with a large number of women employees are required to provide child care facilities. In practice, some urban women who sign a pledge to have only one child are given six months or more of maternity leave. However, these generous benefits are limited to *state-owned* enterprises; collective and private enterprises are more or less free to set benefits at whatever level they wish, including no benefits at all. In addition, in most enterprises women are assigned the lowest-paying jobs and sometimes are paid less than men doing the same job. On that score, it is hard to see how anyone could claim that "hiring women costs more." Yet here too some employers have a rejoinder: "women workers are less reliable." It is usually the woman, not her husband, who takes time off work to nurse a sick child or parent or in-law. And in some households, the woman handles the family budget and so from time to time needs to take time off to do the banking and take care of major purchases. It may be impossible to quantify what this lost time costs the employer, if anything, but it certainly reflects the fact that women bear a double burden: they work outside the home but they are still expected to shoulder the burden of homemaking. Today some younger men are pitching in and helping with the housework, but many older men remain trapped in rigid, traditional ideas about the division between "men's work" and "women's work." In the oppressively hot and humid summer in the city of Wuhan in Central China, men can be seen hanging out on the sidewalk after work, fanning themselves, drinking, smoking, and relaxing. Women are much less in evidence. When a visitor asked a group of men, "Don't women also want to get out of the house and cool off?" an older man snapped back, "Don't be silly! Who'd cook dinner?"[17]

Sexual Imbalance and the Marriage Squeeze

A sign that ought to be posted on telephone poles all across China, but which one will never see, would read like this: "MISSING: Millions and millions of Chinese women." Even the greatest detective could not find these women because they are not missing in the usual sense that they suddenly disappeared. Rather, they are missing in the sense that they should have been born but never were.

Normally in the human species, slightly more boys are born than girls. This is nature's way of keeping things in balance because boy infants have a lower rate of survival. Thus, without any sort of outside intervention, by the time men and women reach reproductive age, their numbers should be about equal. But in China since 1949, and also probably before then, men have outnumbered women. Today the imbalance is a phenomenal 107 males for every 100 females. How is it that China has defied nature, and what does it matter?

The foremost cause of the imbalance has to do with the continuing preference for sons, combined with the one-child policy. If couples may have only one child, and if they strongly prefer to have a son, what can they do? Thanks to modern technology, quite a bit. Ultrasound machines, including inexpensive Chinese-produced models, have been widespread for a number of years. Since a scan often identifies the sex of the fetus, couples can use that information in deciding on an abortion. While there is no way of knowing how many couples choose to abort female fetuses identified by this means, it seems safe to assume that many do. To thwart this, the state has forbidden doctors to divulge the sex of the fetus, but anxious couples often find ways of getting around this. Ultrasound scans are not entirely reliable, and undoubtedly some male fetuses—because they are incorrectly identified as female—are also aborted. This "problem" should fade away as amniocentesis, which identifies sex almost without error, becomes increasingly popular.

There is some talk in the scholarly literature from time to time about another, and brutal, way of controlling the female population, namely infanticide. In traditional times, desperately poor parents sometimes sold their children, knowing that someone who bought a child had the means and the incentive to protect their investment, in other words, to keep the child alive. And sometimes infants, especially girls, died of parental neglect. Even more horrifying, some parents killed their infants, especially the girls. But in China today—a country free of widespread hunger, hopelessness, and utter destitution—the crime of infanticide must be extremely rare, certainly so rare that it cannot play any significant role in the nation's sexual imbalance.

Undoubtedly, an infinitely more prominent role is played by the under-registration of female births. When talking to people, frequently someone will admit to knowing of a family that gave birth to a daughter but, in contravention of the regulations, did not register her with the government. People who get away with this are able to avoid the heavy penalties (a fine of several thousand dollars in some places) of having "too many" children. But the real problem comes later, when the child is ready to start school. As a nonperson, the child would normally be denied all social services.

The obvious result of a shortage of women is that some men are unable to find wives. In the countryside in the 1990s in the age group 20–24 (the prime "getting married" age), for every 100 unmarried women there were no less than 162 unmarried men. The imbalance in the cities is less dramatic, but still troubling. Nationwide, only about 4% of all Chinese between the ages of 28 and 49 are unmarried, but of that group of singles, almost all (94% to be precise) are men.

Understandably, marriageable women have definitely become a hot commodity. This has given them the power, if they choose to use it, to decide whom they will marry and under what conditions. Thus, discrimination against females, manifested in the low rate of female births, has had the paradoxical result of increasing the influence and desirability of women.

Women are taking advantage of the demand for brides by migrating to wealthier regions, where eager, potential husbands await, offering a life better than the one back home. According to census figures, between 1985 and 1990 over 4 million women migrated in order to get married, compared to only about 400,000 men who migrated for the same reason. How do these potential brides and grooms find each other? Lonely heart ads in newspapers and magazines have become popular. The ads, placed mostly by men, read much the same: there is information about the man's age; his housing situation; whether he has been married before, and if so whether he has children; and his height. Matches are also arranged by relatives or friends who are living and working away from home, and by impatient singles themselves. Some men sweep into a town or village on a wife-hunting expedition, interview several prospective brides, draw up a list of those they would consider marrying, and then propose to the first on the list, and if rebuffed, propose to the second, and then the third, and so on until they find a woman who will say "yes."

Many young women migrate to towns or cities to work, and find husbands there themselves. Young, single female workers in Shenzhen in South China are so plentiful that they outnumber the men by 2.5 to one. The government has set up roller-skating rinks, stadiums, amusement parks, and so on to keep these women busy "so they won't think about men."[18] For single men a spot like this ought to be a great hunting ground, but women who have lived in a place like Shenzhen, a stone's throw from Hong Kong and one of the richest and most developed areas of China, are likely to be very choosy. It is hard to imagine that any would be willing to "marry down" by moving somewhere into the dirt-poor countryside. In those rural areas that remain mired in poverty, men can offer almost nothing. For example, in the village of Dachuan in the poor northwestern province of Gansu, in the early 1990s nearly 40% of the households were living below the local official poverty line, which was a per capita income of $50 to $65 *per year*.[19] This kind of abject poverty and the shortage of women has led some rural men to desperate measures.

Official figures indicate that 88,000 women and children were kidnapped and sold into marriage or slavery between 1991 and 1996, although the real number is probably higher. Typically, gangsters arrive in a town and head straight for the marketplace where they lure young women with attractive-sounding offers of jobs in the city. Once in their hands, the women are shipped off to poor rural areas, where they are sold for between $350 and $750. Buyers' families and friends in tight-knit villages usually abet the crime by keeping close watch over the kidnap victims. Their attitude seems to be "well, he paid for the woman so he's entitled to keep her." Besides, many of the victims are themselves poor, illiterate, and fearful. Under these circumstances it is understandable that resistance or escape is more than merely difficult, it is often hopeless.

Recognizing the problem, the government metes out swift and severe punishment to flesh merchants when it can find them. In the northern city of Taiyuan a trial of six kidnappers and their seven accomplices was watched by 10,000 people. The court quickly convicted the six kidnappers, sentenced them to a fine of $2,400, and then shot them. The accomplices were fined $1,200 and sentenced to life in prison.[20] The problem is that many gangsters escape apprehension, and indeed in some places local police have done little to fight kidnapping, perhaps because they are paid off, perhaps because they are reluctant to antagonize neighbors, and perhaps because, in an ironic way, they are community spirited. Especially in poor rural areas, a shortage of marriageable women is a community problem because it threatens the continuity and cohesion of local society.

Even if kidnap victims are able to escape they sometimes face a dim future. In one notorious case, an abducted married woman managed to break free after six months and returned to her home. But her husband and his family refused to take her back. The woman then committed suicide. Her suicide arose not from clinical depression but rather from conventions of rural Chinese society.[21] Her husband said she had slept with another man and that everyone in the village knew it too. The suicide can be interpreted as a reaction to the crushing blow of rejection by the woman's family, but also as an ultimate protest against the monstrous injustice.

This tragic case is all the more disturbing because it is part of a wave of suicide that seems to be washing over the countryside. Estimates of suicides in China range from 13 per 100,000 all the way up to 30 per 100,000. In the Western world, by contrast, suicide rates hover around 10 per 100,000. In China, the large majority of suicides are young rural women. Traditionally, suicide was often a socially acceptable, even honorable, choice for a woman facing humiliation. Today, it may be that it is more often a form of resistance to the crushing weight of old patriarchal norms that young women simply cannot accept. However, for the vast majority of married women resistance takes other forms, including divorce.

Along with almost everything else, divorce has boomed during the reform era. In 1982, toward the beginning of the reform period, according to official figures only about 100,000 couples divorced, an extraordinarily tiny number in view of China's huge population. But by 1986 that figure had jumped to 500,000, and by 1996 it had jumped still again to over 1 million. Furthermore, most divorces—around 70% according to some estimates—are initiated by women. Nowadays, it is obvious that a great many women are not at all hesitant about standing up for their rights. For instance, in 1995 a young rural couple had the woman's dowry notarized just before their wedding. Two years later, the women sued her husband for abuse—he had beaten her and she ended up in the hospital for 10 days. Based on the notarized documents, the court calculated the value of the prenuptial property, and ordered the husband to pay the woman for her medical expenses. The woman explained: "I asked my husband to have all our property notarized before we got married. He initially disagreed, but I persuaded him. . . . I wanted the court proceeding to help him fully realize his mistake."[22] Another young woman, a factory worker, talking about the man she chose to marry, explained: "I was looking for someone who was not going to be as strong as me, because, you know, I have a pretty fierce character. . . . I'm not good at admitting when I'm wrong, even though I am wrong sometimes. So I needed someone who wasn't as fierce as me."[23] It is high time that the image of the women of China as cowed, passive, and timid creatures—which was never quite accurate in any case—be consigned to the dustbin.

NOTES

1. The statistical data in this chapter come from a large number and wide variety of sources. Small-scale, local unofficial surveys and studies are cited in the Notes. However, to avoid a plethora of notes, sources of data from official sources, many available only in Chinese, such as censuses and statistical yearbooks, as well as certain large-scale surveys, all of which are well known to scholars in the field, are not cited.

2. Jun Jing, *The Temple of Memories: History, Power, and Morality in a Chinese Village* (Stanford, CA: Stanford University Press, 1996), p. 42.

3. Meng Yan, "Love More Important in Beijing Marriages," *China Daily* (Mar. 4, 1999), http://www.chinadaily.com.cn (Apr. 6, 1999).

4. Su Wenming, ed., *From Youth to Retirement* (Beijing: Beijing Review, 1982), p. 52.

5. Jiang Hong Li and William Lavely, "Rural Economy and Male Marriage in China: Jurong, Jiangsu," *Journal of Family History* 20, no. 3 (July 1995).

6. Yunxiang Yan, "The Triumph of Conjugality: Structural Transformation of Family Relations in a Chinese Village," *Ethnology* 36, no. 3 (summer 1997): p. 197.

7. Ibid., p. 203.

8. John R. Logan and Fuqin Bian, "Family Values and Coresidence with Married Children in Urban China," *Social Forces* 77, no. 4 (June 1999): p. 1253.

9. *China Daily* (Feb. 9, 1998).

10. Mu Aiping, "To Have a Son: The One-Child Family Policy and Economic Change in Rural China," in Jackie West, Zhao Minghua, and Cheng Yuan, eds., *Women of China: Economic and Social Transformation* (New York: St. Martin's Press, 1999), p. 147.

11. Ibid., pp. 140–41.

12. *World Population Data Sheet* (Washington, DC: Population Reference Bureau, 1989, 1993, 1996).

13. *China: Nationwide Consumer Survey* (Princeton, NJ: Gallup Organization, 1994).

14. *China Tourism*, no. 166 (May 1994): pp. 70ff.

15. Yunxiang Yan, "The Triumph of Conjugality," pp. 204–205.

16. *Beijing Review*, no. 2 (1995): p. 18.

17. David Wakefield, personal communication (July 1998).

18. "China: Sex on Wheels," *Connexions*, no. 38 (winter 1992): p. 4.

19. Jun Jing, *The Temple of Memories*, p. 7.

20. "Wife Enslavers Executed," *Beijing Scene* 6, no. 10 (Dec. 17–23, 1999), http://www.beijingscene.com (Jan. 10, 2000).

21. "Suicide Riddles: China," *Economist* (U.S.), no. 8042 (Nov. 8, 1997).

22. "Spousal Abuse Is Illegal and Punished by the Courts," *WIN News* 24, no. 2 (spring 1998).

23. Quoted in Lisa Rofel, *Other Modernities: Gendered Yearnings in China after Socialism* (Berkeley: University of California Press, 1999), p. 224.

8

Holidays and Leisure Activities

LIKE PEOPLE elsewhere in the world, the Chinese celebrate holidays and festivals as occasions to remember a shared past and to reaffirm traditions as well as to enjoy themselves. Through celebration year after year, holidays create and sustain a sense of community. When the entire nation shares in the same observances and rituals, it affirms that its people belong together, that they hold in common certain fundamental sentiments and values, even if they do not all speak the same language, worship the same gods, or hold the same political beliefs. At a lower level, smaller groups of people identify themselves as members of one community or another by observing holidays or following rituals or activities—such as the Dragon Boat Festival, discussed below—that are local or otherwise not necessarily observed nationwide. At the most personal level, each individual helps create his or her own identity by pursuing avocations and activities that yield personal fulfillment or joy: wood carving, cooking, reading, stamp collecting—the list is infinite.

HOLIDAYS AND FESTIVALS

Official Holidays and Observances

The holidays and festivals observed in China today are a combination of the traditional and the modern, of red letter days officially sanctioned by the government and of folk celebrations whose origins lie deep in the past. The government recognizes 11 holidays, of which four normally involve days off from work and school, and only one of which was also celebrated before the twentieth century. As of mid-1999, legal holidays were:

New Year's Day. January 1 (1 day off);

Spring Festival. A traditional holiday in late January or early February (3 days off);

International Women's Day. March 8, in remembrance of a strike by women workers in Chicago in 1909; in 1910 a socialist congress in Copenhagen declared March 8 "International Women's Day" (some enterprises give their female employees—but not the men—one-half day or one full day off with pay);

Arbor Day. March 12;

International Labor Day. May 1, an ancient springtime festival in much of Europe, and later, during the nineteenth century, appropriated by European socialists as a celebration of workers, and now observed just about everywhere in the world except the United States (1 day off);

Youth Day. May 4, a commemoration of China's first modern mass student movement on May 4, 1919;

International Children's Day. June 1, a holiday to celebrate primary school children, borrowed from the Soviet Union in the 1950s;

Anniversary of the Founding of the Chinese Communist Party. July 1, in celebration of the founding of the CCP, in Shanghai in 1921;

Army Day. August 1, in celebration of the first armed uprising led by the Chinese Communist Party on August 1, 1927, and observed as the establishment of the Red Army (later known as the People's Liberation Army);

Teachers' Day. September 10, introduced in the early 1980s as part of the effort to counter the anti-intellectualism of the Cultural Revolution;

National Day. October 1, to celebrate the founding of the People's Republic of China on October 1, 1949 (2 days off).

In September 1999 the government extended both the National Day holiday and Labor Day to three days each. This, according to the official announcement, was to satisfy the growing need for a better material and cultural life. In the year 2000, May Day fell on a Monday and, with the encouragement of the government, most enterprises gave their employees the entire week off. Some people gossiped that this generosity was prompted less by a concern for the welfare of the people than for the health of the economy. Today's overheated economy has cranked out a glut of products of every description from beer to brass and televisions to tea kettles. The thinking is that with warehouses full, closing factories for a week and encouraging people to open their purses and spend ought to reduce excess inventories. A poll

Figure 8.1. A flea market in front of the Workers' Stadium, Beijing, 1998. The sign on the stadium reads "Whatever New York has, Beijing also has!" *© Jeff Booth.*

conducted in 2000 reported that 83% of urban residents intended to spend more because of the lengthened vacation. A shoe store manager in Beijing's trendy Wangfujing shopping district declared, "We can afford this lifestyle now."[1]

As far as official celebrations are concerned, the biggest is National Day, which in the pre-reform era was marked by parades in most cities, and a monumental parade in Beijing witnessed by China's top leaders standing on a podium at the head of enormous Tiananmen Square. In the past half century, Tiananmen Square—which sits on the southern edge of the Forbidden City, where the emperor lived—has been the focal point of events of the greatest political import. It was there on May 4, 1919, that the famous, nationalistic student demonstrations began; it was there in 1949 that Mao Zedong read the proclamation establishing the People's Republic; it was there in 1966 that Mao reviewed and received the accolades of thousands upon thousands of Red Guards; it was there in 1977 that his embalmed body was put on display in a glass case within a mausoleum; it was there in June 1989 that student democracy activists were bloodily suppressed in front of—thanks to television—hundreds of millions of viewers around the world. If one wants to make a political point and get it noted all across China, Tiananmen Square is the place to do it.

Traditional Holidays and Festivals

Before the twentieth century, although people did not enjoy a regular weekly day (or days) off from work nor did they have annual paid vacations—both are modern inventions—nonetheless, life was normally far from unremitting drudgery. In the first place, people traveled: in search of work or for business, on pilgrimages, or simply for sight-seeing, although the last group was never very large. Furthermore, they attended periodic markets in towns, which were occasions not merely to do some buying and selling but also to have a good time. In the equivalent of modern-day window shopping, anyone, including those with an empty purse, could look over a variety of interesting housewares, farm implements, cosmetics, medicines, musical instruments, books, and even works of art. They could also be amply entertained since marketplaces drew fortune tellers, religious proselytizers, musicians, storytellers, acrobats, and other performers of every stripe. Every month had several festival days, most of which were related to folk religion or to the legendary birthdays of Daoist or Buddhist deities. In the villages in particular, these holidays were usually community-wide celebrations in which everyone was expected to get out and enjoy themselves. In cities too, almost everyone took time off for festivals, either as participants or spectators.

A number of traditional festivals survive to this day as immensely popular celebrations. For several years the Communist authorities tried to put a damper on those happy occasions they considered extravagant and superstitious. However, once that pressure was relieved during the reform era that began around 1979, the principal festivals sprang back to popularity. Even before then, bowing to the inevitable, the state tried to appropriate some traditional holidays and turn them into occasions for celebrating "the revolution." For instance, at the time of the Grave-Sweeping Festival, traditionally a family-oriented day set aside for remembering and honoring one's ancestors, the Communist authorities organized services for the "martyrs of the revolution," such as having schoolchildren place wreaths on the Monument to the People's Heroes in Tiananmen Square. That the state seeks to inject itself into traditions close to the people's heart shows it fully recognizes the immense power and tenacity of popular customs.

Spring Festival

The biggest, longest, and most important holiday by far is the Spring Festival. This is a time for the entire nation to put on its best clothes, eat the best foods, hand out gifts, set off firecrackers (where still permitted), pay calls on friends and neighbors, drink and play games, watch TV specials, and look forward to a better, healthier, and more prosperous new year.

What the Chinese call the Spring Festival (*Chunjie*) is generally known in the West as the Chinese New Year, and indeed it begins on the first day of the lunar year, which falls between January 21 and February 19. In 1912, the infant republican government introduced the Gregorian solar calendar, as used in the West, and tried to get the people to shift their allegiance from the traditional new year to January 1. While everyone was happy to have a new holiday, they still wanted to retain the traditional one, celebrated on the traditional dates. The biggest success of the republican government in this area was in getting January 1 designated as the official New Year and getting the traditional New Year—which was called different things in different places and times—renamed "Spring Festival."

According to the Gregorian calendar, the beginning date of the Spring Festival jumps around from year to year. This is because the lunar calendar contains 12 months but only 354 days, and so is out of sync with the 365-day Gregorian calendar. To complicate matters, both the Gregorian and the lunar calendars need to be adjusted from time to time to get them synchronized with the true movement of the heavenly bodies: as we know, in the Gregorian calendar an extra day is added to the month of February to create a leap year every so often, while in the lunar calendar an entire month is added every third year. With a couple of sharp pencils, a sheaf of paper, and enough time a person could work out a concordance between the Gregorian and the lunar calendar, but most people are sensible enough simply to look in the newspaper or an almanac to find out the dates of traditional festivals.

Before the twentieth century, to have a complete command of the ability to tell dates was beyond the reach of average people in China. Years, months, days, and hours could be designated by a complex combination of two series, one known as the 10 Heavenly Stems and the other as the 12 Earthly Branches. By combining each of the Stems with each of the Branches, a total of 60 named pairs are achieved. Using this system to tell time, especially time over a long duration, such as centuries, was exceedingly challenging. Days and months could also be counted according to an entirely different system, which divided the year into a series of 24 benchmark days (called "nodes" or "joints" in Chinese, reminiscent of the joints on bamboo), spaced at roughly 15-day intervals. The nodes refer to seasonal changes, such as Beginning of Spring, Waking of Insects, Summer Solstice, Great Heat, White Dew. To complicate matters, neither the Heavenly Stems and Earthly Branches nor the 24 nodes were connected with the lunar calendar: the former made up a purely mathematical cycle and had no direct connection with the movement of sun and moon, while the latter were based on a solar reckoning. To make things even more complicated, the Chinese had no single starting point, like the birth of Christ, for counting years. Instead, years were identified according to the reign date of whatever emperor occupied the throne in the year in question. For instance, Baoyuan 2 (i.e., the second year of the reign known as Baoyuan) was the year 1039. Until the Ming dynasty (1368–1644), for magical reasons emperors were in the habit of changing their reign names whenever things were not going well, and thus there were more reign names than there were emperors. The reign name Baoyuan was one of no less than nine used during the 40-year rule of the emperor also known as Renzong. To take a couple of dates at random: eight years before Baoyuan 2 was Tiansheng 9 (i.e., 1031), and 12 years after Tiansheng 9 was Qingli 3 (i.e., 1043). And what was, say, 62 years before Baoyuan 2? If you lived in China at the time, you would have no way of knowing unless you consulted a reference book or had memorized reign names. If you wanted to be able to identify any year back, say, all the way to the birth of Christ, you would have had to master the brain-breaking task of memorizing several hundred reign names. And not just memorize them, but memorize them in order, and memorize how many years were in each reign name. When the republic was established in 1912, it made the Gregorian calendar official, but it also continued this tradition of dating years. The year 1912 became Minguo 1, or the First Year of the Republic. To this day, on Taiwan, to which the Nationalists fled in 1949 (Minguo 38), this system continues. Mercifully, when the Communists came to power in 1949, they adopted the Western way of counting years.

Finally, traditionally years were associated with the Chinese zodiac, represented by 12 animals, one for each of the 12 Earthly Branches: rat, ox, tiger, rabbit, dragon, snake, horse, goat, monkey, rooster, dog, and pig. It was believed that the sign under which one was born influenced one's fortunes. By consulting a fortune teller or looking in an almanac one found that, for example, people born in the year of the rat are talkative and quick witted and harmonious marriage partners with people born in the year of the monkey. Whether many people still believe in astrology of this sort is hard to say, but for everyone it at least remains part of the atmosphere of the Spring Festival.

Since the Spring Festival celebrates the beginning of the new year, it is very much about renewal: completing the business of the old year, re-cementing relationships with family, friends, and associates, and getting everything arranged to start the new year with a clean slate.

Initial preparations begin a month or so before the new year, with the world's largest annual human migration. If at all possible everyone wants to be home for the holiday, and so people working or residing far from the family home begin filtering back, filling up trains, planes, buses, and boats during the 30 or 40 days leading up to the Spring Festival. To cope with the onslaught, extra trains and airplane flights are added, automatic ticket-vending machines are wheeled into factories for the convenience of workers, and every available bus is pressed into service. It has been estimated that in the 40 days before the Spring Festival in the year 2000, some 1.7 billion trips were made, more than one for every man, woman, and child in China. For people who work close to home, the race begins at noon on new year's eve, when offices and plants close and a mass of humanity pours out onto the streets, forming a monumental traffic jam as everyone struggles to get home. By early evening the streets are virtually deserted, with only an occasional harried or smiling pedestrian scurrying off to join the festivities.

Preparations for the holiday get really serious about two or three weeks before the new year. People try insofar as possible to pay off their debts before the close of the old year; they wash their curtains, scrub the floors, and generally spruce up their houses; they lay in a supply of holiday necessities, including foodstuffs and drinks; and toward the end of the 12th month they send off the Kitchen God. This last ceremony is still observed in many households, which keep a picture of the Kitchen God pinned up over the cook stove. On the 23rd or 24th day of the 12th month, the family takes down the picture and burns it, thereby sending the god to heaven where, it is hoped, he will deliver a good report on the members of the family. In some places the family first offers the Kitchen God some *niangao* ("year cakes"), an indescribably sticky mass made of glutinous rice flour, with the thought that the god's lips will be sealed so he cannot make an unflattering report. In other places, before the immolation people smear the god's mouth with molasses, so that he will have only sweet words to report to heaven. On the last day of the old year, once the Kitchen God is safely off on his annual journey, a new picture is posted over the stove and thereby the god is reinvited to watch over and protect the family during the coming year.

Toward the end of the lunar year, people also send out New Year's greeting cards, a custom that dates back several hundred years. Traditionally the cards were red, to symbolize happiness, but today 3-D pop-up cards are also available as are high-tech cards with chips that play a little tune when the card is opened. E-cards have also appeared; given the ease and cost (nothing) of sending e-cards, they seem destined to reach a volume in the billions upon billions.

Also customarily, people buy New Year's pictures (*nianhua*), special colorful prints that portray the Gate God, or cuddly toddlers holding a big peach (a traditional symbol of long life), or some other auspicious image, which they affix to the walls or windows (Figure 8.2). Just about everyone also buys, or writes their own, mottoes called *chunlian* ("spring couplets"), short poems written or printed in black, gold, or silver on red paper, which

鱼 儿 肥 又 大

Figure 8.2. A *nianhua* from the 1980s. The happy, chubby toddler, dressed in a *doudou*, is an exceedingly common theme in nianhua, as is the fish and the lotus plants. The scene is replete with symbolism: the word "fish" (*yu*) is a homophone for "abundance," and "lotus" (*lian*) is a homophone for "repeatedly"; hence the suggestion is "May you enjoy abundance year in and year out." The doudou, lotus flowers, and the fish are all red—*the* auspicious color. The inscription at the bottom reads "The fish and the child are big and fat." *Courtesy of Stefan Landsberger and the International Institut von Sociale Geschiedenis, Amsterdam.*

they paste on gate posts or doorways. The poems express a sentiment appropriate to the season, such as "May your happiness be as wide as the East Sea." Sometimes instead of a poem, the paper contains but a single character, such as "Happiness" or "Virtue." The posting of calligraphy is very characteristic of Chinese culture and is not limited to the Spring Festival. Since calligraphy is an art, putting up attractively written characters is a way of bringing beauty into daily life. It is also a reflection of the importance the Chinese attach to learning, and an opportunity for people to display their love of language, especially their delight in witticisms and puns, which are extremely popular. During the Spring Festival, for instance, the character Good Fortune (*fu*) is often pasted upside down. The word "upside down" (*dao*) is a homophone for the word "arrival," hence the upside down character suggests the idea of wishing for the arrival of good fortune.

On New Year's eve evening, with the family gathered together, the feasting begins. Among the most popular dishes, especially in North China, are *jiaozi*, and especially in South China, niangao. After dinner, the family sits up playing cards and board games, watching TV, chatting, and otherwise having a good time. The television program "Spring Festival Party," which debuted in 1983, has become something of a contemporary tradition. Each New Year's eve, this multi-hour show, featuring a throng of famous singers and actors, draws a huge audience. Trying to telephone someone when the show is on the air is a mistake because many loyal viewers refuse to answer.

In some families, all the lights are kept on in the house and the children are allowed, even encouraged, to stay up to midnight in the belief (at least, it was once believed) that this will contribute to the parents' longevity. The payoff for the vigil comes at midnight when fireworks displays begin in public parks and people gather on the streets to set of firecrackers (except in Beijing and other places where they are prohibited)—not single firecrackers popping here and there, but strings and strings of firecrackers exploding for hours on end. Some Beijingers, nostalgic for the good old noisy days, ride out to the suburbs each year so they can enjoy the deafening sound and pungent smell of exploding gunpowder.

In the morning parents give their children *yasuiqian*, red packets of money, from a few cents to up to $100. Some families also offer sacrifices of food to their ancestors and burn incense (joss sticks, as they used to be called in the West) in their memory. Later in the morning, people pay visits to friends and neighbors, exchanging gifts as they visit, and then go to parks or temples to enjoy traditional activities such as lion dances and stilt walking. After three days, work and school resume. However, in traditional times it was generally considered that the Spring Festival ended only on the 15th day of the first month, with the arrival of still another holiday, the Lantern Festival.

Lantern Festival

The origins of the Lantern Festival, always held on the 15th day of the first lunar month, the first full moon after the Spring Festival, stretch back

Figure 8.3. On a farm in North China, ca. 1990. On the door behind the girls are New Year's decorations: at the center within the diamond is the character Good Fortune (*fu*); immediately above it is a paper decoration with designs and words cut out with scissors. Both the character and the paper decoration were store bought. Pasted on either side of the window in the door are *chunlian*, written at home. *From Qiu Huanxing*, Folk Customs of China *(Beijing: Foreign Languages Press, 1992)*.

some 2,000 years or more. There are several different stories about how the festival got started and of its meaning. For most people, the origins do not matter much; what is important is the delightful beauty of the festival. Children in particular wait excitedly for dusk, when people begin to gather out of doors to take in the sight of thousands upon thousands of paper (and now also plastic) lanterns of all colors, sizes, shapes, and designs decorating streets, shopping centers, and private dwellings (Figure 8.4). Many cities have lantern fairs in parks or stadiums, with impressively huge and magnificent lanterns— dragons were an especially popular motif in 2000, the year of the dragon— containing thousands of lightbulbs and light-emitting diodes.

Figure 8.4. A Lantern Festival, from the late eighteenth century. Beneath the canopy that spans the shopping arcade, a dragon dance is being performed. The ball on the end of the pole held by the man in front of the dragon represents a pearl, which the dragon chases after. *From* Shinzoku Kibun *(A record of Chinese customs), Tokyo, 1800.*

As in traditional times, lanterns are often inscribed with riddles. The answer to a riddle can be a certain Chinese character, an incident from history, the name of a famous person, and so on. Sometimes little objects are hung from the lanterns giving hints to the answer, but even then the riddles can be very challenging.

The Lantern Festival is also a time for outdoor performances and activities, especially various kinds of folk performances such as dancing, singing, stilt walking, story telling, puppet shows, and comic dialogues.

Finally, as in all other Chinese festivals, food plays an important role. The representative food of the Lantern Festival is the *tangyuan* or *yuanxiao*, little balls of glutinous rice flour filled with various kinds of sweets, nowadays orange paste, coconut, chocolate, and so on, and usually served in a soup. So popular are these little dumplings that food companies begin preparing them more than two months before the festival; in the year 2000, more than 200 tons of tangyuan were turned out in Beijing alone. According to the manager of one company, "Most of our products stay on the shelves less than 24 hours before they are sold."[2]

Grave-Sweeping Festival

The holiday known in Chinese as the Festival of Pure Brightness (*Qing-ming jie*) falls on the fourth or fifth of April and is the only principal traditional festival based on the solar, not lunar, calendar. This was a day for worshiping the ancestors and placating their ghosts in the belief that spirits have the power to do the family ill if they are not cared for. The sentiment of Qingming, however, is warm and human, and rarely morbid. For most people it is a time for remembering and honoring deceased members of the family.

Traditionally, after breakfast the family—with rakes, hoes, buckets, and brooms in hand—set out for the local graveyard to scrub and tidy up the family graves. There always seemed to be people who, out of kindness, would also tend to abandoned graves. After cleaning up, offerings of food, tea, and liquor were placed before the grave, along with burning sticks of incense and sometimes candles. The men of the household usually kowtowed before the grave, that is, performed a ritual form of bowing involving kneeling and touching the forehead to the ground in token of homage and deep respect. Ritual paper money was then burnt, since it was thought that in the afterworld the spirit needed the things that are also important in this world. Burning of paper effigies of valuable objects—in other words, sending them off to the deceased—played an important role in funerals as well. This practice is still followed by many families, especially in the countryside. Most limit themselves to ritual paper money and a few other small articles, although from time to time one encounters an ostentatious bonfire, complete with, for example, a nearly life-size paper replica of a Mercedes Benz.

With the ceremonies at the graveyard ended, people sat down, in the cemetery, to have a picnic or strolled off, perhaps to fly kites, an activity once much associated with Qingming, but also enjoyed anytime there was a good breeze. Kites, which are still popular, come in a huge variety of shapes: dragonflies, birds, butterflies, fish, tigers, the moon and stars, and many legendary and historical figures. Adding to the magnificent sight of a colorful kite soaring in the blue sky was its magnificent sound, for very often kites sported a whistle or a tiny aeolian harp (a little bamboo bow, with strings that hummed in the wind). Their clear, pure sound reminded people of the music of the *zheng*, a harp-like instrument—hence the modern name for kites, *fengzheng*, "wind harps."

Not long ago it seemed that kite flying during Qingming might eventually disappear since from the 1950s city people began to be interred in mausoleums rather than buried in cemeteries. Beginning in the 1950s, the government pressed for cremation of the dead, as a way of saving space, promoting public hygiene, and resisting waste and "superstition." Unquestionably, tra-

Figure 8.5. Flying a kite in Tiananmen Square, Beijing, 1998. In the background is the seventeenth-century Gate of Heavenly Peace (Tiananmen), the most photographed spot in China. The signs (partly obscured) on the Gate read "Long Live the People's Republic of China" and "Long Live the Great Unity of the World's People." © *Jeff Booth*.

ditional graves consumed a lot of space. In most areas, each grave consisted of a mound, up to 6 to 8 feet in diameter and 4 or 5 feet high, with a gravestone at the foot. Graves could also be considerably more elaborate, with a larger stone marker and altar or even with a stone (or now sometimes, concrete) mini-mausoleum.

Although cremation is contrary to traditional practice, in the cities, where people suffered from too little living space, there was not much objection to denying the dead their traditionally generous plots. Today in the cities cremation is universal. However, in the countryside burial of the corpse is still most common.

The cremated remains are put in a small cotton bag (most people believe these contain only part of the ashes and ground-up bones and the rest are discarded), which is in turn placed in a wooden box, about 10 × 14 × 8 inches. Some people take the box home. More, however, deposit it in a public mausoleum, which looks much like a library on the inside except that the shelves contain not books but boxed ashes. This lugubrious environment is hardly conducive to the traditional Grave-Sweeping rituals: kneeling in the aisle to kowtow (*ketou*) to remains placed up on the top shelf smacks of the ridiculous. In the past 10 or 15 years, however, enterprising farmers have opened cemeteries, and urban people in large numbers have buried ashes there, in small graves surrounded by young trees. On Grave-Sweeping day, the roads out of cities are clogged with families on a day trip out to the graveyards, there to follow some of the traditional practices, attenuated though they may be. In 1995, Beijing prohibited the burning of paper money, and residents have had to get used to bringing flowers to the graves instead. For people everywhere who cannot get out to the family graves, the Internet offers an electronic solution. In the year 2000 the China-based Web site Netor.com served up virtual veneration: with just a click, surfers could leave a message for the dead, symbolically light a candle, or request a song for the departed.

In 1999, the Chinese press reported on a particularly splashy, recently completed two-story tomb, made of the finest stone and featuring carvings of dragons, swans, and phoenixes, with statues of elephants and lions flanking the entrance. The builder of this towering monument was a Mr. Wang, the Communist Party secretary in the town of Jiaowu, in the province of Zhejiang, who evidently wanted to preserve "his legacy for posterity." When reporters went to interview Secretary Wang, he was defensive, claiming that "all of this construction is legal. I have all the planning approvals to build this tomb. Moreover, I even bought the land-use rights for 125 renminbi [around $15!]."[3] For Chinese readers, this story illustrates much of what they find infuriatingly wrong with their society today. First, the builder of the tomb holds a position of responsibility in the Communist Party, yet the Party has constantly railed against expensive and ostentatious burials. Thus the story reminds readers of the arrogance and hypocrisy of officialdom. It also highlights that while the Party can at times be ruthless in suppressing anything it finds objectionable, at other times it can be incredibly ineffectual, and particularly so when it comes to policing itself. The story also hints at the rampant corruption among China's officials: even without the reporters mentioning a word about it, readers were certain to ask themselves, "And just where would a Party secretary get enough money to build such a magnificent monument?" Readers also must have chuckled over Secretary Wang's statement—which he thought was a defense—that he paid for the land: that the cost was next to nothing surely was the result of backdoor dealing.

"Going through the backdoor," as one suspects Secretary Wang did, is an exact translation of an expression familiar to all Chinese. The idea it encapsulates is simple: to get some special advantage by using one's influence or, as Americans would say, by pulling strings. During the pinnacle of the revolutionary years, in the 1960s and 1970s, the dearth of goods and services made wheeling and dealing a way of life. In those years, trading on one's political power and influence, if one had any, was commonplace. Today, this continues, although the ranks of the influential have expanded with the addition of people who are now able to buy clout. China's tradition of personal connections (*guanxi*) and its elaborate gift-giving customs sometimes blur the line between friendly relations, pulling strings, and out-and-out corruption. For instance, guests are always expected to bring gifts, and hosts sometimes to reciprocate with gifts. This is true even of business meetings, but the gifts normally are trifles, of significance only as symbols of a mutual desire to establish or continue a relationship. People seeking favors also often present a gift (food, drink, cigarettes, and the like), but again this is usually symbolic. If, however, the gift is commensurate in value with the favor being asked, then—depending on the circumstances—it might be considered a bribe. The calculation can be very complicated and discomforting for all concerned. In any event, if officials overstep the line and are found guilty of graft, the consequences can be fatal since egregious cases are punishable by death.

Dragon Boat Festival

The holiday known in China as the *Duanwu jie* (Upright Wu Festival, *wu* being the seventh of the 12 Earthly Branches) is celebrated on the fifth day of the fifth lunar month, which falls anywhere from the very tail end of May to late June. Traditionally, the holiday was marked by races between competing teams in dragon boats—long, narrow vessels rather like large canoes, manned by up to a score of paddlers; hence the term, used in the West but not in China, "Dragon Boat Festival." These races—which were popular in Central and South China, but not in North China, where few people live near suitable waterways—were scarce during the heyday of the revolution in the 1960s and 1970s but have reappeared in the past couple of decades. The heated competition that once characterized them has also resurfaced, with races sometimes ending in shoving and punching, if not an outright brawl. These displays of masculine exuberance are tame compared to the outcome of races related in folktales—of doubtful accuracy—to the effect that centuries ago losing teams ended up on the bottom of the river.

Today the Dragon Boat Festival is a regular workday and for most people the celebrating is limited to eating *zongzi*, a fist-sized pyramid of rice (or, sometimes in North China, glutinous millet) usually with some sort of filling and enclosed in a leaf wrapper. Zongzi, which can be eaten any time of the year, are analogous to the sandwich: they are handy and easy to carry, and if filled with a little meat or some vegetables, they make a quick meal.

Occasionally, magazines and newspapers write of old customs and beliefs associated with the festival, in particular the tale of Qu Yuan (ca. 340–278 B.C.), a leading minister in the ancient state of Chu who lost the confidence of the king through a rival's jealous slander. Unjustly dismissed from office, Qu Yuan wrote a long, magnificent, and bitter lament, "On Encountering Sorrow," one of the masterpieces of Chinese poetry. For his selfless love of his country and people, Qu Yuan earned the devotion of his countrymen, but nonetheless was eventually banished. On his way into exile, on the banks of the Miluo River, clasping a large stone to his chest, Qu Yuan threw himself into the dark water. According to legend, this was on the fifth day of the fifth month. On hearing the tragic news, people rowed onto the river in search of his body, without success. Therein, it is often said (again, with doubtful accuracy), lies the origins of the dragon boat races.

The festival was also associated with warding off pestilence and the "five poisonous creatures" (snake, scorpion, centipede, toad, and lizard), and especially with protecting children from these dangers. A reddish substance was sometimes painted on the noses, ears, and foreheads of small children to repel poisonous creatures. For the same purpose, fragrant herbs were sewn into little cloth sachets and tied with a cord around children's necks. From time to time, children wearing these sorts of amulets can still be seen in the countryside.

People also put up pictures of Zhong Kui, a legendary demon fighter. A stalwart figure with a bushy beard, Zhong Kui was a familiar subject of both popular prints and high art paintings. Frequently depicted surrounded by ugly little demons that he is about to devour, Zhong Kui was also a popular subject of New Year's pictures. In fact, his pictures could be posted any time of the year, for are not demons a constant threat?

Mid-Autumn Festival

The succession of the seasons, with its changes in the weather and in the types of foods that the earth yields up, its cycle of birth, growth, decline, and death, and its constant reminder to man that he is a part of nature, is central to traditional Chinese festivals. Emblematic of man's celebration of nature and his endeavor to harmonize with it is the fact that most of the ceremonies and activities associated with traditional festivals take place out of doors, not within the confines of man-made structures.

The Mid-Autumn Festival, falling on the 15th day of the eighth lunar month (late September or early October), is especially attuned to nature and to the regulator of the seasons, the moon. Indeed, in the West the holiday is often known as the Moon Festival. On that day, people went out to gaze at the full moon, eat moon cakes, and place on the ground offerings of fruit and moon cakes to the moon. In its associations and activities, the holiday resembles the U.S. Thanksgiving: autumn, the harvest, food, and family reunion. To the Chinese, the full moon is a symbol of reunion (*tuanyuan*, the word for "reunion," literally means "a perfect circle"), and indeed the holiday is sometimes known as *Tuanyuan jie* or the Reunion Holiday.

Moon cakes, the characteristic food of the holiday, are still enjoyed all across China, just as they were a century and more ago. In Beijing, in the year 1900 one writer explained that for moon cakes "the Studio of Perfect Beauty . . . is the best place in the capital, whereas those of other places are not worth eating. But as for moon cakes to be used solely as moon offerings, every shop has them. The big ones are more than a foot in diameter, and have portrayed on their tops the images of the three-legged toad and the rabbit of the moon."[4]

The toad and rabbit are characters in a folktale associated with the festival. When her despotic husband was away, Chang E took his pill of immortality and swallowed it. Immediately she began to float in the air. On hearing the approach of her husband, she flew out the window, with her husband in pursuit. Chang E fled across the sky, all the way to the moon. When she landed, for her misdeed she was transformed into a three-legged toad, but not before, panting from her exertions, she spit up the pill casing, which was immediately transformed into a jade rabbit. To this day, if you look up at the moon you will see the rabbit, with a large pestle in hand, pounding out the elixir of immortality.

LEISURE ACTIVITIES

With China's growing prosperity, its people have ever more wealth to spend on *zuole*—having fun. In 1997, mean annual family income was $1,250, a puny figure by standards of the industrialized world, but enough to sustain a consumer culture that in some respects is sufficiently spirited, freewheeling, and profligate to qualify as "world class."[5] Furthermore, not since 1949 have people had so much time to fritter away. In May 1997, China passed a milestone on the march to prosperity when it officially adopted the five-day workweek. As always, perhaps the best measure of a people's consumption is the quantity and quality of what they waste and throw away. By this yardstick, China is moving ahead by leaps and bounds: in the cities, where these sorts of things are easiest to measure, in 1995 China's citizens churned out over 107 million tons of garbage, a great step upward from the 31 million tons of 1980.[6]

Leisure also is something to be consumed. From the unlimited variety of personal, pleasant indulgences we take up below a few of the most popular and revealing.

Television

Of all the changes that China has undergone in recent decades none can quite compare with its television revolution. In China today, as in so many other places in the world, when it comes to leisure activities, television is king.

In 1978, on the eve of the reform, China still had but one television network, the official China Central Television (CCTV), which began limited broadcasting in 1958 and by the early 1980s was on the air only about 40 hours a week. Today, CCTV, broadcasting about three-score programs on eight channels, airs 138 hours *per day*. Furthermore, it has been joined by several other networks, including cable networks (80% of the households in China's largest cities subscribe to cable TV), with more than a thousand stations, serving around a billion viewers nationwide. One of the truest statements about contemporary China is best put in the negative: just about nobody doesn't watch TV.

Television sets, which before the reform were owned by only a few privileged households, are now ubiquitous. In Shanghai in 1981 there was only one private TV per 100 households; 15 years later, in 1996, there were no less than 109 TVs per 100 households.[7] Put another way, in 1995 93.6% of Shanghai households owned at least one color TV.[8] The vast countryside is not far behind, with 83% of rural households owning a TV in 1997.[9]

The most popular program in the early years was the CCTV evening news, which remains a favorite although the style of delivery has been spiffed up in recent years. Originally, newscasters and TV hosts spoke in telecast-style Mandarin and wore a serious, professional, straight face. Now, to appeal to a wider audience, "television personalities" with a relaxed, even chatty, delivery have taken over. Furthermore, programming has moved into areas that would have been unimaginable 20 years ago.

To Tell the Truth, which started around 1993, became a model of sorts. Among its several segments—including in-depth news reports and interviews—is *Space of Life*, which explores the everyday life and problems of everyday people. Building upon this formula is *True Encounters*, a syndicated Jerry Springer–like program that brings troubled couples together on stage to work—or fight—out their differences in front of an enthusiastic in-studio audience. These gladiatorial contests run against Chinese tradition "by having people show their emotions openly," according to the producer Chen Xiaodong.[10] It is precisely this flaunting of conventions that gives the show its appeal.

On a higher plane, one of the most popular programs today is *Focal Point Inquiry*, a 10-minute show aired daily on CCTV after the evening news. In its purpose, the show—which draws an audience of 300 million—is similar to *60 Minutes*, the long-running program in the United States that exposes corruption, abuse of power, sale of shoddy and fake products, and other shady activities. Since China's legal system is still weak and its consumer organizations are in their infancy, a program like *Focal Point Inquiry* serves a strongly felt need among viewers that there be some recourse for injustice. People line up at the entrance to the CCTV studio in Beijing to plead that the program air their grievances. But, as critics point out, the program "can only go after 'flies' not 'tigers' or corrupt high officials."[11] When it comes to corruption among top officials, the Communist Party handles matters internally, or occasionally stages a trial, but in all cases brooks absolutely no "outside interference."

Despite China's self-professed "opening," the Party's innocuous-sounding Central Publicity Department still exercises censorship over the media. In May 2000 the censors banned the airing of a 35-part series *Dangerous Events in the Capital*, which dramatized the corruption scandal surrounding Chen Xitong, the former mayor of Beijing, and his deputy, Wang Baosen, whose suicide in 1995 brought the scandal out into the open. Reportedly, the drama ran afoul of the censors because it suggested the involvement of other high officials, who still remain in power.[12] Just a month before the censors axed *Dangerous Events in the Capital*, they passed the novel, with the same title, on which the TV drama was based—another example of the inconsistency and capriciousness of officialdom.

Still, subversive ideas creep into television in ways the censors can hardly anticipate. A North China resident had the audacity to object that he could not be convicted of the crime with which he was charged because the police failed to read him his rights. When the court asked where he got the strange idea that the police had to advise people of their rights, he said he saw it on *Hunter*, a U.S. detective program of the 1980s that has become immensely popular in China.

The government is not entirely insensitive to these sorts of dangers, and it limits imported programming to 15% of prime-time viewing. Nonetheless, foreign influence makes itself felt even in programs produced in China. Several domestic shows have taken their inspiration from abroad, including a Chinese-produced version of *Sesame Street*, which debuted in 1998. Celebrity game shows, following established Japanese and Taiwanese formulas, have proliferated to such an extent that top stars are reportedly getting tired of being invited to appear.[13] Even more popular are serialized dramas that began to appear after a couple of long soap operas from Mexico and Brazil became big hits in 1986 and 1987. These "indoor dramas" as the Chinese call them (because they consist mostly of indoor scenes shot in a studio) are the sorts of programs about which tens of millions of viewers feel exceedingly passionate. One of the first, *Yearning*, which aired in 1990 and 1991, in no time spawned a craze, or "fever" (*re*) as the Chinese term it. Thousands of people called the stations to demand the program be aired every night; in many cities, streets were deserted when it played; people everywhere hummed its theme song; in the city of Wuhan, a scheduled power cut in the middle of one episode sent an angry crowd to the power plant, which the mayor quickly ordered back into operation.[14]

In the past couple of decades, the nation has been gripped by one fever after another, and not only in entertainment. Is China particularly susceptible to fads? Perhaps. The first three decades of rule by the Communist Party certainly prepared people for moving in lock step with the crowd. The Party tended to lead society through campaigns, such as the infamous campaign to build backyard steel furnaces during the Great Leap Forward (which resulted in lots of useful pots and pans being melted down to make brittle, worthless steel) or the campaign to "plant grain everywhere" (which resulted in pitiful yields from land more suited to other crops). Political campaigns were very fadlike: they exploded on the scene, usually with no warning, and overnight everyone all across the nation became (or was supposed to become) passionately gripped by the message. Of course, under the Party's leadership, campaigns were well orchestrated, with the printing of editorials and news articles in all the press, the unfurling of posters and banners, and the staging of rallies. But the degree of central control was probably always much less than outsiders assumed. The development of campaigns was like a man pulling a rail car: to get the car moving takes a lot of straining and sweat, but once it is moving the car rolls along easily on its own momentum. And if it hits a decline, unless someone puts on the brakes quickly enough, it can become a runaway, as happened during the Great Leap Forward and the Cultural Revolution. The big difference today is that fads, so far as one can tell, are not orchestrated: the rail car is pulled here and there by invisible forces. The Party still makes attempts, increasingly feeble, to launch political campaigns from time to time, but nowadays nobody is listening.

Instead, people are gripped by things like *Yearning*, or in more recent years by two popular serials dealing with recent Chinese emigrants in America. The first, *A Beijinger in New York*, which aired in 1993, painted an unflattering portrait of life in America. At one point, the protagonist Wang Qiming growls his contempt for Americans: "They were still monkeys up in the trees while we were already human beings. Look at how hairy they are; they're not as evolved as us. Just 'cause they've got some money!" The second, *Chinese Restaurant*, a 40-part comedy that aired in 1999, dealt with emigrants in Los Angeles and was generally kinder in its treatment of Americans. Might this be because the series was financed by Sony's Columbia TriStar and sponsored by FedEx and Coca-Cola?

Also popular, particularly among younger viewers, are sports programs, especially foreign soccer matches and NBA basketball games. A recent survey of middle school and high school students in five coastal cities asked them to name their favorite athlete: tops was Michael Jordan (with 26.5%, far ahead of the second most popular sports star, a Chinese, who garnered only 7%). Among high school students, Michael Jordan also scored in the top five on a list of the "most successful" people. Who was number one? Bill Gates (at 14.9%), followed by Deng Xiaoping (at only 7.4%).[15]

Movies

What is China's biggest grossing movie of all time? *Titanic*. Its second biggest? *True Lies*. Its third? *Saving Private Ryan*. All are recent products of Hollywood. American movies now account for more than half of the Chinese box office. In fact, their popularity is even greater than box office receipts suggest. In the first place, Beijing, struggling to protect domestic film producers and counter what some Chinese vilify as "cultural colonialism," strictly limits imported movies. Each year, the authorities impose an informal quota that permits in only around 10 foreign movies on a revenue-sharing basis; several more, but still not many, are allowed in if the foreign producers agree to take a small fixed fee, rather than share in the box office receipts. Second, in some cases all seats for Chinese-made movies are subsidized by the *danwei* (the "work unit" or "workplace"), that is, the enterprise to which workers in state-owned industries and offices are attached. The biggest grossing Chinese-produced movie in 1996, *Kong Fansen*, about a deceased Han Chinese cadre who had worked selflessly in Tibet, brought in around $3.5 million, but very few paying customers. Nationally, paying customers made up only 5% of viewers. In big cities, that percentage was even smaller; in Beijing, for instance, it was only 0.5%.[16]

The admission for nonsubsidized screenings, including all Hollywood productions, is steep by Chinese standards at $3.50 to $5 for a first-run movie in an upscale urban theater. Still, annual movie attendance is said to be about 15 to 17 billion, which if true means that on average each person in China goes to the movies around 15 times a year. But only 10% of middle school and high school students regularly watch Chinese-made films.[17] That people in droves are willing to pay a hefty admission fee suggests just how much they prefer imported entertainment—but not all imported entertainment. Disney's *Mulan* was a flop, probably because the authorities did not permit it to be aired until after the Spring Festival, when school had resumed (so it would not compete with Chinese-produced kiddie features), and because many viewers had already seen it on pirated videos (the pirating of videos and CDs is a huge business in China, and one which the authorities are only recently making sporadic and desultory efforts to suppress), and because, finally, its portrayal of traditional Chinese social relations—a subject about which even some Chinese children know a thing or two—was laughably inaccurate. On the other hand, audiences do not automatically reject Chinese productions. Films that are entertaining, and free of heavy-handed patriotic themes calculated to please the authorities, do well. Among the many recent domestic movies that have competed successfully with American megaproductions is *Be There or Be Square*, a romantic comedy released in 1999 and featuring two big stars, Xu Fan and Ge You. Shot in Los Angeles, and dealing with recent emigrants, *Be There or Be Square* is presumably less popular with the authorities than with paying audiences.

Physical Culture

"Think of the starving people of China." With those words, American parents once urged their finicky children to eat all the food on their plate. How downright archaic that sounds today. "Obesity obsesses 70 million people in China." Those words, in a report on CCTV in March 2000, describe what really troubles many people in China today. According to the report, one-third of all adults in Beijing and Shanghai are overweight, as are 11% of the children.

This is a novel development in a country that traditionally valued physical culture. Chinese martial arts, involving a multiplicity of forms of both armed and unarmed combat, was for centuries practiced by warriors, by Chinese opera performers, and by common people as a form of exercise and physical development. *Taijiquan* (which can be roughly translated as "ultimate boxing" and is often rendered as "t'ai-chi ch'uan" in the West), an offshoot of Chinese karate, over the past couple of centuries evolved into a slow motion form of shadow boxing that is now practiced mostly by the elderly. Mornings, groups of oldsters gather in parks to go through the slow, circular, graceful movements of taijiquan, which are somewhat akin to dances in that they follow a set pattern or routine. Taijiquan is of little, if any, value for fighting, but is practiced in order to promote the flow of and develop control over *qi*. Qi, which we have mentioned in conjunction with fengshui, is a fundamental concept in Chinese culture. It is a vital force or energy that suffuses all living things and many inanimate objects also. In the human being, the center or generator of qi is thought to reside in the belly, an inch or two below the navel. Through taijiquan and other techniques, the practitioner is able consciously to stimulate and direct the flow of qi, and even to project it outside the body, through the soles of the feet or through the tips of the fingers for instance.

The government has been of two minds about taijiquan. On the one hand, the authorities in principle oppose any organized activity, no matter how nonpolitical or benign it may appear, that they themselves do not regulate or control, out of fear that uncontrolled activity can potentially lead to oppositional activity. Furthermore, in some minds the concept of qi is evidence of backward, superstitious, unscientific thinking. On the other hand, taijiquan evidently promotes the physical and mental health of its practitioners, and the government certainly supports good health. Qi is also an essential concept in traditional Chinese medicine, which the government has also generally supported.

The government is similarly conflicted over *qigong*, another form of physical culture. Qigong (which can be translated as "qi skills") is a variety of meditative, breathing, and gymnastic exercises aimed at controlling and manipulating the qi. Many claims are made about qigong, including that it promotes good health and a sense of well-being, and, at the most extreme, that it cures cancer and can endow its exponents with the power of levitation, clairvoyance, and X-ray vision. (A man in his thirties, an acquaintance of the author, as he practiced qigong with a self-styled "master," tripped, fell, and broke his arm. So much for levitation and clairvoyance!) The origins and history of qigong are unclear. A silk scroll dating back to the second century B.C. portrays 40 postures that may be related to an early version of qigong, and over the centuries several medical texts have mentioned qigong. But it remained obscure until the 1980s when it burst forth into one of contemporary China's most astonishing crazes. Today estimates of the number of its practitioners run from 20 or 30 million all the way to 100 million or more. It is, as one report described it, "perhaps the largest mass movement in modern China not under direct government control."[18]

To bring the phenomenon under its control, the government has insisted that qigong organizations register with the appropriate official organs, as all voluntary organizations are required to do. However, one particular out-growth of qigong has managed not merely to run afoul of the authorities, but to strike fear in their hearts. That outgrowth is Falun Gong (sometimes called Falun Dafa, lit. the Universal Principles of the Falun). Established in 1992 by Li Hongzhi (b. 1951), before then an obscure practitioner of qigong, Falun Gong originally joined the officially approved Qigong Scientific Re-search Association, which gave it legal standing and also made it subject to government control. In 1996, Li withdrew from the association, saying that Falun Gong was essentially unlike organizations that treated qigong merely as a method of promoting health. When he tried to re-register Falun Gong with the government in some other capacity, he was rebuffed. Around that time he began traveling abroad, and in 1998 he settled in New York with his wife and daughter. When asked why he chose to live in the United States, he replied, "My daughter wanted to go to the States. I also wanted her to study more English language. I heard U.S. education was pretty good."[19]

Because Falun Gong was not officially registered, in the eyes of the gov-ernment it had no right to exist. It came under heavy official criticism, which stimulated it, in April 1999, to respond by putting on a display that, in the Chinese context, was truly extraordinary. Around 10,000 Falun Gong ad-herents gathered in Beijing before Zhongnanhai, the residential compound of China's top leaders, where they stood—in silence—in ranks 10 deep, to protest the government's harassment. Although after several hours the police convinced the Falun Gongers to leave, the consternation among China's leaders must have been palpable. Thereafter, despite a government ban im-posed in July 1999 and despite a vigorous campaign to crush it, the move-ment has shown no evidence of disappearing. On the contrary, every few weeks Falun Gongers show up in Tiananmen Square, where they try to unfurl banners. But now the uniformed and plainclothes police who patrol the square quickly pounce on them, and with kicks and punches whisk them off to jail. Reportedly, several arrestees have met their death in jail, at the hands of the police.

What exactly is Falun Gong? Who are its adherents? And why has it become anathema to the government? The official Falun Gong Web site (www.falundafa.org) claims that the movement is neither a cult nor a religion, but rather "a powerful cultivation system based on the essential characteristics of the universe." In fact, a glance at the *Zhuan Falun*, the movement's bible, written by Li Hongzhi in 1994, and other documents shows that it is a quasi-religious pastiche consisting of borrowings from Buddhism and Daoism, combined with many of the common claims of qigong (that it promotes health, for example) together with Li's own idiosyncratic, antiscientific beliefs and assertions. As an example of the last, in the *Zhuan Falun* Li discusses a uranium mine in the African country of Gabon. He writes that "scientists" verified that this mine was actually once "a large-scale nuclear reactor with a very rational layout. Even our modern people cannot possible create [something like] this, so when was it built then? It was constructed 2 billion years ago and was in operation for 500 thousand years."

Li Hongzhi himself has claimed over 100 million followers in 30 countries. This is surely a grossly inflated figure, but even if the movement had several tens of millions of adherents by the end of the year 2000, that still represents a phenomenal growth in eight short years. It appears that the movement has attracted a wide variety of followers, including doctors, professors, and other intellectuals; working-class people; many middle-aged people of all backgrounds, especially women; and even high-ranking cadres in the Communist Party. These are hardly the sorts of people that one would think of as a threat to social order; on the contrary, most of them are average, stable members of society. Indeed, Falun Gong consistently denies that it has any political agenda at all. Its adherents claim that they are attracted to Falun Gong as a means of easing physical and mental distress. Unlike Western cults that fixate on death and Armageddon, Falun Gong promises its followers a long and healthy life. This fits in perfectly with the Chinese tradition of searching for longevity.

Falun Gong has a simple, innocuous ethical message—"truth, kindness, and tolerance"—which is also part of its appeal, and its leader, Li Hongzhi, despite his unusual, if not bizarre, statements, is in many ways simple and low key. Its central dynamic is also simple: Master Li, as he is called, implants a falun—a "wheel of law"—into the follower's belly, where it constantly spins, generating and radiating qi. Practice of its exercises is not demanding, and in fact if one does not regularly exercise, that is not a problem: Li says, "If I plant the wheel in you, you don't have to worry."[20]

What probably makes tens of millions of people receptive to Falun Gong is a feeling, especially among those over age 50, that China is adrift. During the heyday of socialism, the Communist Party seemed genuinely to believe its own ideology, and despite the sharp and unsettling turns in the road to revolution, among the common people a faith in revolution itself was genuine and widespread. Today the Party's overriding interest seems to be merely to survive in power, and for this the revolutionary ideology of "Marxism-Leninism–Mao Zedong Thought" is of little relevance. Where once the revolution called for selfless devotion to society and self-sacrifice, today everyone is encouraged to get rich, and if that is at the expense of other people, so be it. In almost every sphere of society, stability and certainty have evaporated. In such an environment, a movement offering comfort and something to believe in, as does Falun Gong, finds a ready home. In addition, in the reform era, with the state in headlong retreat from the socialist welfare system, medical care has become increasingly expensive and problematic. The press frequently reports on patients who are kept hospitalized longer than necessary in order to run up a big bill, quacks who perform needless surgery, and other irregularities. This has triggered fear and concern among the public, and prompted many people to turn to Falun Gong, or other of the qigong movements, for a very practical purpose: to maintain good health.

The government's absolute and uncompromising struggle to smash Falun Gong is a measure of its insecurity. Although the movement has no discernible political message, that it has attracted a huge following and that it has created an effective and efficient organization, despite its pariah status, suggest it has the potential to challenge Communist rule itself. That it could bring 10,000 people to Beijing, get them all to Zhongnanhai at the same time, and have them act in concert—all this evidently without the government knowing about it in advance—is abundant proof of the movement's strong organization. Chinese history records many rebellions arising from movements with striking similarities to Falun Gong and the qigong movement in general, movements that had a vaguely Buddhist ideology, emphasized physical culture, were organized underground, and believed in magic and supernatural power. Today, the state has good reason to be wary of the entire qigong movement and to be fearful of groups like the Falun Gong in particular.

Tourism

From 1949 to the beginning of the reform era in 1979, travel within China except on official business was difficult. Transportation was expensive and hard to arrange, tourist facilities were poor, and in any case, city people had little time for travel, working as they did six days a week, 12 months a year. Travel overseas for pleasure was out of the question. A typical Chinese had about as much chance of visiting, say, Paris as he did the moon.

High-class hotels, of which there were not many, were reserved for Party big shots and foreign visitors (of which there also were not many). Average citizens not only could not stay there, they could not even enter them. There is a delicious story that in the mid-1980s when Jiang Zemin was the mayor of Shanghai, his wife, pushing their grandson in a stroller, walked up to a hotel. The doorman, thinking she was just another grandmother, would not let her in.

In the past 20 years—and especially since the 1990s—tourism, like so many other things, has boomed. With living standards and disposable income rising, the government has encouraged domestic travel and hundreds of millions of people have eagerly responded. In 1999, 719 million Chinese traveled within the country and 4.3 million went abroad on private trips. More than 10% of all Chinese adults have flown in an airplane; in the largest cities, that figure increases to around a third.[21] The most popular "foreign" destination is Hong Kong (technically a part of China, but Chinese who are not residents of Hong Kong require special permission to travel there). The most visited domestic sites remain the "five peaks" and the "four most famous mountains"—altogether sometimes known as China's sacred mountains—the first five associated for the past 1,500 or so years with Daoism, and the latter four with Buddhism. For century after century people have been climbing these mountains and they still continue to trudge up them.

More recent is travel by large numbers of people to exotic destinations. In the past couple of decades, the majority Han people of China have become enamored of the country's minority nationalities, particularly those in the far southern province of Yunnan. The scenery there is beautiful, the weather pleasant, and the indigenous people attractive. Tourists daily pour into some towns by the busload, taking pictures of the local people in native costume, buying souvenirs, and doing the other things that tourists the world over do. Some Western observers have criticized the patronizing attitude of the tourists. Many of them may be patronizing, but no more so than tourists elsewhere in the world, at least tourists who have not yet learned the strictures of political correctness. Besides, they bring in money. For tourists who would like to sample the culture of all of China's minority peoples in one easy trip there is the China Folk Culture Villages in the city of Shenzhen. This attraction features 24 villages spread over four acres, and presents entertainers from the minority nationalities living in Yunnan, Guizhou, Sichuan, Tibet, Hunan, Xinjiang, Inner Mongolia, and elsewhere. English-language advertisements of the Folk Culture Villages gush, somewhat unidiomatically, "Enjoying primitive, graceful song and dance."

Many tourists turn to domestic tourist agencies offering package tours. Such agencies have proliferated, to the extent that the competition has kept prices down. At the same time, quality seems to have suffered, and complaints about poor food, abusive "service," and mandatory stops at gifts shops have mounted. In any case, these may be indignities disproportionately suffered by relatively wealthy travelers. A survey undertaken in 2000 revealed that 90% of tourists with a family income of less than about $240 per month plan their own travel and eschew group tours.[22]

Pets

In a few marketplaces of Beijing on winter days one can see peddlers squatting on the ground next to little drums. What they are selling is not *in* the drums, but *on* the drums, almost invisible until the buyer gets close: crickets. The drums are heated, and the contented little creatures sit there on top, clever enough not to jump off into the freezing air. For a couple of dollars one can buy a pet cricket, either to keep for its pleasant chirping song or for its fighting ability (half a century or more ago cricket fights were popular among some men, but today they are rare). After putting the cricket in a tiny gourd or other suitable container, the buyer tucks it into his shirt, next to the skin, to keep it warm on the trip home.

Crickets have been popular pets, particularly among men, for centuries. Birds and fish have also traditionally been favorites. Since time began, and still today, among children, especially in the countryside, almost any animal they can get their hands on can be a pet: crickets, grasshoppers, beetles, turtles, even silkworms. Dogs and cats, however, have to be classified as "new" pets since it is only in recent years that city people could even consider keeping them as pets. Before the reform era, when meat was rationed, few people were willing to share their meager allotment with a four-legged friend. Besides, for centuries city dwellers tended to raise dogs and cats for practical purposes—dogs to guard the house and cats to catch mice. In most cases, they were not viewed as pets. In the 1960s and 1970s, the authorities preached that keeping a dog was decadent, antirevolutionary, and bourgeois—in other words, almost criminal. Like so many other aspects of life, this has changed in recent years, and today many city people evidently want a dog. In 2000, in a survey of residents of eight major Chinese cities, of those who said they actually wanted a pet, 54.4% preferred a dog; in second place came cats (39.6%). However, those who wanted any kind of pet at all were in the minority: more than 50% of urban residents said they are opposed to owning a pet.[23]

Games and Toys

The noted twentieth-century scholar Hu Shi once calculated that each day in China 4 million man-hours are spent playing mah-jongg (*majiang*), a popular game vaguely similar to dominoes. If you multiplied that by the number of days in a year, and then multiplied the resulting product (1.46 billion) by the number of years mah-jongg has been played since it was invented, you would quickly find your calculator running out of zeros for, according to legend, the game—like so many other things Chinese—goes back to the time of Confucius. While it is hard to substantiate that, it is clear that over the centuries mah-jongg has become one of China's favorite ways of whiling away idle hours.

Mah-jongg is played in many families from time and time, and by some devotees seemingly all the time. The rules, which vary a bit from family to family and place to place, are not difficult, so players (there are always four) can joke, chat, smoke, and drink while they play. But serious players treat the game almost as if it were a sporting competition, and play it with great concentration and speed—above all, speed. They do not just lay their mah-jongg tiles (which are made of wood, or bamboo, or bone, or—of course today—plastic) down on the table as they play, but slap them down with a sharp "clack." And at the end of each game, eight hands reach out and vigorously "wash the tiles"—that is, put them all facedown and then mix them up. The rustling, clicking, and clacking sound is marvelous and stimulating.

More refined, and slower, are *xiangqi* and *weiqi*. The former is often called Chinese chess, and with good reason since it and Western chess share the same Indian ancestor and bear many family resemblances (Figure 8.6). In fact, xiangqi literally means "elephant chess," a name derived from the term *Xiangzhu*, "Elephant Lords," a traditional name for India, a land famous for its elephants. Weiqi (which could be translated as the "surrounding game" and is perhaps better known in the West through its Japanese variant, *go*) is played on a board with 19 horizontal lines and 19 vertical lines (= 361 intersections) and 361 little pieces or stones (180 white and 181 black) that are placed on the intersections. The rules are deceptively simple and so is the object—to stake out as much territory on the board as possible. But to play with success requires an ability to develop a complex strategy and to analyze an astronomically huge number of possible board positions (said to number 10 to the 750th power). This is definitely a game for serious adults and the rare, precocious youngster.

What do China's 100 million nonprecocious children play after school? Most turn to the same sorts of games and toys that delight Western youngsters, but many also enjoy folk toys. Drums, bamboo flutes, plastic or clay bird-shaped whistles, and other musical toys are favorites. Shadow puppets are also popular, as are glass marbles. And as all children know, food is something to be played with. Sugar figurines—made by pouring melted sugar into molds in the shape of pigs, fish, tigers, and lions—are still enjoyed by

Figure 8.6. Playing *xiangqi* in a teahouse in Chengdu, ca. 1985. All the older men are dressed in *zhifu*. On the table by the hand of the bald gentleman is a smoking pipe with a thimble-sized bowl of the type that first appeared when China began to cultivate tobacco in the seventeenth century. Some older smokers still prefer this sort of pipe. *From Qiu Huanxing,* Folk Customs of China *(Beijing: Foreign Languages Press, 1992).*

children, as they have been for centuries. Even more fun are candy figurines made right on the spot. In parks, village lanes, or street corners the candy artist sets up a little table and then takes a bit of molten candy or wheat gluten and with tweezers or a spatula quickly forms a horse, a dragon, or almost any other creature you can think of. For children the greatest pleasure comes from telling the man exactly what they want, and then watching how, with a few deft strokes, he transforms a blob of candy into, say, a unicorn. The end result looks like a delicate figurine of glass but is, of course, good to eat.

NOTES

1. Reuters (May 1, 2000).

2. *China Daily* (Feb. 17, 2000), http://www.chinadaily.com.cn (Mar. 5, 2000).

3. *Beijing Scene* 6, no. 5 (Nov. 12–18, 1999), http://www.beijingscene.com (Dec. 5, 1999).

4. Tun Li-ch'en, *Annual Customs and Festivals in Peking*, trans. Derk Bodde (Hong Kong: University of Hong Kong Press, 1965), pp. 65–66.

5. Gallup Organization, *1997 Survey: The People's Republic of China—Consumer Attitudes and Lifestyle Trends*, http://www.gallup.com/poll/reports/china.asp (June 8, 2000).

6. Guojia tongji ju [State Statistical Bureau], *Zhongguo tongji nianjian* (China statistical yearbook) (Beijing: Zhongguo tongji chubanshe, 1996).

7. Hanlong Lu, "To Be Relatively Comfortable in an Egalitarian Society," in Deborah S. Davis, ed., *The Consumer Revolution in Urban China* (Berkeley: University of California Press, 2000), p. 137.

8. Ibid., p. 134.

9. Gallup Organization, *1997 Survey*.

10. Terry McCarthy and Jaime A. Florcruz, "Uncanned Laughter," *Time International* 154, no. 19 (Nov. 15, 1999).

11. *Beijing Scene* 7, no. 5 (Feb. 18–24, 2000).

12. Fong Tak-ho, "TV Series on Capital Graft Scandal Banned," *Hong Kong Standard* (May 6, 2000).

13. McCarthy and Florcruz, "Uncanned Laughter."

14. Jianying Zha, *China Pop* (New York: New Press, 1995), p. 27.

15. Horizon Research Company, *Xun Cool yidai* (Looking for the cool generation), Research report (Dec. 15, 1999).

16. Stanley Rosen, "Chinese Youth in the Year 2000." (Paper presented at the annual meeting of the Association for Asian Studies, San Diego, CA, Mar. 9–12, 2000), p. 14.

17. Horizon Research Company, *Xun Cool yidai*.

18. Zhu Xiaoyang and Benjamin Penny, "Editors' Introduction," in *The Qigong Boom. Chinese Sociology and Anthropology*, no. 1 (fall 1994): p. 3.

19. Agence France Presse, cited in *China News Digest*, Global News no. GL99–058 (May 5, 1999).

20. *Christian Science Monitor* (Jan. 6, 2000).

21. Gallup Organization, *1997 Survey*.

22. Xinhua News Agency (Mar. 3, 2000).

23. "Pets Less Popular in Major Cities," *China Daily* (Apr. 7, 2000).

Epilogue: Culture in Crisis? China and Its Future

WHAT DO THE CHINESE think of their own culture? Most undoubtedly do not give the question of culture much thought. Their concerns are coping with daily life and making decisions about the family budget, what brand of television to buy, what clothes to wear, what apartment to buy or rent and how to furnish it, and the myriad other quotidian matters that face almost everyone, everyday.

Intellectuals are an entirely different matter. Their role, of course, is to interpret and criticize society, and here Chinese intellectuals have performed in such an exemplary manner that at times they seem not merely concerned with their country's culture, but preoccupied with it, even obsessed with it. If this were not enough, the character of the discourse on culture today, down to its rhetoric, is remarkably reminiscent of the debates that stretch back to the late nineteenth century: the same old, familiar, and by now tedious, tunes, played on the same worn record, going round and round but getting nowhere.

At one extreme are melodramatic songs of loathing of Chinese culture. In the 1920s, the poet Xu Zhimo (1896–1931), then probably China's best known author after Lu Xun, wrote an essay (in English) in which he excoriated his country: "My almost brutal imagery of the society we know [i.e., China] would be a deadly stagnant pool of water, dark with mud and noisy with base insects and worms swarming over and about it. . . . Here in China one finds a magnificent nation of physical weaklings, intellectual invalids, moral cowards, and withal, spiritual paupers."[1] Sixty years later, in the 1980s, the author Bo Yang (b. 1920), who had fled to Taiwan in the Nationalist debacle of 1949 and later became a dissident there for which he was imprisoned for a decade, published a collection of diatribes under the title *The Ugly Chinese* (which the publisher of the English-language translation made even more sensationalistic by calling it *The Ugly Chinaman*). In this book, which was reprinted on the mainland in 1986, Bo Yang declared that Chinese "culture, from the time of Confucius onwards, hasn't produced a single thinker" and went on to paint China with exactly the same black pigment spread by Xu: China is, Bo Yang declared, a "pool of stagnant water. . . . This stagnant water . . . is such that, if dropped in it, even a honey peach would come out a turd ball."[2]

At the opposite extreme is a chauvinistic chorus singing paeans of praise for Chinese culture. In the 1990s "patriotic" writers extolled China's unique "national essence" and "greatness." This cultural puffery also has a radical nationalist element, evident in, for example, the book *China Can Say No*, published in 1996 and written by a group of five young previously unknown authors. This book, which caused a sensation in China, denounces the United States as a "hegemon" plotting against China in a new cold war and spreading a moral toxin that has—to pick one of the more provocative accusations—seduced innocent young Chinese women into "unhesitatingly rushing into the embrace of white men."[3]

The literature on the so-called cultural crisis in China implicitly or explicitly draws comparisons with the West. Again, the comparisons hardly differ from those made throughout the twentieth century, and even during the latter half of the nineteenth century. In those decades, thinkers wanting to buck up Chinese spirits made the argument that the West was a materialistic civilization (evidence of its material richness was there for all to see, of course) but that the East was a spiritual civilization, and so Chinese could console themselves with the thought that at least in that respect their culture was superior. The same sort of simplistic argument is still being made today. In the 1990s, Ji Xianlin, a professor at Beijing University, argued that the strength of Western thought is analysis, while that of the East is synthesis. In Ji's mind, the era of Western primacy has reached a dead end and now, in the twenty-first century, it is time for the East to dominate.[4]

The view that the West is materialistic and the East is spiritualistic and the belief (which is really merely a desperate hope) that, in the end, the East will triumph over the West reflects one aspect of a central notion in Chinese culture—a notion very much evident in Mao Zedong's thinking, by the way—that right makes might. If only the people of China persevere in following the "right [Chinese] path," then they cannot fail to triumph.

Most Chinese intellectuals do not subscribe to either extreme: that Chinese culture is either a "turd ball" to be flushed away or a jewel to be held up "for the world to behold in awe." Nonetheless, the intellectual atmosphere in

China, even among those who reject extreme positions, is permeated with a miasma of cultural crisis. Liu Binyan (b. 1925), a noted journalist who has been exiled in the United States since 1988, considers China's present "spiritual crisis" the worst since the reform began at the end of the 1970s, a "fact" he blames on the failure of the Communist system.[5] The Communists too talk as if the country were grappling with a moral crisis, but they of course put the blame entirely elsewhere, on bourgeois ideas and lifestyles and on "spiritual pollution" from the West.

Just what are the dimensions of this supposed cultural/spiritual/moral crisis? As we have suggested, there is a very wide range of opinion on the character of the crisis, its sources, and its solutions. But looking at the many conferences organized by the government, universities, and think tanks, the countless surveys of public attitudes and beliefs, and the mountains of books and articles written on cultural crisis, it appears that the rot or threat of rot has penetrated into every recess and corner of Chinese society. There is one issue on which almost all critics and observers can agree: a weakness of public morality. In a celebrated incident in 1991, two middle school students in the province of Guangdong, riding on a rented motorbike, had an accident in which one of them sustained serious head injuries. People stopped to stare, but then walked or drove off. It was not until 2 hours and 20 minutes later that someone finally took the injured boy to the hospital. He was dead on arrival. Does this incident reveal a flaw in Chinese culture? Do Chinese simply have no sense of public, moral responsibility? In the early years of the twentieth century, the thinker Liang Qichao argued precisely that: China had a tradition of private morality, but it lacked public-spirited citizens. In fact, it would be difficult to agree since this tragedy in Guangdong generated a storm of public outrage. *Southern Daily*, the major newspaper in the province, sent reporters to the scene after the boy's death to interview bystanders, who offered one excuse or another for not "getting involved." The newspaper then invited its readers to write in with their reactions. The hundreds of letters received amounted to a debate on the moral and ethical questions involved.[6]

The range of reactions to this single incident—from the bystander who defended his inaction by saying, "When you bring someone to the hospital, you'll be asked to pay a fee before they're admitted; why get into all that trouble?" to the readers of *Southern Daily* who expressed their outrage—is indicative of the diversity of views and values among the people of China. Is that not to be expected? Culture is rarely an either/or proposition. Chinese culture is complex, diverse, and rich in contradictions. It leaves ample room for the exercise of individual choice. Like all other cultures, it is made up of countless elements, taken from here and there, and accumulated and shaped over years, centuries, and millennia. Trying to boil it down to its "essence" is bound to result in nothing but a bunch of platitudes and stereotyped banalities, a little heap of no value for reasoned analysis and understanding.

The many surveys that ask Chinese about their values confirm that there is certainly no uniformity nor consistency across time, place of residence, and generation. In a 1997 Gallup survey of 3,700 households throughout China, respondents were asked to rank six values. By far the most common response, given by 56% of those surveyed, was "work hard and get rich." By contrast, only minuscule percentages in any demographic group put in first place "never think of yourself, give everything in service to society."[7] This would seem to confirm Liang Qichao's pessimistic judgment of nearly a century ago. However, a closer look reveals the matter is not so simple. The "work hard and get rich" response comes overwhelmingly from rural residents (69%). Among urban residents, 38% (and 51% in Beijing) put in first place "don't think about money or fame, just live a life that suits your own tastes." Furthermore, this latter value is becoming more and more widespread. Compared to 1994, in 1997 nearly twice as great a percentage of respondents, both urban and rural, assigned it first place. And younger adults, aged 18–29, in particular increasingly put self-fulfillment through nonmaterial means in first place: in 1997, 18% of rural young adults and 47% of urban young adults ranked in first place "don't think about money or fame, just live a life that suits your own tastes."[8]

Living a "life that suits your own tastes" is a manifestation of individualism; so too, for that matter, can be striving to get rich through hard work. An American author of a survey of 512 students in 15 colleges and universities conducted in 1991 seemed surprised by the finding that "at the cultural level, students exhibit a strong tendency toward individualism, rather than toward the collectivism generally associated with traditional Chinese society."[9] This finding should be no surprise in view of the deep vein of individualism that runs through Chinese culture. Sun Yat-sen, early in the twentieth century, complained about what he thought to be the negative aspect of this individualism: Chinese, he remarked, were like a sheet of loose sand. But it is too easy to categorize the people of China as a collection of egoistic individualists. The ethos of being a responsible member of groups—all the way from the family to the nation—is also strong.

Evidence of what some have called the "group centeredness" of Chinese might be seen in the rising tide of nationalism. Yet, even there, public sentiment is complicated. In a survey conducted in Shanghai and surrounding areas, 700 youth were asked to rank 18 values. In 1984, "patriotism" (a category that the Gallup poll did not include) ranked fifth.[10] In 1994, it had jumped up to second overall, and among workers, rural residents, and science students, it ranked first. In a large-scale survey of reading habits covering the entire reform period from 1978, respondents were asked to rank books that had the greatest influence on them. Of books published since 1993, *China Can Say No* was ranked in second position (2.4%), just barely behind a general category of "books on economics," and just ahead of the liberal journal *Dushu* (Reading). These results might suggest nationalism is rampant in the Chinese public. But a closer look reveals that to be a much too facile conclusion. If one considers *all* books, not just those published since 1993, then among respondents 20 years of age or younger, *China Can Say No* falls to 23rd place, with just 1.82% (and 0.9% among readers of all ages), far behind such classics as the eighteenth-century novel *Dream of the Red Chamber* (20%), or *Romance of the Three Kingdoms* (14.55%), a novel variously dated to the fourteenth to sixteenth centuries, and far, far behind a catch-all category of "foreign literature by famous authors" (47.27%).

There is no question that surveys and anecdotal evidence indicate patriotism is rising, especially among younger people, and that the United States is understandably the main target of criticism. But patriotism in this case is not the same as chauvinism or parochialism. On the contrary, large numbers—probably the majority—of college and university students would like to study abroad. In a survey of students at five well-known universities in Beijing in 1999, 70% of the respondents said they intended to study abroad, with 73% choosing the United States. Since the reform program began, around 300,000 Chinese students have gone abroad to study (and only around 100,000 have returned). That kind of evidence, combined with the abiding interest of youth in international popular culture (movies, sports, etc.), explodes the myth that the young people of China are ultra-nationalists.

In general, the people of China are not just eagerly receptive to "foreign" culture and ideas, but they are also tolerant of other belief systems. In a recent survey of 2,000 respondents in four provinces, 65% agreed with the statement "A person's belief system is his/her own affair." In the same survey, among respondents who identified themselves as atheists, 85% said they could tolerate religious beliefs in others. At the same time, people are not about to let someone else do their thinking for them. In the Shanghai survey of 700 youths mentioned above, the value consistently ranked lowest—last in 1984 and last again in 1994—was "obedience to authority."

Taken together, all these diverse responses in various surveys are indicative of what some observers have described as the graying of Chinese culture. Values have become mixed and indistinct, no longer (if they ever were) black-and-white, and no longer "red" (Communist). Particularly among youth, there is a marked mood of uncertainty, ambivalence, and skepticism. A recent study of ideals among 2,000 respondents in four provinces found that 36%

of those asked said they had no ideals. If one added to this the response "I used to have ideals, but I have none now" the total would be more than 58%.

Far from being a cause to wring one's hands, a widespread lack of ideals, especially among youth, may actually be encouraging and may bode well for China's future. China's transition to a modern, wealthy, stable society which began a century and a half ago, has not yet ended. Living standards are still far lower than in the West, the search for a stable polity continues, and the debate over what China's culture should be and how China should come to terms with the outside world, especially the West, drones on. During this long transition, China has suffered at the hands of true believers who thought they had the answers to all of the country's woes, who arrogantly were convinced of their rightness, and who sought to impose their "solutions" on the nation. The country has been pulled violently left, and then right, and then left, and right again, and torn apart by the most incredible violence. Millions have died for the sake of campaigns and pipe dreams that were so ill-conceived and destructive as to be criminal. To confront the huge problems facing China today, and those that are certain to arise in the coming decades, will require all the wisdom and energy that the people of China can muster. If the youth of today are not ready to put their faith in abstractions, to blindly follow authority, to try to impose their way of thinking on others, to turn their back on the cultural wealth of China's past and the cultural richness of the outside world, then there is reason to be optimistic about China's future.

NOTES

1. Xu Zhimo, "Art and Life," *Chuangzao jikan* 2, no. 1 (1922), in Kirk A. Denton, ed., *Modern Chinese Literary Thought: Writings on Literature, 1893–1945* (Stanford, CA: Stanford University Press, 1996), p. 169.

2. Cited in Richard W. Bodman, "From History to Allegory in Art," in Su Xiaokang and Wang Luxiang, *Deathsong of the River* (Ithaca, NY: East Asia Program, Cornell University, 1991), pp. 28–29.

3. Song Qiang et al., *Zhongguo keyi shuo bu* (China can say no) (Beijing: Zhonghua nong-gong-shang lianhe chubanshe, 1996), p. 23.

4. Ji Xianglin, in *Chunyan* (Popular tribune), no. 5 (1991); idem, *Ershiyi shji* (Twenty-first century), no. 3 (Feb. 1991), cited in "Fragmented Fractals: Towards Chinese Culture in the Twenty-first Century," *China News Analysis*, no. 1462 (June 15, 1992).

5. Liu Binyan, "Zhongguo dalu de jingshen weiji" (The spiritual crisis in mainland China), *Zhengming* (Contention), no. 164 (June 1991): pp. 64–66.

6. The incident is discussed in "Moral Education," *China News Analysis*, no. 1441 (Aug. 15, 1991).

7. Gallup Organization, *1997 Survey: The People's Republic of China—Consumer Attitudes and Lifestyle Trends,* http://www.gallup.com/poll/reports/china.asp (June 8, 2000).

8. Ibid.

9. June Rose Garrott, "Chinese Cultural Values: New Angles, Added Insights," *International Journal of Intercultural Relations* 19, no. 2(1995): p. 211.

10. Where a specific source is not cited, the survey data in this chapter are taken from Stanley Rosen, "Chinese Youth in the Year 2000." (Paper presented at the annual meeting of the Association for Asian Studies, San Diego, CA, Mar. 9–12, 2000).

Glossary

ao	襖	surcoat
baicha	白茶	"clear tea" (hot water as a beverage)
baihua	白話	"plain speech" (the vernacular language)
baozi	包子	steamed stuffed bun
bayin	八音	"eight timbres"
cai	菜	meat, vegetables, fruit and all other foods, excluding cereals
Changjiang	長江	Yangzi River (lit., Long River)
changpao	長袍	men's long gown
chashaobao	叉燒包	steamed bun stuffed with barbecued pork
cheongsam	長衫	*see* qipao
chifan	喫飯	to have a meal
chunbing	春餅	"spring pancakes"
Chunjie	春節	Spring Festival (Chinese New Year)
chunlian	春聯	Spring Festival couplets
danwei	單位	work unit
Dao	道	"the way" (Daoist concept; a term also used by Confucians)
dao	到	arrival
dao	倒	upside down
Daodejing	道德經	*The Classic of the Way and Virtue* (alternate title for *Laozi*)

dianxin	點心	dim sum
didi	弟弟	younger brother
dizi	笛子	bamboo flute
doudou	兜兜	an undergarment covering the chest and abdomen
doufu	豆腐	bean curd
Duanwu jie	端午節	Dragon Boat Festival (lit., Upright Wu Festival)
erhu	二胡	2-stringed fiddle
Falun Dafa	法輪大法	"Universal Principles of the Falun" (alternate name for Falun Gong)
Falun Gong	法輪功	"The Practice of the Wheel of Dharma" (a spiritual movement)
fan	飯	cooked rice or other cereals
fengshui	風水	geomancy (lit., wind and water)
fengzheng	風箏	kite (lit., wind harp)
fenjia	分家	division of the household
fu	福	good fortune; happiness; prosperity
fu	蝠	bat
fushi	副食	"secondary food" (nonstaple foodstuffs; same as cai)
gaoliang	高粱	sorghum
gege	哥哥	elder brother
guanxi	關係	connections; relations
guo	鍋	wok (frying pan)
guohua	國畫	painting in the traditional Chinese style (lit., national painting)
guqin	古琴	alternate name for the qin (harp)
Han	漢	the ethnic majority of China
Huanghe	黃河	Yellow River
huangzhong	黃鐘	"yellow bell"
huntun	餛飩	wonton (a kind of dumpling)
Jiangbeiren	江北人	people from north of the [Yangzi] River
jiaozi	餃子	shallow-fried or boiled dumplings
jiejie	姐姐	elder sister
junzi	君子	superior man
kang	炕	heatable brick bed

kowtow (ketou)	磕頭	ritual obeisance
kuaizi	筷子	chopsticks
lao	老	old
laonianren	老年人	old people
laoshi	老師	teacher
Laozi	老子	ancient philosophical text; also the name of its reputed author
li	禮	rules of proper behavior, civility
liang	涼	cool; cold
magua	馬褂	short jacket
majiang	麻將	mah-jongg
mantou	饅頭	steamed bun
meimei	妹妹	younger sister
minguo	民國	republic
niangao	年糕	glutinous New Year cake
nianhua	年畫	New Year's pictures
pailou	牌樓	ceremonial archway
pinyin	拼音	official form of romanization (writing Chinese with the Latin alphabet)
pipa	琵琶	4-stringed fretted lute
putonghua	普通話	common speech (of the Chinese language); standard pronunciation
qi	氣	vital force
qigong	氣功	"qi skills" (a form of physical culture)
qin	琴	7-stringed zither (*see* guqin)
Qingming jie	清明節	Grave-Sweeping Festival (lit., Festival of Pure Brightness)
qipao	旗袍	woman's form-fitting dress
re	熱	hot; heat; fever; craze
ren	仁	human-heartedness
shan	衫	jacket
shan-shui	山水	"mountains and water"
shaomai	燒賣	steamed dumpling, usually pork filled, with the dough gathered at the top
Shijing	詩經	*Book of Songs* (classic from ca. 12th to 6th century B.C.)

shenfen	身份	class status
sheng	笙	mouth organ
shu-hua	書畫	calligraphy and painting
shui-mo	水墨	"water and ink" (an alternative term for guohua)
suona	嗩吶	double-reeded horn
taijiquan	太極拳	traditional form of shadow boxing
tangyuan	湯圓	filled, sweet rice dumplings
tuanyuan	團圓	reunion; a perfect circle
Tuanyuan jie	團圓節	Mid-Autumn Festival
tu	土	local; parochial; traditional
weiqi	圍棋	"surrounding game" (a board game)
wenyan	文言	classical style of writing
wok		*see* guo
xiangqi	象棋	Chinese chess (lit., elephant chess)
Xiangzhu	象主	"Elephant Lords" (a traditional name for India)
xiaochi	小喫	snacks
yang	陽	male principle (half of the yin-yang dyad)
yang	洋	foreign; sophisticated
yangge	秧歌	folk dance
yasuiqian	壓歲錢	money given to children at the Spring Festival
yi	義	righteousness (Confucian concept of how one ought to act)
yi, shi, zhu, xing	衣食住行	clothing, food, shelter, transportation
yi jin ye xing	衣錦夜行	hidden talent (lit., to wear a silken robe but walk by night)
Yijing	易經	*Book of Changes* (ca. 6th century B.C.)
yin	陰	female principle
youtiao	油條	"oily sticks"
yu	裕	abundance
yu	魚	fish
yuanxiao	元宵	*see* tangyuan
zhifu	製服	uniform
Zhongguo	中國	China
Zhongshanzhuang	中山裝	Sun Yat-sen suit (aka Mao suit)

zhushi	主食	"primary food" (rice and other forms of fan)
Zhuangzi	莊子	3rd century B.C. text; also name of its reputed author
zongzi	粽子	fist-sized pyramid of rice with a filling
zuole	作樂	to have fun

Suggested Readings

GENERAL

Barmé, Geremie. *In the Red: On Contemporary Chinese Culture.* New York: Columbia University Press, 1999. A collection of essays, some superb and all fascinating, on various aspects of contemporary culture.

Dutton, Michael. *Streetlife China.* Cambridge, UK: Cambridge University Press, 1998. A collection of articles and vignettes, taken from Chinese sources, on daily life in the late 1980s and early 1990s, informative and revealing albeit marred by the fact that the selections are unbalanced (tending to be sensationalistic) and the commentary is weighed down with postmodernist "cultural studies" jargon.

Lin Yutang. *My Country and My People.* London: Heinemann Educational, 1977. Originally published in 1935, and available in several editions, both in English and Chinese, this is an idiosyncratic, brilliant, and marvelously written interpretation of life in traditional times and during the transition to modernity.

Wu Dingbo and Patrick D. Murphy, eds. *Handbook of Chinese Popular Culture.* Westport, CT: Greenwood Press, 1994. Essays, of widely varying quality, on popular culture, especially contemporary culture. Many of the essays are most useful for their annotated bibliographies.

Zha, Jiangying. *China Pop: How Soap Operas, Tabloids, and Bestsellers Are Transforming a Culture.* New York: New Press, 1995. A witty, engaging, and personal account of popular culture in the late 1980s and early 1990s.

LAND, PEOPLE, AND HISTORY

Gernet, Jacques. *A History of Chinese Civilization*, 2d ed. Cambridge, UK: Cambridge University Press, 1996. The best single-volume history of China in English, unequaled in its thoroughness and erudition.

Ropp, Paul S., ed. *Heritage of China: Contemporary Perspectives on Chinese Civilization*. Berkeley: University of California Press, 1990.

Smith, Christopher J. *China: People and Places in the Land of One Billion*. Boulder, CO: Westview Press, 1991.

THOUGHT AND RELIGION

Creel, H.G. *Chinese Thought: From Confucius to Mao Tse-tung*. New York: New American Library, 1960.

Fung Yu-lan. *A Short History of Chinese Philosophy*. New York: Free Press, 1966.

Hsu, Francis L.K. *Americans and Chinese: Passage to Difference*. Honolulu: University of Hawaii Press, 1981.

Thompson, Laurence G. *Chinese Religion: An Introduction*, 5th ed. Belmont, CA: Wadsworth Publishing Co., 1996.

Yang, C.K. *Religion in Chinese Society*. Berkeley: University of California Press, 1961.

LITERATURE AND ART

Clunas, Craig. *Art in China*. Oxford: Oxford University Press, 1997.

DeFrancis, John. *The Chinese Language: Fact and Fantasy*. Honolulu: University of Hawaii Press, 1984.

Hsia, C.T. *A History of Modern Chinese Fiction*, 3rd ed. Bloomington, IN: Indiana University Press, 1999.

Lai Ming. *A History of Chinese Literature*. New York: John Day and Co., 1964. Reprint. New York: Capricorn Books, 1966.

Lau, Joseph S.M., and Howard Goldblatt, eds. *The Columbia Anthology of Modern Chinese Literature*. New York: Columbia University Press, 1995.

Link, E. Perry. *The Uses of Literature: Life in the Socialist Chinese Literary System*. Princeton, NJ: Princeton University Press, 2000.

Liu Wu-chi. *An Introduction to Chinese Literature*. Bloomington: Indiana University Press, 1966. Reprint. Westport, CT: Greenwood Press, 1990.

Mair, Victor H., ed. *The Columbia Anthology of Traditional Chinese Literature*. New York: Columbia University Press, 1994.

Sullivan, Michael. *Art and Artists of Twentieth-Century China*. Berkeley: University of California Press, 1996.

MUSIC AND DANCE

Jones, Andrew F. *Like a Knife: Ideology and Genre in Contemporary Chinese Popular Music*. Ithaca, NY: East Asia Program, Cornell University, 1992.

Jones, Stephen. *Folk Music in China.* New York: Oxford University Press, 1995.

Liang Mingyue. *Music of the Billion: An Introduction to Chinese Musical Culture.* New York: Heinrichshofen Edition, 1985.

Mackerras, Colin, ed. *Chinese Theater: From Its Origins to the Present Day.* Honolulu: University of Hawaii Press, 1988.

Scott, A.C. *An Introduction to the Chinese Theatre.* New York: Theatre Arts Books, 1960.

Wang Kefen. *The History of Chinese Dance.* Beijing: Foreign Languages Press, 1985.

FOOD AND CLOTHING

Anderson, Eugene N. *The Food of China.* New Haven, CT: Yale University Press, 1988.

Chang, K.C., ed. *Food in Chinese Culture: Anthropological and Historical Perspectives.* New Haven, CT: Yale University Press, 1977.

Garrett, Valery M. *Chinese Clothing: An Illustrated Guide.* Hong Kong: Oxford University Press, 1994.

Roberts, Claire, ed. *Evolution and Revolution: Chinese Dress, 1700s–1900s.* Sydney: Powerhouse Publishing, 1997.

Scott, A.C. *Chinese Costume in Transition.* New York: Theatre Arts Books, 1960.

ARCHITECTURE AND HOUSING

Hannan, Kate, ed. *China: Modernisation and the Goal of Prosperity.* Cambridge, UK: Cambridge University Press, 1995.

Kirkby, R.J.R. *Urbanization in China: Town and Country in a Developing Economy, 1949–2000 A.D.* New York: Columbia University Press, 1985.

Knapp, Ronald G. *China's Vernacular Architecture: House Form and Culture.* Honolulu: University of Hawaii Press, 1989.

Liu, Laurence G. *Chinese Architecture.* New York: Rizzoli International Publications, 1989.

Steinhardt, Nancy. *Chinese Traditional Architecture.* New York: China Institute of America, 1984.

FAMILY AND GENDER

Croll, Elisabeth. *Changing Identities of Chinese Women: Rhetoric, Experience, and Self-Perception.* Hong Kong: University of Hong Kong Press, 1995.

Davis, Deborah, and Stevan Harrell, eds. *Chinese Families in the Post-Mao Era.* Berkeley: University of California Press, 1993.

Watson, Rubie S., and Patricia Ebrey, eds. *Marriage and Inequality in Chinese Society.* Berkeley: University of California Press, 1991.

West, Jackie, Zhao Minghua, and Cheng Yuan, eds. *Women of China: Economic and Social Transformation.* New York: St. Martin's Press, 1999.

Holidays and Leisure Activities

China Tourism. A monthly pictorial, published in Hong Kong in both Chinese and English editions, with lavishly illustrated articles on culture and customs.

Davis, Deborah S., ed. *The Consumer Revolution in Urban China.* Berkeley: University of California Press, 2000.

Latsch, Marie-Luise. *Chinese Traditional Festivals.* Beijing: New World Press, 1984.

Index

About the Author

RICHARD GUNDE is the assistant director of the Center for Chinese Studies at UCLA. He was the associate editor of the journal *Modern China* for more than 20 years.